Imagery and Text

Imagery and Text

A Dual Coding Theory of Reading and Writing

Mark Sadoski

Texas A&M University

Allan Paivio

University of Western Ontario

LAWRENCE ERLBAUM ASSOCIATES, PUBLISHERS

2001 Mahwah, New Jersey   London

Lawrence Erlbaum Associates, Inc., Publishers
10 Industrial Avenue
Mahwah, NJ 07430

Cover design by Kathryn Houghtaling Lacey

Library of Congress Cataloging-in-Publication Data

Sadoski, Mark.
Imagery and text : a dual coding theory of reading and writing /
Mark Sadoski, Allan Paivio.
p. cm.
Includes bibliographical references and index.
ISBN 0-8058-3438-9 (cloth : alk. paper)
ISBN 0-8058-3439-7 (pbk. : alk. paper)
1. Cognition. 2. Psycholinguistics. 3. Imagery (Psychology).
4. Meaning (Psychology). 5. Reading—Psychological aspects.
6. Writing—Psychological aspects. I. Paivio, Allan. II. Title.
BF311 .S25 2001
302.2'244'019—dc21
00-047612
CIP

Books published by Lawrence Erlbaum Associates are printed on
acid-free paper, and their bindings are chosen for strength and dura-
bility.

Printed in the United States of America
10 9 8 7 6 5 4 3 2 1

For our families

CONTENTS

PREFACE

This book presents an overall theory of cognition in literacy and an assertion of that theory. It offers both an exposition of the Dual Coding Theory of reading and writing and an argument for it.

Theories of cognition in reading and writing have developed separately. Microtheories of specific aspects of reading or writing also have developed separately. Overarching, unifying theories that provide a general architecture to frame these separate theories are timely and necessary. Dual Coding Theory is an established theory of general cognition that provides one such framework. Furthermore, it provides specific accounts of reading and writing in its own terms.

Dual Coding Theory is about the nature of two great symbolic systems of cognition: language and mental imagery. Fascination with the roles of language and mental imagery in thought and memory dates back more than two millennia. The reader will be introduced to that history (chap. 2) and frequently reminded of it in coverage of more contemporary issues. Many of these issues have rich and varied histories in philosophy, rhetoric, literature, education, psychology, linguistics, and other disciplines.

This theory is also presented as an empirical and pragmatic alternative to the formal rationalism of current computer-based theories of cognition. At the heart of Dual Coding Theory is an explanation of the essentially human concept that is at the heart of literacy: meaning. We frequently emphasize the difference between Dual Coding Theory and theories that explain cognition and meaning in terms of computational concepts such as abstract propositions and schemata. Detailed contrasts with specific theories are given in several chapters. Dual Coding Theory has roots in the humanistic traditions of the disciplines mentioned above, but it also has firm roots in science. Empirical research studies are regularly reviewed in making the case for the theory.

Coverage in this book includes chapters on the development of Dual Coding Theory (chap. 1), its historical and philosophical background (chap. 2), an explanation of the theory proper (chap. 3), meaning and comprehension (chap. 4), memory (chap. 5), the reading process (chap. 6), and the writing process (chap. 7). More than most theories, Dual Coding Theory offers rich and practical implications for education. Such implications are woven throughout the book, and the final chapter (chap. 8) is dedicated to a review of research on educational applications of concreteness, imagery, and verbal processes as covered by the theory.

This book is designed for a broad audience of theorists and researchers interested in literacy including educators, literacy's foremost proponents. We have made efforts to be theoretically precise, yet readable to that broad audience. The value of a theory is perhaps best seen in its application, basic knowledge in the service of informing and directing human learning.

We would like to acknowledge the many people who have been encouraging and supportive during the writing of this book. We particularly acknowledge our families, especially Carol Sadoski and Sandra Paivio, who read and responded to our drafts. The original graphics for the book were done by Kameshwari Viswanadha at Texas A&M University. Some material in the book was previously published in journals of the International Reading Association and is used with permission. Permissions for figures and tables are given with their captions. Naomi Silverman was our helpful editor. We extend special thanks to Lawrence Erlbaum for his personal encouragement of this project.

—Mark Sadoski
—Allan Paivio

CHAPTER 1

Introduction: A Unified Theory of Literacy

This book presents a unified theory of reading and writing that derives from, and is completely consistent with, a well-established general theory of human cognition. Few such unified theories of literacy have been proposed, and even fewer with the historical, empirical, and practical support presented here.

Unifying reading and writing under the aegis of a theory of general cognition is a timely and inevitable scientific step. The importance of this step can be stated simply: Any theory of reading or writing that does not eventually align with a broader theory of general cognition will not endure. Reading and writing are cognitive acts, but there is nothing about either of them that does not occur in other cognitive acts that do not involve reading or writing. That is, we perceive, discriminate, analyze, synthesize, interpret, anticipate, comprehend, compose, imagine, remember, and express ourselves without text as well as with text. Stated differently, cognition in literacy is a special case of general cognition involving written language. Any theory of reading or writing that does not eventually align with some theory of general cognition will either require revision or languish as the fields of psychology and literacy advance.

Accounting for reading and writing through corresponding cognitive processes is a consummate goal for both theoretical and practical reasons. In the final analysis, the receptive and productive faces of literacy must be interpreted as complementary parts of the same cognitive system, deriving from the same basic mental representations and processes, sharing the same sources. Such an approach to literacy has considerable practical value for education, where the development of certain cognitive capabilities could efficiently serve both ends.

Dual Coding Theory is the general theory of cognition that provides our unifying framework for literacy. This theory offers a combined account of both verbal and nonverbal cognition. The inclusion of nonverbal aspects of cognition such as mental imagery is the most novel facet of this approach in a modern context, but it provides a comprehensive account of the verbal, linguistic aspects of cognition as well. Accordingly, it provides an explicit psychological account of literacy's most central but elusive ingredient: meaning.

While we make efforts in this book to keep theoretical explanations simple, the theory itself is hardly simplistic. Dual Coding Theory originated in observable, everyday phenomena in thought and memory and has developed to account for a complex variety of both everyday phenomena and specialized laboratory phenomena. It is an empirically based theory; its complexity is determined by our ever-widening knowledge of human cognitive behavior. The constellation of testable predictions derived from its basic principles has been programmatically explored through decades of studies, but this program is far from complete and new questions arise regularly. For the most thorough understanding of this theory, the interested reader needs to study the key references cited in this chapter. Our purpose in this book is to explain the theory in commonsense terms and then show how it addresses major issues in literacy.

In the rest of this chapter, we briefly sketch the development of Dual Coding Theory and its extension to literacy, touch on some current philosophic connections, and overview the treatment of the theory presented in the remaining chapters of the book.

The Development of Dual Coding Theory

Dual Coding Theory is relatively new to the literacy field, but its origins can be traced to the cognitive revolution of the 1960s and 1970s. That revolution came as a reaction to radical behaviorism and heralded a return to the study of inner mental processes after years of exclusive attention to external stimuli and their external responses.

Behaviorism classified reading as one kind of verbal operant, which means that the occurrence of a verbal response was tightly controlled by the printed stimulus word. Thus, behaviorism held that subvocal speech and other covert and overt behavior was the medium of human thought and memory, to the extent that such a medium was theorized at all. Meaning posed no problem: The meaning of a written word was fully explained when all of the stimulus conditions that controlled its occurrence had been specified, as well as all of the overt or covert responses it controlled. Literacy was a matter of being conditioned to written language.

Cognitivism shifted attention to the inner world of mental experience; it focuses attention on internal representations and processes as well as external stimuli and responses. These mental representations and processes include verbal ones. However, some current cognitive and linguistic theories interpret language and meaning in terms of completely abstract verbal entities such as abstract lexical nodes, propositions, and schemata. Some of these computer-based theories propose that a single, abstract, verbal code and its computations ultimately explain all of our inner experience. Others distinguish between verbal and nonverbal representations at the superficial level of input or output, but assume that deeper levels of cognition are carried on exclusively through an abstract verbal code.

But cognitivism rekindled interest in another form of mental experience that has fascinated thinkers since antiquity: mental imagery. Dual coding, in fact, evolved from an imagery-based mnemonic technique, rooted in the ancient method of loci described in chapter 2, which takes current form in the memory systems taught in public speaking (see Paivio, 1991a, for the roots of the theory).

One common system uses words that rhyme with numbers as memory pegs for related objects. Examples of the numbered pegs include one-bun, two-shoe, three-tree, and so on. If you were shopping for a few odd items such as toothpaste, batteries, and a picture frame, you could remember mental images of a tube of toothpaste in a bun, a shoe full of batteries, and a tree growing through a picture frame as an alternative to a shopping list. Going through the numbers would remind you of the rhyming peg word and the items in turn.

This mnemonic technique makes use of verbal-imaginal dual coding. The rhyme and memory targets (if presented as words) are verbal. These are transformed to nonverbal images, and the novel components of the images are transformed back to verbal responses at recall. This dual-coding kernel gradually evolved into Dual Coding Theory through a systematic program of research covering more than 30 years.

From the outset, the research program involved convergent operations including (a) varying of stimulus materials such as the concreteness of the language presented, (b) experimental instructions such as directions to form mental images or verbal associations, and (c) measurements of individual differences in imagery and verbal ability. Data from introspective reports of the use of imagery or language supplemented these operations. This systematic research program had already tested concreteness (ease of imagery) against more than 20 other variables as predictors of verbal recall by the time of the theory's initial publication (Paivio, 1969).

The theory and its empirical record were first presented more comprehensively in *Imagery and Verbal Processes* (Paivio, 1971). It was updated and extended in *Mental Representations: A Dual Coding Approach* (Paivio, 1986) and updated again in a comprehensive review (Paivio, 1991b). The theory has been applied to various domains including motor learning, bilingualism, neuropsychology, and the philosophy of science, among others. By the mid-1990s, Dual Coding Theory had become recognized as "one of the most influential theories of cognition this century" (Marks, 1997, p. 433). The research program continues to investigate new and unresolved issues.

Dual Coding Theory differs from the other theories noted above in important ways. It assumes that mental representations retain properties derived from perceptions in our various sensory modalities, rather than being amodal and abstract. These modality-specific representations can be verbal, such as representations derived from speech or writing, or they can be nonverbal, including images of nonlinguistic things we have seen, heard, felt, tasted, or smelled. These modality-specific units retain some of their original, holistic properties even when they are associated parts of a larger mental structure, much as pebbles in an aggregate or particles in a suspension.

This associational characteristic of the theory bears comparison with older associationist theories (e.g., Osgood, 1953) and newer connectionist theories (e.g., Seidenberg & McClelland, 1989). Accordingly, Dual Coding Theory is basically an associationist or connectionist theory, but it differs from all other members of that class in its emphasis on the functional difference between the interconnected verbal and nonverbal codes. Verbal associationist theories did not take imagery into account, and newer connectionist and computational theories either ignore the difference between verbal and nonverbal encoding or recognize it without attributing any functional significance to it. In .Dual Coding Theory, the strength of the connections between units is important, but the difference in the qualities of the verbal and nonverbal units that get connected is also important.

Chapter 3 describes the current theory and explains these distinctions along with material in other chapters. We next turn to the extension of the theory to explaining literacy.

Extending Dual Coding Theory to Literacy

The role of imagery in reading had been of interest to researchers in literacy and education for decades before the 1970s (e.g., Durrell & Murphy, 1963). One of the earliest theorists to propose a central role for imagery and the nonverbal in reading was Huey (1908, discussed in chap. 2). Huey was unable to resolve the apparent impasse in his theory created by the difficulty of imaging to relational words such as prepositions and conjunctions. However, others extended Huey's theory, suggesting that such words are imaged when associations are brought together in phrases and sentences (e.g., Bugelski, 1971; Paivio, 1971). Thus, imagery could derive from, and contribute to, contexts as well as individual words.

Interest in imagery in reading and education burgeoned throughout the 1970s and into the 1980s. Pressley (1977) presented a review of dozens of studies on imagery and children's prose learning by various researchers between 1970 and 1977 (see also reviews by Alesandrini, 1985; Denis, 1984; Levin, 1985; Rasinski, 1985; Suzuki, 1985). Dual Coding Theory captured early attention as a potential explanation of text comprehension and individual differences in reading (Jacob, 1976).

The potential of Dual Coding Theory to explain reading gained more direct attention in the 1980s, with some reading researchers invoking it specifically as an explanation for their results (e.g., Sadoski, 1983, 1985). An analysis of the use of both imagery and verbal processes in reading was presented by Paivio and Begg (1981, chap. 14). A fuller extension of the theory to reading came about when it was posed as an alternative to schema theory in explaining reading comprehension (Sadoski, Paivio, & Goetz, 1991). That article questioned schema theory on various grounds and argued that Dual Coding Theory could more parsimoniously and consistently account for the research results claimed as support for schema theory in reading. Shortly afterward, the dual coding view of reading was proposed more comprehensively to include comprehension, learning, appreciation, and reader response (Sadoski & Paivio, 1994). It was also introduced as a plausible theory of written composition (Sadoski, 1992).

The unified theory of literacy presented here covers the basic processes of reading and writing with an emphasis on reading comprehension and written composition. The theory also provides accounts of meaning, memory and remembering, and an array of educational applications to literacy that have been well researched. These accounts are framed in a historical context of literacy, tracing the roots of the theory from ancient rhetoric through its fruition in contemporary cognitive and educational science. Its historical foundations in philosophy are covered therein, but the theory also has current philosophical connections, which we touch on next.

Philosophical Approach

Paivio (1986, chap. 1) discussed the empiricist and pragmatic approach that is implicitly expressed in Dual Coding Theory. It is empiricist, as opposed to rationalist, because adequacy and consistency in explaining observable things and events in the world is a primary criterion rather than satisfying formal, logical coherence rules. It is pragmatic because theoretical truth is tentative and dependent on empirical outcomes in particular contexts, such as reading and writing behavior. The extension of the theory to literacy is consistent with this general approach, with perhaps even more emphasis on pragmatism's view of meaning as the imagined completion of acts, including speech acts (Sadoski, 1992). In short, the philosophical approach here owes much more to empiricism and pragmatism than to rationalism and idealism.

Recently, "empirically responsible" philosophies have been introduced that challenge traditional approaches such as Kantean idealism as well as current aspects of analytic philosophy, linguistic philosophy, and poststructuralist philosophy (e.g., Lakoff & Johnson, 1999). The asserted basis for such a philosophy is that what we have learned from the scientific study of cognition must inform our understanding of knowledge and reason.

For example, Lakoff and Johnson (1999) maintained that all knowledge and reason is inherently embodied—rooted in sensual experience. Our conceptual system is grounded in, and shaped by, our sensorimotor systems. Conceptualization is therefore fundamentally concrete. Abstract conceptualization and reasoning are based in metaphors that are rooted in sensorimotor experience (e.g., time is movement in space, cause is physical force; see chap. 4). Lakoff and Johnson rejected the rationalistic notions of Kantean schemata, Chomskyan autonomous syntax and other strong versions of mental modules, as well as poststucturalist views of the arbitrariness of signs and the relativism of signification. They extend their philosophy beyond epistemology to morality and metaphysics.

Without necessarily accepting the entire philosophy and its implications, the kinship between the embodied philosophy of Lakoff and Johnson and the Dual Coding Theory approach is evident. Both suggest an empirical approach to mind and mental abstractions that is pragmatically determined by our individual and common concrete experiences and our scientific understanding of cognition.

Some philosophical accounts of the evolution of human intelligence are also akin. The evolutionary perspective in the natural philosophy of Bronowski (1977, 1978) is a case in point. Bronowski likewise rejected the innateness assumptions of Kant and Chomsky, proposing that human culture, including all our art and science, is based in the advanced mental imagery and imagination that has evolved in humans. Natural language, he contended, emerged from evolution in the areas of our brains that provide the ability to analyze signaled messages into constituents that represented separate things or actions in the outside world. The concurrently emerging mental ability to apply imagination or foresight to these constituents allowed humans to speak of things in their absence, to speak of things that had not occurred: to go beyond signals in the here and now to symbols unbounded in time and space (cf. Langer, 1962). Among other human traits, this evolutionary confluence accounted for consciousness and free will.

Bronowski further maintained that abstract concepts derive from concrete ones metaphorically and that algorithm derives from metaphor. That is, the scientist seeks descriptive sentences or formulas that refer to the concrete world in the most efficient and generalized way; the poet and playwright likewise use concrete descriptions to symbolize abstract themes. Both scientific and artistic language attempt to elegantly express the world as it is imagined to be; hence, the interaction between imagery and language is the basis of all art and invention.

This philosophical approach is a profound story that is enjoying considerable current attention. However, we turn now to the extension of Dual Coding Theory to literacy as presented in the rest of the book.

Overview of the Rest of the Book

Chapter 2 chronicles how the fundamentals of dual coding have been of interest throughout intellectual history from ancient times through the Middle Ages, the Renaissance and Reformation, the Enlightenment, the Romantic Period, and the Modern Period through the mid-20th century. This chapter establishes the historical foundations for the theory and investigates the way imagery and verbal processes have interacted in philosophy, rhetoric, literature, psychology, and education. The story tells of conflicts between the verbal and the imaginal, but also between teacher and student, church and state, the divine and the occult.

Chapter 3 presents the Dual Coding Theory of cognition proper. Included are exposition of the basic assumptions of the theory, its basic units, the systematic organization of those units into two different codes, the basic processing operations within and between the codes, and the main functions served by the codes. A general model is also provided, and discussions are related to literacy with clear examples given. Efforts have been made to make the theory approachable and understandable to those unfamiliar with it.

Chapter 4 presents the dual coding analysis of meaning and comprehension. The meaning of language is defined through a series of examples. Three levels of meaning are presented that derive from the operations of the two codes separately and the interconnection between them. The dual coding view of mental models is presented including the joint roles of imagery and grammar. Finally, the roles of direct experience, metaphor, and affect in meaning are discussed. Illustrative examples are provided for those topics as well.

Chapter 5 deals with the crucial role of memory and remembering in text processing. Semantic and episodic memory are distinguished as meaningful long-term memory and memory for specific episodes, respectively. Semantic memory is discussed in terms of the roles of language and imagery in traditional and current views of concepts and concept formation. Episodic memory is discussed in terms of the cooperative activity of language and imagery in representing events. Key research studies of episodic memory in reading are examined and interpreted from a dual coding perspective. Code additivity and the conceptual peg hypothesis, both central aspects of the theory's account of memory, are explained.

Chapter 6 presents the dual coding account of the reading process. The theory is an interactive one, accounting for bottom-up, print-driven processes, and top-down, memory-driven processes. An extended analysis of the reading of a concrete sentence and a similar analysis of an abstract sentence are provided as illustrative examples. Sections detailing the bottom-up processing of features, letters, and words are provided, including a theoretical account of the role of phonetic recoding in reading. Sections dealing with top-down processing follow, including accounts of context effects, coherence, and inferencing. Finally, the theory is compared and contrasted with selected other contemporary theories of the reading process.

Chapter 7 presents the Dual Coding Theory of the writing process. An extended analysis of the composition of a simple example of everyday writing is provided to explain the process. Another cognitive theory of the writing process is compared with the dual coding analysis. Relevant empirical studies using various research methodologies are presented in detail. Anecdotal evidence from noteworthy writers of fiction and nonfiction that is consistent with the theory is presented. Finally, a dual coding analysis of the key rhetorical concept of persona is presented.

Chapter 8 lets the empirical record speak on the application of Dual Coding Theory to literacy education. Numerous references are reviewed, covering a period of more than 30 years of relevant research by a wide variety of researchers. Topics involving reading include decoding or recoding, sight word learning, vocabulary acquisition, spontaneous imagery in text comprehension, using concreteness to enhance comprehension, induced imagery, using pictures with text, evoking interest, verbal-associative learning techniques, and remedial reading. Some controversial issues and challenges to the dual coding approach to reading education are presented. Topics involving education and written composition include the effects of using concrete materials, audience effects, induced imagery, and verbal-associative learning techniques.

This book is addressed to a broad audience meant to include psychologists, educators, teachers, higher education students, and literacy researchers and theorists. Theoretical accounts are often austere because of the frequently abstract nature of the concepts and principles involved. In keeping with Dual Coding Theory's emphasis on concrete experience and language, we have attempted to phrase our explanations in familiar, concrete examples as much as possible. The phrase "for example" is one of the most common phrases in the book; we apologize in advance for our redundancy.

CHAPTER 2

Historical
and
Philosophical Background

In order to construct a history of the role of mental imagery and its relationship to verbal processes in literacy, we must interweave threads from such diverse disciplines as philosophy, rhetoric, literary study, psychology, and education. Our tapestry will still be incomplete, however, because our history in these areas is incomplete and because the concepts of imagery and literacy have been treated differently at different times. Imagery has been a controversial topic, sometimes seen as the divine human faculty, sometimes as mystical and occult—it might be called "the concept from heaven and hell." In particular, the imagistic and the concrete have been in a continuing tension with the verbal and the abstract, reflecting intellectual movements across the ages.

In fact, the historical record reveals a recurrent waxing and waning of the concept of imagery, despite the common intuition that imagery pervades all aspects of our mental lives including what we experience when we read and write. The methods of many literacy practitioners throughout history tended to emphasize either imagery or verbal memory and study methods rather than trying to marry the two. Much of the rest of this book presents a scientific perspective on resolving this puzzle and on more recent ones that could not have been anticipated by the philosophers and educators of earlier times.

Though fragmented, the history of imagery and verbal processes in literacy is nonetheless a fascinating story. We will briefly trace its outline over the centuries.

The Ancient Method of Loci

The philosophical roots of imagery in literacy run deep into the oral period before literacy had become a common practice. In the absence of print, paper, publishing, or convenient writing instruments for recording notes for speaking or listening, memory was crucial to the communication of spoken rhetorical discourse. The ancient connection between memory, mental images, and rhetoric has been well documented (Carruthers, 1990; Yates, 1966).

About 86–82 B.C., an unknown Roman teacher of rhetoric produced a treatise for his students called the *Rhetorica Ad Herennium* (Caplan, 1944). This text records much of what was practiced in oratory in ancient times. The author held that memory was the custodian of all aspects of rhetoric. Memory was held to be of two types: the natural and the artificial. Natural memory was spontaneous and occurred simultaneously with thought. Artificial memory, on the other hand, was gained through disciplined training and allowed the orator to deliver long speeches with unfailing accuracy.

Memory training, or mnemotechnics, employed locations (loci) and images. Loci were real places such as the rooms of a house, a series of shops on a familiar street, or other locations well known to the orator. Images, in turn, could be divided into images of things and images of words. Images of things were of concrete objects that reminded the speaker of topics, whereas images of words were of concrete objects or verbal associates that reminded the speaker of specific words. The whole technique was compared to literacy by analogy. Places were compared to wax tablets or papyrus, images were compared to letters, the arrangement of the images was compared to script, and the delivery of the speech was compared to reading.

Speeches were organized through the loci. Each main point of the speech was associated, in order, with the familiar set of locations. Into each of these locations were placed images representing particular points of the speech. One historical example is provided by the Roman teacher and rhetorician Quintilian (30–96 A.D.). An anchor and a spear were placed in adjacent rooms, presumably to remind the orator of two of the parts of a speech about naval matters and military operations, among other topics (Quintilian, 1921). The organization of the speech was recalled by going from room to room, taking a mental tour of the house, as it were. The images placed in the rooms then brought to mind the specific content, and even key words, of each part of the speech.

The loci method remained the model of rhetoric for centuries. The method was detailed in many particulars: Images were best if vivid and emotionally stunning; the loci should be distinct places, not too dark or too bright; an image of a hand was placed after every fifth locus, possibly so that the organization of the discourse could be traced on the fingers, gesturally. Vestiges of these practices remain today, as when speakers or writers organize their discourse using the transitional phrases, "in the first place . . . in the second place . . . on the other hand," and so on.

The loci method is consistent with some psychological principles that have been supported in modern research: the idea that memory and thought employ traces left by the perception of external objects and events; that the visual sense is mnemonically powerful; or that mental representations, such as images and words, can be mentally exchanged for each other. However, other aspects of the loci method have not found support: Vividness, novelty, and bizarreness have met with mixed results in predicting memory performance, and memory organization may not be as linear and sequential as assumed.

Quintilian noted some of the limitations of loci mnemonics including the difficulty of imaging abstract ideas, particular words, and the overloading of memory if one had to image every word. He therefore stressed verbal rehearsal and rote memorization as well. This alternative proposal has had great impact over time. But apparently no resolution to the implied contrast between the imaginal and verbal codes was proposed.

Imagery in Greek Philosophy, Rhetoric, and Literacy

The loci mnemonic method has been traced back historically to the ancient Greeks, where it is linked to major philosophical traditions (Hermann & Chaffin, 1988). The loci method is generally first attributed to Simonides of Keos (c. 556–468 B.C.), a lyric poet and teacher of rhetoric known for equating the methods of poetry, painting, and mnemonics because all drew on intense mental visualization. Simonides is said to have called painting silent poetry and poetry painting that spoke. Aristotle (384–322 B.C.) was familiar with mnemonics and artificial memory and gave imagery a prominent place in his philosophy of mind. On this point he was at odds with his teacher, Plato (427–347 B.C.), who held mental images to be counterfeits of knowledge. Their disagreement on the role of imagery is central to understanding virtually all ensuing debates about the roles of imagery and language in cognition and literacy. We shall therefore briefly summarize their positions.

Plato, in the *Theaetetus,* proposed that mental images were metaphorically like the impressions of a signet ring on a wax tablet. However, he believed that knowledge did not derive from such sensory perceptions but was innate and changeless, held latent in memory as essences, pure forms, or ideas. Sensory images were mere objects of sensation, whereas ideas were objects of pure reasoning; any image was only an approximation or an instantiation of its idea, an imperfect and flawed copy. Every general term such as *good, beauty, redness, circularity,* and so forth, had a corresponding abstract idea.

Interestingly, Plato compared memory and recollection to literacy and mental imagery. In the *Philebus,* he metaphorically likened the soul to a book. On its pages, an internal scribe wrote discourses of memory, sense impressions, and feelings. Sometimes these experiences were recorded truly, sometimes falsely, accounting for true or false opinions. Also at work in the soul was a painter who came after the scribe and painted images of these discourses, also truly or falsely, depending on their concordance with ideas. For Plato, memory and thought appeared to progress from innate abstractions to language to images. Hence, cognition in literacy would be based in the abstract, with language being closer to the source than imagery.

Aristotle, on the other hand, took a realist philosophical position in his *De Anima* and *Parvia Naturalia*. He held that all knowledge came about from sense impressions, which he also compared metaphorically to impressions on a wax tablet. Knowledge arose from a process of grasping the connections among the particular things experienced. For example, we are led to understand bravery not by thinking of bravery in the abstract, but by holding in mind images of bravery made up of images of brave individuals and brave deeds.

For Aristotle, thought never occurred without a mental image. But as opposed to simple memory of isolated images, thought could organize, through memory search, sets of images by means of associations such as contiguity, similarity, contrast, and order. Thought controlled all the effects of language; words stood for things. For Aristotle, psychology was based in empiricism, and memory and thought appeared to progress from images to constructed abstractions to language. Hence, cognition in literacy would be based in the concrete, with imagery closer to the source than language.

Aristotle's philosophy was congruent with the loci method, although historical evidence suggests that this was not recognized until much later. Mental imagery could be used to organize discourse for delivery and to create both a reasoned and a perceptual effect on the audience. In both his *Poetics* and *Rhetoric,* Aristotle exhorted the use of mental visualization in composing coherent plot and action, in evoking emotions, and in creating clear and rapid realizations in the mind of the audience. Plato, on the other hand, discouraged the use of such methods and also of note-making, because these techniques invoked base forms of knowledge and worked against higher intellect. These contrasting philosophical positions are so basic that most subsequent philosophy related to cognition, rhetoric, and literacy grew out of one or the other.

Imagery in Roman Rhetoric and Literacy

As already noted, both the Roman author of the *Ad Herennium* and Quintilian seemed to have adopted the views of Simonides and Aristotle on the role of mental imagery in rhetorical discourse. Quintilian insisted that education in literacy should interrelate memory, speaking, listening, writing, and reading. Imagery made memory easy; memory made speaking easy; speaking made writing easy; writing made speaking precise; and the reading of written texts for purposes of recitation, paraphrase, or transliteration was associated with hearing the reading voice (Murphy, 1990). Quintilian recommended that students learn their speeches by heart from the same tablets on which they committed them to writing so that they could visualize not just the pages, but individual lines, and at times would be speaking as if reading aloud. Quintilian further admonished his students that it was the feeling and force of imagination that made for eloquence in rhetoric. Another famous Roman orator, Cicero (106–43 B.C.), also was a proponent of these views; his teachings had a great impact on the later views of medieval scholars.

Another first-century Roman, Longinus, took a similar view of the effect of imagery in written discourse as well as oral discourse. In one of the seminal works of literary criticism, *On the Sublime* (Fyfe, 1960), he maintained that images were mental representations that gave birth to speech and writing. He further maintained that imagery had one purpose for the poets and another for the rhetoricians: The purpose of the poetic image was enthrallment whereas the purpose of the rhetorical image was the vivid description of reality. Both, however, persuasively stirred the emotions of an audience. Longinus held that weight, grandeur, and energy in writing were largely produced by the use of images.

An important imagery and memory theorist of this time was St. Augustine (354–430 A.D.). In his *Confessions* he alluded to the distinction between he concrete and the abstract, leaning toward the Platonic view. He found countless sensory images in the chambers of his memory, but he wondered about images for notions such as forgetting and remembering. He could not find an image of God and so concluded that the idea of God must be innate. Augustine was trained in rhetoric and used vivid imagery in his arguments. Shuster (1979) noted that Augustine's central image was of a ladder (also a tree) by means of which one could ascend to a desired height. As we shall see, other writers from Lull to Dante to Darwin used a central image of steps in an ascension.

The classical use of imagery had become firmly established in Roman education by the time Rome and North Africa were sacked in the fifth century. Rhetoric and its memory techniques had spread with Roman schools and Roman garrisons throughout the

Western world. Basic to the Latin educational system were the seven liberal arts (grammar, rhetoric, logic, arithmetic, geometry, music, and astronomy). This Latin educational system was allegorized by Martianus Capella in his curiously titled work *The Marriage of Mercury and Philology* (Stahl, Johnson, & Burge, 1971). The work itself is full of vivid images in which a wedding is taking place and the liberal arts are personified as handmaidens being given to the bride. For example, grammar is portrayed as an old crone with knife and file with which to remove grammatical errors. Rhetoric is portrayed as a tall, beautiful woman wearing a rich dress decorated with the figures of speech and carrying weapons to wound her adversaries. The vividness of the images was in keeping with the admonitions of the *Ad Herennium* that striking, emotionally charged images be used for their memorability.

Like Quintilian, Martianus Capella held that what one wished to remember should be written down. What was fixed by letters on wax or papyrus was also consigned to memory by impression on loci, and memory was fixed by the images as though they were a text to be read. The popularity of *The Marriage of Mercury and Philology* as a guide to rhetoric extended far beyond the time and place in which it was written.

The Imagery Tradition in the Middle Ages

No consistent theory of mental images or imagination existed during the thousand years referred to as the Middle Ages (Bundy, 1927). Divergent, often conflicting, views could be traced back in one form or another to Plato or Aristotle. The medieval scholastics were heavily concerned with abstract, rational, and linguistic inquiry primarily for religious ends. Several noteworthy scholars employed the classical imagery tradition and related it to the philosophical, theological, and rhetorical trends of the times. Chief among these were Albertus Magnus (1193–1280) and his student, Thomas Aquinas (1225–1274).

Albertus Magnus in *De Bono* and Thomas Aquinas in *Summa Theologica* both discussed the imagery techniques of the *Ad Herennium* and determined that they would be useful in remembering abstract and universal theological precepts for sermonizing. Aquinas likened images to sense perceptions or "corporeal similitudes," concrete objects including people that were the basis of reasoning and remembering. Understanding could not occur without images because universals were abstracted from particulars. In this matter, Aquinas appeared to adopt the main points of Aristotle's theory of knowledge and association.

Aquinas' memory system was spread throughout Europe by the Dominican order, to which he belonged, for use by their preachers in composing and delivering sermons and in religious instruction. In contrast, the Franciscan order adopted the memory system of Ramon Lull (1232–1316). Lull's system was based on verbal associations and abstract formulae and derived more from the Platonic tradition. It made use of alphabetic notations for basic concepts and set them down in a combinatory framework such as a ladder or a tree, probably after Augustine. His most famous framework was a set of concentric circles that could be revolved to produce different formulaic combinations of the basic concepts. This system did not achieve popularity until later, but it stands as an example of the historical tension between abstract, verbal views of mind and concrete, imaginal views in the production and reception of spoken and literate discourse. As with the ancients, no theoretical resolution to this tension was apparently proposed during the Middle Ages.

Imagery and the Nature of Literacy in the Middle Ages

Literacy was an exclusive commodity in medieval times, held mostly by clergy. Books were few and inspired awe, but gradually they began to be collected into libraries to be used as reference material by the educated few. At the time of the Norman Conquest in 1066, books were still special objects treasured as shrines and stored with religious relics, but by 1300, King Edward I expected them to be available for perusal whenever he wanted (Clanchy, 1979). The invention of the printing press, the production of relatively inexpensive paper, and the invention of eyeglasses contributed to a broad and secular spread of literacy in the later Middle Ages.

Some medieval scholars became superb readers, despite the probability that they saw less written matter in a year than an ordinary person today does in a week (Chaytor, 1950). Three distinct techniques of reading were known and used for different purposes: silent reading, reading in a murmur, and reading fully aloud. Silent reading and murmur reading were primarily done privately whereas oral reading was done publicly. Silent reading was employed largely for purposes of literal textual analysis, internal recitation, or as a companion to external reproduction in writing, whereas fully oral reading was delivered in a loud voice to listeners in the ancient rhetorical tradition (Petrucci, 1995).

Reading in a murmur was associated with rumination, meditation, and memorization. This was reading for digestion, like a cow chewing its cud. Reading material was memorized through the murmur, mouthing the words as the text was turned over and over in memory. Both Quintilian and Martianus Capella had noted that murmuring accompanied meditation, and even suggested various physical postures and gestures to aid the process. The purpose of this type of reading was to make the text one's own by digesting and re-experiencing it in memory (Carruthers, 1990). Thus, when medieval scholars murmured a text this way, they consumed and memorized it.

Mental imagery was the rationale for ruminative reading. An appropriate mental image was both a likeness and a response to a text as it was reheard, reseen, refelt, and reexperienced. Reading was to be made corporeal, to be literally incorporated into the reader's senses. Reading in this manner was thought of as a dialogue between two memories, for as long as the reader was attentive in murmuring meditation, the other member of the dialogue would be held in mind as if actually present. The voice of that memory would speak through the written letters and evoke images from memory (Carruthers, 1990). The ancient imagery methods of Greece and Rome thereby endured and were perhaps given new purchase by medieval scholastics.

Rumination based in mental imagery was also central to the process of composing a text. Invention or prewriting was a murmuring, gesturing act in which organized memory images stored in various loci were brought together or "recollected" in new arrangements. Invention involved visiting appropriate imaginal places where other images had been stored and selecting among them, not logically, but on the basis of association.

As composers mentally walked the paths of their carefully organized memories, they might be led down interesting sidestreets by these associations. Although some insightful creativity may have occurred as a result, for medievals composing was seen as a memory search for what had been read into memory as well as some personal experience that had also been stored. "New" knowledge came about from taking existing knowledge from its familiar places (i.e., "commonplaces") and rearranging it together in a new place.

Although modern interpretations of this process refer to abstract memory structures and rational thought, for ancients and medievals the composing process was the sensory and emotional activity of putting images together in a deliberately recollected way (Carruthers, 1990; Crowley, 1993). Hence, reading-writing and composing-learning connections were very real in medieval times, and steeped in mental imagery.

The drafting, revising, and polishing aspects of composition were secondary processes. Composing did not necessarily result in writing in ancient and medieval times, but often it did either as a record for those who would be absent from the oration or for purposes of aiding the student composer's memorization. Drafting (i.e., drawing) was tried out mentally or on wax or parchment as an aid to revision and digression. Extensive revision was uncommon and thought to be a sign of weak invention. Rather, glosses were added to the drafts. Such annotated drafts were what students attempted to imprint as a mental image of a page before delivering it orally; this procedure invited digression and commentary without losing one's place (Carruthers, 1990).

Scribes were sometimes employed to do the physical act of writing while the composer dictated. However, by the twelfth and thirteenth centuries, writing had become closely bound to reading. People read and wrote together for commenting and annotating (Petrucci, 1995).

The commentary book resulted from the reading-writing connection. Handwritten texts and later published books came to be printed with the text centered between wide margins. In the margins were printed elaborate glosses written by educated commentators, who explained the organization and meaning of the text for others. Mortimer Adler, in his classic *How to Read a Book* (1940), noted that he adopted his system of reading and study from the medieval commentators, who, he believed, read better than anyone today.

The illuminated manuscript or book was a form of commentary that more directly involved imagery. The margins of these works were frequently illustrated in ways designed to make the pages more memorable than what the words alone could do. The earliest illuminations, colored initials, occurred at the beginning of text sections to mark major memory divisions (the spaces left for the painted letters eventually became paragraph indentations). Later, painted figures, objects, and scenes in the margins served as "word pictures" to cue or illustrate the key words or themes in the accompanying text, somewhat after the method of loci. The artistry was often memorably ornate using beautiful figures such as crowned saints or angels and grotesque figures such as demons or dragons. Visual alphabet books derived from this tradition: A is for apple (picture of an apple), an so on (Yates, 1966). The illustrated book that derived from the imaginal memory tradition led to important changes in literacy instruction in the Renaissance.

The Imagery Tradition in the Renaissance and Reformation

The Renaissance occurred from the fourteenth to the sixteenth centuries and marked the transition from the medieval world to the modern. It was a time of revived interest in classical art, literature, and learning in Europe and beyond. C. S. Lewis (1954, cited in Covino, 1994) referred to this period as a time when high, austere abstractions commingled with earthy, concrete particulars, and the distance between them was much smaller than now. Many of the imagery traditions of the ancients and the medievals found great fruition during this period, and also new opposition.

Imaginative memory systems rose to a high status. Many treatises on memory were written. Not only was imagery elevated to the status of a divine and mystically powerful form of cognition, it was seen as the means to create new secular knowledge and understanding. Some Renaissance scholars believed that through the faculty of imagination and elaborate imaginal memory systems, the entire universe could be understood. This change in attitude toward imagination—from a mnemonic training device to the source of the highest human power for understanding—formed a basic difference between the Middle Ages and the Renaissance (Yates, 1966). This was imagery as the concept from heaven.

A famous medieval literary epic serves as an example of this emerging change. The *Divine Comedy* by Dante Alighieri

(1265–1321), with its emphasis on the faculty of imagination, is often seen as the literary culmination of the Middle Ages and the herald of the Renaissance and Reformation. Familiar with medieval scholastic philosophy, Dante appreciated the value of the rational intellect as well as the senses in understanding all knowledge. His subject in the *Divine Comedy* was the universe, both secular and divine, plus his own personal politico-religious messages.

He structured his epic poem in a rational, unified form based on the mystical numbers 3, 7, 9, and the decimal system. But he also believed that the senses were the avenues to the mind. He combined images of sight, sound, hearing, smell, and touch with fear, anger, horror, joy, love, ecstasy, and other emotions to bring the text vividly to life for the reader. Dante was much concerned with imagery and imagination as a means to understanding abstractions such as good, evil, beauty, prudence, justice, and so on (Bundy, 1927; MacAllister, 1954).

The *Divine Comedy* can also be seen as an elaborate system of loci. The poem is based on locations in hell, purgatory, and heaven in which the descending levels of hell are the ascending levels of heaven in reverse. At each level is a vividly imageable example of the respective vice or virtue that resided there. Hence, the scheme of the universe could be held and traced in memory using the loci method (Yates, 1966).

Perhaps as a result of the spread of literacy during this period, both images and letters were combined in some memory systems. The most elaborate memory system ever devised may be that of Giordano Bruno (1548–1600). Bruno's system included elements of the loci method as well as the more verbal, abstract system of Ramon Lull, mentioned previously. Like Dante, he used mystical numbers. He also employed the stars and planets (as had Dante), the zodiac, the horoscope, phases of the moon, and letters from several alphabets. All these symbols and more were arranged on a set of concentric Lullian wheels that, when revolved in imagination like a giant decoder ring, conjured up combinations to remind the user of all human knowledge and then magically generate new knowledge. The commonplaces of memory became enormously elaborated. However, Bruno's system was associated with the mystical, the magical, and the occult, and he died at the stake in the Inquisition (Covino, 1994; Yates, 1966).

Peter Ramus (1515–1572) introduced a memory system that stressed verbal abstractions and rejected imagery as part of the iconoclasm of the Protestant Reformation. He broke from the Aristotelian and scholastic traditions, eschewing loci and images and instead basing his system on logical reasoning (i.e., dialectic). His aim was to abolish memory as part of rhetoric and to reform education by providing a simpler way of memorizing subject matter. Every subject was arranged in hierarchical, schematic order with the general, inclusive words and categories of the subject presented first. These were then dichotomized into subclassifications, which were in turn dichotomized into subclassifications in an inverted tree structure with binary branchings (literally, ramifications) at each node. Once a subject was set out in such an epitome, it was memorized from the printed pages. Although memorizing such a layout could involve spatial visualization, the content was primarily verbal.

Ramism became very popular in Protestant countries such as England along with the Reformation's general iconoclastic movement against religious icons and other nonverbal representations. Just as statues and images had been torn from cathedrals and smashed, so idolatry of the mind was attacked; this was imagery as the concept from hell. Ramus' influence was perhaps intensified when he was martyred in the St. Bartholomew's Day massacre of French Protestants; in any case, Ramism can still be felt today in the subject organization of most textbooks. This system emphasizes the verbal transmission of information, logical categorization, and linear cognitive processing, and deemphasizes mental imagery (Speidel & Troy, 1985; Yates, 1966).

Memory systems began to decline in influence after the Renaissance and Reformation. Besides the destructive impact of iconoclasm, advances in print technology made books more available and reduced the need for holding organized information in memory. Neoplatonism rose to dominance in philosophy, emphasizing abstract ideas over mental images (Wittrock, 1977). However, imagery came to find a place in literacy education during this time and introduced one of its first changes since the methods of the ancients.

Imagery and Basic Literacy Education From Ancient Times Through the Renaissance and Reformation

Whatever its status in memory systems or as a literary or rhetorical device, mental imagery played little role in basic literacy education in ancient or medieval times. The imagery mnemotechnics taught as a part of the rhetorical tradition were advanced techniques mastered by relatively few. But the Renaissance brought a renewed interest in classic texts and methods. Humanistic education based on classical Latin and Greek ideas of eloquence and wisdom became the norm for the educated elite as well as some of the emerging middle class. The humanistic curriculum revolution was so successful that it lasted well into the 20th century (Grendler, 1989).

The rediscovery of manuscripts by Quintilian and Cicero in the early 1400s formed an important part of this revolution. These ancient scholars had recognized the difference between images for things and images for words. The humanistic education of the Renaissance translated this difference into content and language; "things, not words" became a slogan of humanistic education for centuries. The "things" were the concrete experiences of real life, both in the present and as recorded in classical texts. "Words" proceeded from the things they named; just as clothes were worn for different occasions, words fitted content with eloquence appropriate to it (Grendler, 1989).

The things-words distinction had an influence on teaching materials in literacy. This distinction converged with the traditional use of mental imagery in memory systems, most notably in the work of the great Moravian educator Johan Amos Comenius (Komensky) (1592–1670). He designed materials to teach reading, and his method is generally credited as the first significant revolution to occur in this field.

The method of teaching beginning reading in ancient and medieval times was the spelling or alphabet (ABC) method (hence the term *abecedarian*). Ancient and medieval tutors required their students to learn the alphabet by rote, reciting it over and over, forward and backward. When this was accomplished, students learned syllabaries made up of various vowel-consonant combinations such as *ab, eb, ib, ob, ub* and consonant-vowel combinations such as *bla, ble, bli, blo, blu* in succeedingly larger letter combinations until some words were mastered. Spelling drill preceded pronunciation drill until spellings were well known. Lists of words containing names and places were next memorized to prepare the student to read literature and scripture; these usually took the form of nominalia, vocabularies, and glossaries of terms. With few exceptions, this method was employed well into the 19th century.

Until this time, no other approach was widely accepted, and few were proposed (Huey, 1908; Mathews, 1966; Smith, 1986). The rote memory method was applied to learning grammar and other basic subjects as well.

Visual alphabet books were introduced in medieval times, as noted earlier. Nominalia, vocabularies, and glossaries were sometimes illustrated as well. Whether illustrated or not, they often employed concrete, imagery-evoking vocabulary such as lists of farming tools, parts of the house, the limbs of the body, cooking terms, garden plants, trees, fish, animals, and so forth. In 1562 a literacy practice book by Alexander Lacy was published in England that presented in verse the words of a merchant, who shouted aloud a range of goods that people might buy. Children learned to read and write the occupations, tools, and commodities being advertised. In 1614, a German professor, Lubinus, advocated the use of illustrations in learning words and sentences (Davies, 1974). These medieval innovations are consistent with the view of imagination as a vehicle for understanding as well as memory, and of the Renaissance emphasis upon things before words.

Comenius published the *Orbis Sensualium Pictus* with the subtitle: *A World of Things Obvious to the Senses Drawn in Pictures* in Nuremburg in 1658. The first fully illustrated reading book, it was hugely successful for more than a hundred years, running through editions as late as 1810 in New York (Broudy & Palmer, 1965). It has been heralded as the first significant challenge to the alphabet method, the first attempt at object lesson instruction, and the beginning of the word method in reading (Huey, 1908). The *Orbis* was instrumental in introducing content and meaning to beginning reading, going beyond the rote study of letters. It was an astonishingly original pedagogic method at the time (Yates, 1966).

The *Orbis* stressed sense experience before logical, verbal classification and correlated words with things, reading with writing, Latin with vernacular, and amusement with serious study (Laurie, 1972). The text was topically organized around a unity in nature, which Comenius saw in creation. It referred to the world, the sun, the heavens, eclipses, fire, birds, cattle, the flesh and bowels, cooking, printing, and various other observables. For example, one section of the *Orbis* is called "The Barbers-Shop" and presents a copper cut of Renaissance barbers trimming the hair and beards of customers. Objects in the illustration are numbered. Beside the illustration are parallel columns of Latin and vernacular translation labeling and describing the numbered objects including the barber, hair, beard, scissors, razor, basin, soap, suds, lather, towel, comb, and a penknife for occasional bloodletting (Fig. 2.1).

Each subject had its picture and explanatory sentences; Comenius contended that by matching things with words learning to read could be accomplished without the tedium of the spelling method. However, the *Orbis* also included a picture alphabet that cued phonic associations, for example a picture of a growling dog for the sound of *r* or a picture of a person vigorously exhaling for the sound of *h*. In addition, Comenius suggested that students write down in their notebooks whatever they heard or read to enrich the imagination and assist memory.

The *Orbis* seems to have been directly derived from a memory system similar to Giordono Bruno's that was based on a city of the

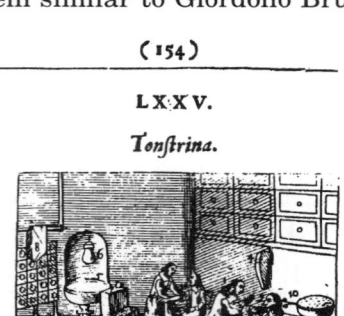

(154)

LXXV.

Tonſtrina.

The Barbers-ſhop.

(155)

The Barber 1.	*Tonſor* 1.
in the Barbers-ſhop 2.	in *Tonſtrinâ* 2.
cutteth off	tondet
the Hair and the Beard	*Crines* & *Barbam*
with a pair of Sizzars 3.	*Forpice* 3.
or ſhaveth with	vel radit
a Razor,	*Novaculâ*,
which he taketh out of	quam è *Thecâ* 4.
his Caſe 4.	depromit;
and he waſheth	& lavat
one over a Baſen 5.	ſuper *Pelvim* 5.
with Sud,	*Lixivio*
running out of	defluente
a Laver, 6.	è *Gutturnio*, 6.
and alſo with Sope, 7.	ut & *Sapone*, 7.
and wipeth him	& tergit
with a Towel, 8.	*Linteo*, 8.
combeth him with	pectit
a Comb, 9.	*Pectine* 9.
and curleth him with	criſpat
a Criſping-Iron 10.	*Calamiſtro* 10.
Sometimes he cutteth a vein with	Interdùm Venam ſecat
a Pen-knife 11.	*Scalpello* 11.
where the blood	ubi Sanguis
ſpirteth out. 12.	propullulat. 12.
The Chirurgion	*Chirurgus*,
cureth Wounds.	curat *Vulnera*.

The   Equi-

FIG. 2.1. *Adjacent pages from a 1659 English version of the* Orbis Sensualium Pictus *illustrating a contemporary barber shop (smudges in the original). Note the catchwords at the bottom of each page. Some old books printed a word at the bottom of a page that began the text of the next page to hold the reader's attention. "Equi-" is short for "Equile," The Stable, the subject of the next section. Facsimile reprint from the series* English Linguistics, 1500–1800, *No. 222, published by the Scolar Press, Ashgate Publishing Ltd, Aldershot, UK, 1970.*

sun, with a sun temple painted with images of the heavens at its center and surrounded by the concentric walls of the city on which were displayed the world of human activity (Yates, 1966). It is very likely that the organization of the book also borrowed from the loci tradition, the ancient distinction of images for things and images for words, the Aristotelian and Renaissance views of imagination as a means of conceptual understanding, and the medieval illuminated manuscript and visual alphabet books, among other sources.

Despite its popularity, the *Orbis* did not replace more purely verbal methods. Hence, the alphabet method was the most widely used method still in colonial America (Johnson, 1904; Mathews, 1966; Smith, 1986). This distinction was perhaps another form of the now longstanding tension between an abstract, verbal emphasis and a concrete, imaginal emphasis in cognition and learning.

Imagery, Philosophy, and the Teaching of Literacy During the Enlightenment

Sometimes called the Age of Reason, the Enlightenment occurred in the late 17th century and the 18th century. The movement championed rationalism, science, natural laws, and universal order. Philosophers of the time held a clockwork conception of the universe, the mechanisms of which could be studied and understood through human reason. The discovery of universal natural laws and their mechanisms, such as Newton's laws of physics, was of great interest.

The imagery tradition in memory persisted during this period although the emphasis on innate reason was somewhat of a reaction against the medieval scholastics and occultists and the Aristotelian tradition. Francis Bacon (1561–1626), Rene Descartes (1596–1650), and Gottfried Leibniz (1646–1716) were influential philosophers of this period who drew on the classical tradition of imagery in memory. They all generally held that imagery in memory would be useful in symbolically organizing and categorizing scientific thought in encyclopedic fashion for use in arriving at true, universal knowledge through reasoning. It was seen as part of a universal language or method, based in concrete reality, that could be applied to the solution of all problems. For example, Leibniz's invention of calculus may have resulted from his search for universal symbols for things (Yates, 1966). The effect of these ideas on imagery in literacy was a continuing emphasis on concrete, meaningful experience as a basis for literacy and learning.

Comenius' *Orbis* may be seen as the early emergence in literacy of a more rational method of Renaissance and classical associations for learning. The literacy learner was introduced to an organized world of practical experience with pictured objects and events associated with their words and sentences. Natural sounds were associated with letters to illustrate their phonic values. Learning and literacy were done according to nature and its order, with an emphasis on observation and the new methods of science.

Other literacy scholars of the Enlightenment period promoted this emphasis. Friedrich Gedike (1754–1803), one of the most influential Prussian educators of his day, was philosophically akin to Comenius. In learning to read the traditional way, spelling out words, the child was working in a manner contrary to natural learning, Gedike reasoned. The more appropriate procedure would be to start with whole, meaningful words and learn letters through seeing them in those words (Mathews, 1966). The words to be used denoted common concrete objects that would be known to children and could be presented or pictured and related to memory images.

Jean Joseph Jacotot (1790–1840), a French scholar and educator, expanded Gedike's ideas of analyzing wholes. Endorsing Gedike's method, he went beyond it, entertaining larger and larger "wholes," consistent with the Enlightenment view of understanding the universe and all its related workings. Jacotot proposed reading an interesting and vivid literary work to students (e.g., a young person's version of the *Odyssey*), perhaps several times, until its entirety had been imaginatively realized. The book was then analyzed section by section into successively smaller units until each sentence and each word had been analyzed for meaning, structure, pronunciation, spelling, etymology, and so on.

However, some German teachers disagreed that the entire book was the appropriate starting place or "whole," and felt that the sentence was a more appropriate and manageable unit. In actual practice, shorter and shorter sentences were used until the single word was again proposed as the "whole." This language unit became the most accepted for reading instruction, and the technique became known as the "normal words" method, later to be called the "sight vocabulary" or "look-and-say" method. The notion of "normal" words employed in this method was that commonplace, concrete objects could be presented or at least pictured for children as the word itself was presented. In this sense, it was similar to Comenius' emphasis on concrete, picturable, and imageable content. This method spread throughout Europe and America in the 1800s, competing with and eventually replacing the alphabet method (Huey, 1908; Mathews, 1966).

Philosophy, Imagination, and Literacy in the Romantic Period

The Romantic period, which occurred approximately from the mid-18th century to the mid-19th century, was marked by a return to nature and belief in the natural innocence of humankind, the rediscovery of the artist as an individual creator, and the exaltation of the senses and emotions over reason and intellect. It formed a reaction against classicism and the mechanistic rationalism of the Enlightenment. There was a transcendental blending of the idealistic and the imaginative.

In Germany, the intellectual force of the age came from the German idealists, particularly Immanuel Kant (1724–1804). Kant, like Plato, held that the true nature of reality is inaccessible to the mind, and that the mind impresses schematic, conceptual order on sensory data. He held that individuals had the mental power to weave together sense perceptions such as images and become the creative interpreters of nature and society. The idealistic transference of authority for knowledge from the external world to the internal world was a liberating force for the romantics.

In France, Jean-Jacques Rousseau (1712–1778) was the most famous philosopher of the spirit of Romanticism. In his book *Emile* (1762), Rousseau decried the early teaching of reading as a scourge on childhood emphasizing extensive sensory experience first. For example, literacy would be learned only after the desire to produce and receive written messages appeared naturally, as when Emile began to receive written invitations from friends to birthday parties. He felt that when such needs emerged naturally in human development, restrictive educational methods would be largely unnecessary.

The ideas of Kant and Rousseau were far-reaching. They influenced Johann Heinrich Pestalozzi (1746–1827), who was also influenced by the Enlightenment view of scientific natural laws. That is, the laws of human nature were the laws of human development. Intellectual development proceeded from the particular to the universal, from the simple to the complex, and from the concrete to the abstract. The key to efficient learning was a set of images, concepts, or sensorimotor patterns that served as internal standards for the learner and from which could be induced abstract principles. These vivid images, prototypes, or intuitions were best provided by immediate, familiar objects. For Pestalozzi, as for Aristotle, concrete sense impression was the foundation of all knowledge (Broudy & Palmer, 1965; Green, 1969).

Pestalozzian education is best known for the object lesson. The use of real objects for observation, verbal description, and verbal definition was central to his teaching method. Along with the use of a concrete object, the object lesson included a discussion that moved from sense impressions to abstract principles, verbal definition, and concept formation. Einstein, one of the great visual thinkers, attended a Pestalozzian school and claimed that it had a profound influence on his thinking (Miller, 1984).

However, the Pestalozzian method as applied to initial literacy learning posed a contradiction between concreteness and simplicity. When it came to words and letters, what was concrete, simple, and particular, as opposed to abstract, complex, and general? Letters seemed simpler than words, and words simpler than sentences, but letters were also more abstract than words, and an act of abstraction was necessary to separate letters or syllables from the concrete perceptual wholes used in spoken or written language.

This problem was recognized by Pestalozzi but was not resolved; his initial literacy teaching seemed to have focused on combining letters into meaningless syllables prior to reading and practicing curves and straight lines prior to writing (Broudy & Palmer, 1965). The appropriate method for teaching basic literacy had by now become a full-blown philosophical and psychological problem. It was an educational manifestation of the unresolved historical tension between the abstract and the verbal and the concrete and the imaginal.

Influential literary figures of the Romantic period provided both theories and some actual evidence regarding the place of imagery and imagination in literacy, particularly composing. William Blake (1757–1827) claimed to experience images so vividly that they invaded perception and bordered on hallucination. He gave them simultaneous expression in his poetry and his engravings and paintings, which he often used on the same page, after the tradition of the medieval illuminated manuscript. Blake's works expressed his mystic inner vision of the whole of human life, in which the forces of energy and imagination battled with the forces of mental and social oppression. Blake saw the supernatural and the divine as inseparable from imagination and often depicted and described divine and supernatural beings in his works in the exacting detail in which he imagined them.

Samuel Taylor Coleridge (1772–1834), the English poet, critic, and metaphysician, was influenced by the Neoplatonists and Kant. Like other philosophical thinkers of his era, he was interested in unity in the universe, wholes, and the ordering of their parts. He also believed in the individual mind's ability to organize sensory experience creatively through imaginative power into transcendent forms that could be understood by reason. The human mind could interpret nature and its laws and see divine order in the world of sense experience; it could also shape and create in light of that insight (Richards, 1950).

Lowes (1927) analyzed Coleridge's composing of two of his most famous poems, *The Rime of the Ancient Mariner* and *Kubla Khan*. Through primary research in Coleridge's extensive notebooks, Lyons showed that Coleridge was a voracious reader and what he read about often appeared in his works. Through extensive mental associations, images and wordings were combined into imaginative new presentations that retained much of their source content and organization.

For example, in the fourth part of *The Rime of the Ancient Mariner,* the mariner finds redemption in feeling love toward multicolored water snakes writhing in a luminescent, becalmed sea. Lyons was able to trace the content of those lines and even specific wordings to seven different books on travel and exploration that Coleridge was known or believed to have read from comments in his notebooks. Several of these books described luminescent plankton or jellyfish, others described sea snakes or other coiling sea creatures. Their reported colors were the same as those used by Coleridge. These natural phenomena were not widely known at the time. Many other passages in both poems were similarly attributed.

This account of Coleridge's composing is somewhat at odds with his public claims. For example, *Kubla Khan* was supposedly inspired by images in a dream. When Coleridge awakened from this vivid dream, he spontaneously and feverishly began to compose the poem and accounted for its brevity by noting that an interruption occurred when someone came to the door and the spell was broken. However, this account is suspect. As documented by Lowes (1927), much of the content and language of this poem can be traced to travel books known to Coleridge. The discovery of an earlier manuscript of the poem suggests that the poem went through more than one draft (Schneider, 1953). Coleridge's own vivid imagery, verbal eloquence, extensive memory, and associative thinking were well known from his own public theories and from the testimony of his colleagues. He appears to have based his theories on his own intertextual, imaginative reading and writing processes and his metaphysical ideas.

Intense, imaginative states of mind approaching trance are not uncommon in the composing episodes of poets and other literary figures (McCabe, 1971; McKellar, 1957). As noted earlier, Aristotle advocated visualization, gesture, and physical action when composing poetry, drama, or rhetoric. Medieval scholars and clerics were known to go into such states when composing, even becoming prostrate and tearful (Carruthers, 1990). However, it may be an exaggeration to claim that these states are mystical events that occur only to great minds. Contemporary theories of psychology that include both imagery and verbal processes may be able to explain them as intensified and creative versions of the composing processes common to all writers. We deal with this issue in chapter 7.

Imagery and Literacy in the Modern Era

The role of imagery in literacy in the era from the mid-19th century well into the 20th century was affected by the continuing influence of science, especially the new scientific studies of psychology and reading, and the introduction of pragmatist philosophy. However, influences from the Enlightenment and Romantic periods, and even ancient and medieval times, could still be seen in literacy education.

As noted, the spelling method was still the most common practice for teaching beginning reading in the early to mid-1800s. This method retained the medieval tradition of letter-by-letter reading that was requisite before the emergence of standardized spelling, punctuation, spacing between words, and other labor-saving print conventions, when every letter stood for a speech sound and writers spelled as they pronounced in an unbroken string of capital letters.

Reading under those conditions was a ponderous, ruminative process that involved much rereading and the assistance of an oral rendering to help fix the text in memory. Reading performance in primary schools into the 19th century was largely an act of public oral interpretation, emphasizing accurate pronunciation, distinctness, voice tone, reading posture, and the other trappings of ancient oral rhetoric.

The influences of Comenius, Jacotot, Rousseau, Pestalozzi, and others succeeded into this period. These influences took the form of a more meaningful approach to literacy education with an emphasis on meaningful words, sentences, and texts as well as letters. Meaning and comprehension became more frequently mentioned in teaching materials, and imagery, both pictorial and mental, played an important part in this emphasis. Reading textbooks became illustrated as a matter of course. Some primers even used pictures instead of words in the lines of print, as in the line, "See the (small picture of a dog) run after the (small picture of a cat)." They were referred to as "object exercises," derived from object lessons. Educational journal articles emphasized the use of words that would evoke distinct images of things or actions that would be readily remembered by young readers. The same discussions suggested arranging words in naturally associated groupings such as *bird, tree, wings, feathers, fly,* and so on (Fries, 1962). Thus, both imagery and verbal associations became inherent parts of meaningful reading instruction.

A teaching method used widely through the late 1920s advocated reading literary stories to children as the first step in literacy instruction because children had already acquired the ability to translate spoken words into meaning and to visualize situations described by them (Elson & Runkel, 1921, cited in McGill-Frazen, 1993). After listening to the story and visualizing it several times, students acted the story out physically. Next, extensively illustrated story books with simplified text were used to teach sentences, words, and phonic elements. Mental, physical, and pictorial imagery were combined with verbal learning in a literary encounter.

The teaching of phonics was influenced similarly. In medieval times, picture alphabets had been introduced to cue letter pronunciations. For example, Comenius in the *Orbis Pictus* had provided pictures to cue the sounds associated with letters. In 1889, a system of synthetic phonics was developed by Rebecca Pollard in America, which stressed the blending of the phonetic sounds of letters as a precursor to reading. This system used environmental sounds and auditory imagery to suggest the phonemes to be associated with letters, as the growling of a dog for the letter *r*, or the sound of a train for the digraph *ch*. Kinesthetic imagery was used to remember the position of the teeth, lips, and tongue for discriminating pronunciations. Her method was controversial, but may have been the first systematic attempt to make the learning of English phonics interesting and appropriate to children (Huey, 1908; Smith, 1986).

European educators also attended to imagery in various modalities in the teaching of literacy. One of these, Rudolf Steiner (1861–1925), began the Waldorf schools in Germany. Steiner placed mental imagery at the center of comprehension and developed a system in which all instruction was devised in a pictorial, imagistic way. Teaching in all content areas relied heavily on the observation of objects, pictures, and the use of concrete, imageable language from which abstract principles were later derived. In literacy instruction, writing was taught before reading through drawing pictures. For example, in learning how to write the letter *M*, students would draw or paint a mouth. The top ridge of the upper lip was then accentuated into the shape of an *M* and associated with the first letter and sound in the word *mouth* (Speidel & Troy, 1985).

Maria Montessori (1907–1952) began the Montessori schools in Italy. She attempted to develop a scientific pedagogy based on systematic sensory observation, the development of mental images, and the abstraction of concepts and principles from concrete experience. Her method of literacy instruction involved a multisensory approach to learning the identification of letters, sounds, and words. Large letters covered with textured materials such as sandpaper were used for visual and tactile stimulation; writing letters with large crayons while producing associated speech sounds was used for auditory and kinesthetic stimulation. Letters were associated with pictures of objects whose name began with a given letter and its pronunciation. Letters were blended into new words and sentences. Montessori stressed that through these exercises the child, upon hearing a word or thinking of a word, would see with the mind's eye the letters in the appropriate arrangement; the auditory, tactile, and kinesthetic images would support the visual image (Speidel & Troy, 1985).

Although he was not directly concerned with literacy education, the developmental theories of Jean Piaget (1896–1980) gave imagery an important place in learning. For Piaget, imagery served both representative functions and, along with language, symbolic functions. Imagery was also used in mental transformations or anticipations necessary for interacting with the environment, solving problems, and developing abstract principles. Such imagery functions would have to play some role in comprehending text, learning from text, and composing text.

The influence of such educational theorists and practitioners during the late 19th century and early 20th century formed another landmark in literacy instruction and in our conception of literacy practices. Reading came more and more to be silent thinking and less and less oral translation. Comprehension, content, and silent reading for meaning gained increasing emphasis. A series of research investigations in the period from 1915 to 1918 indicated that silent reading was superior to oral reading in both speed and comprehension, and an immediate and sweeping reform substituted silent reading methods for oral reading methods (Smith, 1986). Hence, the longstanding historical emphasis on oral reading and subvocalized, ruminative reading for memorization gave way to an increased emphasis on silent reading for comprehension and critical analysis.

Perhaps the most noteworthy advocate of the day for learning to read meaningfully was Edmund Burke Huey (1870–1913), who published *The Psychology and Pedagogy of Reading* in 1908. This book was among the earliest scientific explanations of reading with implications for educational practice. After reviewing the existing psychological studies of reading and the history of reading and reading instruction, Huey concluded that reading and writing should not be primary subjects but should be learned secondarily, as they served the growing needs and interests of the pupils, and that reading should always be for meaning.

Huey's concept of meaning was heavily imbued with both imagery and language. Meaning in reading, he felt, was the affective feeling states and motor attitudes that were fused with the inner utterance of sentences. Apparently, he did not recognize affective or motor imagery as cognition, although contemporary psychological theorists often refer to cognitively represented affective states as a form of imagery (Lang, 1979; Leventhal, 1980; Mandler, 1975). Huey believed that meaning was not visual imagery or words, but that both were used as conscious signs or instruments of meaning. He felt that imagery occurred primarily to phrases or sentences because many individual words, such as conjunctions and prepositions, evoked no imagery except as a part of a larger language unit. Paivio (1971, 1986) commented that images could theoretically be experienced for isolated relational words if they were mentally elaborated through common verbal associations (e.g., *in* elaborated to *in the house* or a similar familiar phrase), but imagery experienced in reading text would typically derive from the context.

Imagery and Literacy in Pragmatist Philosophy and Progressive Education

The advent of pragmatist philosophy and progressive education occurred during the modern era, bringing with it a concern for meaning, imagery, and language as central elements in cognition. Pragmatism was concerned with the act; it held that knowledge and truth derived from action, practice, and experience. Ideas were referred to their consequences for their truth and meaning; the meaning of an idea was the same as its consequences and implications. Cognition was a guide to action through the imaginative reconstruction of experience to confront problems. The work of the pragmatist philosophers George Herbert Mead (1863–1931) and John Dewey (1859–1952) can be seen as complementary. Mead was most concerned with the operation of the mind and its development, whereas Dewey was more concerned with solutions to social and educational problems.

The centrality of imagery and the imagined event in cognition found its most fundamental place in Mead's philosophy. Like other pragmatists, Mead centered on the act. He held that we exist in an action-oriented, ongoing present with an eye to the past and an eye to the future. Mental images remembered from the past and mental images projected into the future were a vehicle for the transaction of reality (Mead, 1934). Mead's positions on imagery have been reviewed and found to be consistent with the role of imagery in current cognitive psychology (Count-van Manen, 1991; Meltzer, 1991).

Mead was also centrally concerned with language. He held that language takes its meaning from the imagined completion of an act. Language incites imaginings of the physical or mental events it signifies and, by extension, the consequences of those events. The one who produces the language and the one who receives it each in imagination completes the acts of which the words are the incipient motions. Meaning arises from the imagined consequences and implications of the acts, whether or not they are ever realized in actuality. Hence, in both oral and written language acts, imagery and imagination are central to meaning in Mead's philosophy (Sadoski, 1992).

John Dewey had a profound influence on the theory and practice of American education. Advocating concrete learning, experimentation, and practice before abstract learning, he believed that imagination was the medium of mental realization and appreciation in every field. He was concerned that learning be based in representative experience and that excessively symbolic learning, such as through formal literacy, could become unrepresentative of experience, mechanical, and meaningless. However, Dewey went beyond the pure sense activity he saw in object lessons and advocated programs of active inquiry and both real and imaginal experimentation to build abstract concepts from concrete experience. According to Dewey (1916), experience, both direct and imagined, was the basis of meaning and learning.

The most direct application of Dewey's principles to literacy occurred in the activity-centered progressive education movement, which was also influenced by Comenius, Rousseau, Pestalozzi, and others. Literacy learning derived from concrete and imageable content that was of concern to learners and stressed the understanding and analysis of meaningful wholes such as words, sentences, and texts. The language experience approach, in which children had a concrete experience and subsequently dictated sentences to be recorded and used as instructional text material, was common in progressive schools. Children often illustrated their texts (Huey, 1908; Smith, 1986). This approach was promoted in America by the progressive educator Francis Parker (1837– 1902), who credited its development to Comenius and Pestalozzi. However, progressive education and the activity approach in literacy learning were never widely practiced and remain controversial (Mathews, 1966).

The Influence of Behaviorism on Imagery and Verbal Processes in Literacy

Although imagery played a role in literacy learning during this period, a more exclusively verbal emphasis supervened. Much of the increasing emphasis on verbal skills came with the advent of behaviorist psychology. Hence, the object lesson and the experience chart became secondary to the flash card, the workbook, and the sequential organization and teaching of verbal skills. Content area learning came to be delivered through textbooks organized around a linear outline of verbal and numerical subheadings, classrooms became dominated by still more verbal explanation, and standardized tests that were heavily reliant on verbal ability became institutionalized.

Behaviorism was introduced into American psychology by John Watson (1878–1958) and others. Watson broke from his teacher, George Herbert Mead, in declaring that internal mental states such as imagery were without functional significance and that thought and memory were predominantly verbal. The approach to psychology taken by the behaviorists was to focus predominantly on verbal stimuli and verbal responses to them while ignoring or rejecting any intervening mental processes. The mental functions that had been attributed to images became the burden of words; habitual overt and covert verbal responses were the vehicle of thought and the definition of meaning. This view of psychology dominated during the first half of the 20th century.

Behaviorism in early literacy education soon prompted attempts to condition appropriate verbal responses to verbal stimuli such as orally responding to words on flash cards or correctly copying sequences of letters from a model. By the 1950s, the popular "Dick and Jane"-style primers were strongly influenced by behaviorist principles. Each page of the primers introduced a small number of new words, which were systematically repeated on that page and at specific intervals throughout the rest of the book. Careful counts were made of the number of uses and reported in the teacher's manuals. Reinforcement was provided through the children's external and internal verbal responses. Additional practice with the words was provided in ancillary flashcards and workbooks. Systematic introduction of vocabulary progressed through Grade 6.

However, the teaching method proposed was eclectic and not entirely behaviorist. For example, the "Dick and Jane" teachers' manuals also called for stimulation of mental imagery in various modalities and integration of text and pictures for the purpose of forming vivid, interpretive images (Gray, Artley, Arbuthnot, & Gray, 1951). However, in practice this often received little emphasis.

Other reading systems of the day emphasized attention to vivid, imaginative realization only after spelling patterns and word recognition were mastered (Fries, 1962). Materials used in this system had no illustrations. For a time, imagery was neglected in the scientific study of psychology and the heavily verbal literacy instruction that was influenced by it.

Imagery in Modern Literature

Literary figures in the early 20th century took profound interest in imagery. Imagist poets such as Ezra Pound, Amy Lowell, and William Carlos Williams (circa 1912–1917) concentrated on the writer's response to a visual object or scene by using vivid descriptions, metaphors, and the ironic juxtaposition of diverse objects. Their poems were often brief, concentrated snapshots, which evoked nature after the style of the Japanese haiku. Imagism as a literary movement was short-lived, but it is credited with beginning modern poetry. Virtually every poet up to the present has been influenced by the imagists and employs vivid images that are juxtaposed without specifying their relationship (Abrams, 1993).

The school of literary thought known as the New Criticism stressed imagery as an essential element in literature and a major clue to symbolism, meaning, structure, and effect. This school of thought influenced literary criticism and education well into the 20th century. T. S. Eliot (1960) concluded that the only way to express emotion in poetry was find an "objective correlative," a set of concrete objects, situations, or events that evoked the emotion in the reader without directly stating that emotion. The poet C. Day Lewis (1948) contended that a poetic image is a picture made out of words and that a poem may itself be an image composed from a multiplicity of images. Caroline Spurgeon, in *Shakespeare's Imagery and What It Tells Us* (1935), produced frequency counts of various types of imagery used in Shakespeare. She pointed out image clusters that provided the atmosphere, motif, or central theme of each play, such as animal imagery in *King Lear* or images of light as manifested by the sun, moon, stars, and fire in *Romeo and Juliet*. Paivio (1983) discussed the effects of imagery in literature in terms of Dual Coding Theory. We return to the subject of imagery in literary response in later chapters.

We end this historical review in the mid-20th century. The resurgence of cognitive psychology and the role of imagery and verbal processes in theories of psychology and literacy since that time will be the subject of the next several chapters. Dual Coding Theory, the subject of chapter 3, is prominent among those theories. From a historical perspective, this theory can be seen as an important step toward resolving the longstanding and at times destructive tension between imaginal and verbal processes in cognition and literacy that has been evident in the record since ancient times.

Summary

Even though the tapestry is incomplete, it is clear that mental imagery has played a powerful role in literacy throughout history. Ancient philosophers such as Aristotle believed that all cognition involved imagery and therefore gave imagery a prominent place in composing or comprehending discourse. Others, such as Plato, were more cautious of imagery but still compared cognition to literacy, at least metaphorically. Mental imagery was central to composing in the loci method of the ancient and medieval rhetoricians. It was central to reading in the ruminative practices of the medieval scholastics. Renaissance scholars and educators gave imagination a central place in their world view and introduced pictorial imagery and emphasized concreteness in literacy learning. Romantic philosophers, educators, and literary figures emphasized natural, concrete, meaningful experiences and imaginative processes in all cognitive activity including composing and reading. Modern philosophers, educators, and scientists have theorized that imagery is important in cognition and literacy. Literary scholars during every historical period have seen imagery as central to both the composing of literature and reader response to literature.

Mental imagery and verbal processes have often been at odds in philosophy, psychology, rhetoric, and education. The prominence of either concrete experience or verbalized abstraction has been somewhat competitive, and a historical tension has evolved between them. While Plato stressed the abstract and verbal, Aristotle stressed the concrete and imaginal. Aquinas stressed imagery and corporeal similitudes, whereas Lull stressed verbal association and abstract formulae. Comenius stressed the concrete and pictorial while Ramus stressed verbal dialectic. Imagery was extolled by Renaissance and Romantic figures but denounced by iconoclasts and behaviorists. The alphabet method vied with the use of concrete words and objects as a vehicle for basic literacy. Pestalozzian education encountered the dilemma between the abstract and the concrete and the simple and the complex in structuring literacy education. Pragmatism and the experience approach of the progressive educators vied with behaviorism's exclusive concern with verbal learning and behavior. This polarity persists today, although promising theoretical efforts that include both imaginal and verbal processes in cognition and literacy have been introduced. Dual Coding Theory is such a theory.

CHAPTER 3

Dual Coding
in Literacy

The workings of the mind while reading and composing have been of interest since ancient times, and the roles played by mental imagery and language have long been sources of fascination, but the objective rigor provided by the scientific study of cognition is a relatively recent development. The theory of cognition in literacy presented in this chapter is a specific application of a scientific theory of general cognition, Dual Coding Theory (DCT).

Here we introduce DCT as it applies to literacy, referring to the broader aspects of the theory as appropriate. We first present an overview of the basic assumptions of the theory, and then we elaborate them in sections on (a) the theory's structural units; (b) their organization and interconnections; (c) processing operations, or the activation of the units; and (d) functions, or the purposes served by the units and processes. Subsequent chapters provide more specific theoretical accounts of meaning and comprehension, memory for text, the reading process, the composing process, and other topics related to literacy.

OVERVIEW: BASIC ASSUMPTIONS OF DCT

The most basic assumption of DCT is that cognition in reading and writing consists of the activity of two separate coding systems of mental representation, one system specialized for language and one system specialized for dealing with nonverbal objects and events. Mental representations refer to internal forms of information used in memory. Coding refers to the ways the external world is captured in those internal forms. The activation of representations within and between the systems is referred to as processing.

Through experience, we develop a remarkable ability to understand and use language, based on a specialized linguistic code, as well as a remarkable ability to retain, manipulate, and transform the world around us mentally using a nonverbal code of mental images. In DCT, the linguistic coding system is referred to simply as the verbal system; the nonverbal coding system is often referred to as the imagery system because its main functions include the analysis of external scenes and the generation of internal mental images.

These systems are organized hierarchically. The organization is sequential in the verbal system and nonsequential (e.g., spatial) in the nonverbal system, resulting in characteristically different constraints on processing. The structuring and processing of these mental representations, or encodings, is the basis of all cognition in this theory.

Other contemporary theories of cognition assume that mental representations are abstract and amodal structures, usually called *propositions* or *schemata,* which are governed and coordinated by equally abstract monitoring mechanisms and executive processes. Language and imagery are presumably generated from this abstract base, and no functional distinction is made between them. DCT does not presuppose such abstract mechanisms. Instead, all meaning and knowledge is explained through direct interconnections between the modality-specific mental representations in the two systems, so that we can switch from one form of representation to another, or recode, both within a system (e.g., speech to writing) or between systems (e.g., language to mental images). Any monitoring functions occur within and between the systems themselves, not from a separate source. For example, we can regulate our cognitive behavior through self-regulatory inner speech and/or through imagining alternative scenarios and different points of view.

STRUCTURAL UNITS

Codes and Modes

DCT shares the common assumption in psychology that there is a continuity between perception and memory. External experiences are perceived through the stimulation of our various sense modalities, including the visual, auditory, haptic, gustatory, and olfactory sense modalities. Patterns for motor responses in various modalities such as speech articulation or writing must also be stored as part of our cognitive representations, so that our modalities can be described as sensorimotor.

In DCT, all of our mental representations retain some of the original, concrete qualities of the external experiences from which they derive, so that representational structures and processes are modality-specific rather than amodal. This implies that our mental encodings themselves are concrete rather than abstract although they can easily deal with abstract information and concepts such as language symbols, charts, or diagrams.

Let us elaborate on this point. The modality-specific character of mental representations is maintained across the two codes. This means that for the visual sensory modality, for example, there can be both verbal and nonverbal encodings. A visual verbal encoding might be a mental representation of a visual letter form such as **C** or visual word form such as **cup.** A nonverbal visual encoding might be a mental representation of an object or scene such as a coffee cup or a table setting with a cup and saucer.

In the auditory modality, an auditory verbal encoding might be a phoneme such as /k/ or word pronunciation such as /kup/. A nonverbal auditory encoding might be an environmental sound such as the clinking of cups on saucers or the sound of coffee pouring into a cup.

A haptic verbal encoding might be the sensation arising from actively touching the raised dots in Braille or the motor activity of handwriting, say, writing the cursive form of *cup*. A haptic nonverbal encoding might be the heft, smoothness, and warmth of a cup of coffee.

There are no verbal representations in the chemical (olfactory and gustatory) sensory modalities, although we have nonverbal representations in these modalities. That is, we do not have language forms that come directly from smells or tastes, but we can experience smells and tastes and encode them as olfactory and gustatory images. For example, we can have images of the aroma and flavor of a good cup of coffee, but these representations are not linguistic in nature. Similarly, various affective experiences can be imaged, but language is not constructed from affective representations. Table 3.1 provides a diagram of the orthogonal relationship of mental codes and sense modalities.

These mental "codes and modes" are somewhat modular. That is, they form separate subsystems whose units are structured differently and can function independently. We can recall a visual image of a cup of coffee without necessarily recalling its aroma, flavor, warmth, word spelling (*c-u-p*), pronunciation (/*kup*/), or the motor activity used to write *cup*, although these may all have close connections in memory.

These subsystems are localized in different parts of the brain. Just what neurological form they may take is a fascinating subject in itself about which much is being learned. (See Paivio, 1986, chap. 11, and Paivio, 1991b, for a review of neuropsychological evidence for codes and modes and other aspects of DCT; for direct neu-

TABLE 3.1. *Diagram showing the orthogonal relationship between mental codes and sense modalities as theorized in DCT. The examples within the diagram are types of modality-specific representations in each subsystem. Adapted from Paivio (1986, p. 57). Reprinted by permission of Oxford University Press.*

	Mental Codes	
Sense Modality	*Verbal*	*Nonverbal*
Visual	Visual language(writing)	Visual objects
Auditory	Auditory language (speech)	Environmental sounds
Haptic	Braille, handwriting	"Feel" of objects
Gustatory	—	Taste memories
Olfactory	—	Smell memories

ropsychological evidence supporting the theory in reading, see Holcomb, Kounios, Anderson, & West, 1999; Kounios & Holcomb, 1994; West, O'Rourke, & Holcomb, 1998.)

Everyday evidence for modality specificity can be seen in the phenomenon of modality-specific interference. Attempting to perform two different tasks in one modality causes a disruption in one or both of the tasks, but performing two tasks in separate modalities does not interfere. For example, we can listen to music (auditory task) while exercising (motor task) without interference; in fact, the two may harmonize. But it is difficult to listen to two conversations simultaneously (two auditory tasks); we must shuttle back and forth between the two (the "cocktail-party effect"). Similarly, silent reading (visual task) may be disrupted by experiencing related visual images (visual task) at the same time. A qualification here is the degree of activity—barely perceptible imagery will probably not cause a ripple in the reading process, but intense visualization may interfere until rereading is necessary.

Basic Units: Logogens and Imagens

Cognitive theories usually specify basic units or "building blocks" of cognition. These units in DCT are not abstractions without concrete form; they are assumed to have some physical form in neural structures and pathways. The basic representational units in the verbal system are called *logogens,* a concept introduced by Morton to deal with visual word recognition but later expanded by him to include other modalities as well (Morton, 1979). Analogously, the basic representational units in the nonverbal system are called *imagens.*

These terms are theoretical shorthand or jargon used for convenience to distinguish between the underlying neurological representations and their conscious expression in language and imagery. Logogens and imagens can also be otherwise described: Logogens are alternatively called verbal representations, verbal encodings, mental language, and inner speech; imagens are alternatively called nonverbal representations, nonverbal encodings, mental images, or imagery. We often use these more common alternatives in the book. Where theoretical precision is required, however, the technical terms are useful, so we next define them. (For a fuller discussion of logogens and other representational concepts frequently used in cognitive psychology, see Paivio, 1986, pp. 22–32.)

The morpheme *logo-* is Greek for word, speech or discourse, and the morpheme *imago-* for imitation, copy, or image; the morpheme *-gen* means that which generates. Hence, logogens are language generators and imagens are image generators; both are also useful in recognition. More specifically, logogens are modality-specific (visual, auditory, etc.) units in the verbal system that are activated by external stimuli or internally by other, previously activated mental representations. Likewise, imagens are modality-specific units in the nonverbal system that are activated by external stimuli or internally by other, previously activated mental representations.

In DCT, logogens and imagens are not limited to any particular size, although some empirical evidence suggests that logogens are word-like and imagens are object- or scene-like. Logogens in the visual modality refer to whatever functions in visual perception as a language unit; that is, something that has been learned by someone as a separate unit of visible language. Thus, visual logogens may consist of familiar written units with consistent features such as letters, numbers, or punctuation marks (e.g., a straight line and a loop in different orientations can form a *p, q, d,* or *b*); common subword combinations of letters such as affixes; whole written words; and familiar written phrases. Logogens in the auditory modality could refer to phonemes, syllables, word pronunciations, familiar spoken phrases, and even memorized extended passages such as poems or prayers, which are stored (represented) as wholes for the person who can recite them.

Logogens of different sizes may not have equal status because some sizes are more familiar than others (e.g., words). But by assuming that logogens vary in size, the theory does not privilege any particular language unit. This is necessary in explaining the reading and writing processes because the attention of the reader or writer may shift among features, graphemes, phonemes, words, punctuation, phrases, and larger familiar units from moment to moment as the situation requires.

Likewise, imagens are not limited to any particular size, although familiar objects and scenes may be the most common units. An image of a face can be decomposed into images of the eyes, a nose, a mouth, and so on. Or an image of a face can be part of a larger image of a head, which is part of a still larger image of a body. Even an image of an eye can be decomposed into the iris, pupil, white, eyelid, and eyelash. In imagery, we can switch rapidly among these parts and wholes without much regard to size.

The maximum size of logogens and imagens in the visual modality is an empirical question, but there seem to be some limits, at least in our everyday experience. These imaginal size constraints seem to reflect visual perception in the physical world. For example, if we attempt to read a newspaper headline from an increasing distance, most of the individual features of the letters soon become indistinct but the overall shapes of the words are still recognizable. That is, the overall configuration of words may help in their recognition as well as the features and arrangements of their parts.

Likewise, simple introspection suggests that we can experience clear, detailed visual images of words (i.e., activate visual word logogens) up to three or four letters in length. If there are more letters, we may (a) mentally scan the letter sequence; (b) experience the word image as an overall shape with few distinct features, as from a distance; or (c) pronounce or spell the word while imaging word parts sequentially. For example, the word *cup* might be imaged in full featural detail, but longer words or familiar phrases pose more difficulty.

Nonverbal mental imagery apparently reflects similar limitations. Visual images seem like "grainy" photos with much out of focus; detail is lost with imagined distance; and they fade rapidly, needing to be "rejuvenated," or reactivated, frequently. For example, imagine a pirate with a wooden leg. Was the pirate wearing a hat? Logically, the pirate either wore a hat or did not. However, because our focus was on the wooden leg, we may not have clearly envisioned the head and must mentally scan upward, take a wider angle, or refabricate the image to clearly "see." Mental representations in other modalities are similarly imperfect, and our refabrications and rejuvenations can introduce elaboration, distortion, and interpolation.

Experienced readers develop large stores of logogens. There may be multiple representations for the same phenomenon. For example, our visual logogens for the letter *A* may be as many forms of that letter as we have learned (e.g., **A, a,** *a*). Thus, we may have different logogens for uppercase and lowercase letters, script and block formats, and various other formats and fonts as well as familiar handwritings. Unfamiliar or barely legible handwriting is hard to read because we lack the logogens for it; that is, we have not encountered such forms with sufficient consistency to have encoded them.

Despite the diversity of functionally equivalent representations, when asked to think of a language unit of any size, we often think of a typical one. If asked to think of the letter *A,* people often report visualizing a block letter as opposed to a script letter or an italic letter. This suggests that we operate for efficiency around prototypical exemplars. A "good" exemplar acts as a symbol of a larger group of similar instances; it serves as the central tendency in a multidimensional distribution. The other members of that distribution are variants that have been experienced or are interpolated. In this way we can recognize atypical instances, such as a letter in Old English. However, it may be difficult for us to write such letters because we are not used to the motor formation of their complex featural details. This not only suggests the experience-based nature of these encodings, but demonstrates as well that we have logogens in different modalities for reading (visual) and writing (haptic).

Logogens for auditory units such as words, syllables, or phonemes are similarly formed and stored. These units are derived from speech through perceptual similarity and discrimination, and auditory logogens are thereby encoded. In producing speech, the voice and articulatory apparatus finds a way to produce syllables and phonemes and articulatory-motor logogens are thereby formed. Some theories suggest that phoneme units are perceived by reproducing them in this motor fashion (Liberman & Mattingly, 1985). In DCT, speech logogens are not encoded in an abstract, amodal code, but as concrete encodings in the auditory and articulatory-motor modalities.

The idea that we have separate, multiple, modality-specific logogens accommodates the fact that literate people can recognize variations of the same written and spoken forms and relate them to each other in flexible, adaptive ways. For example, we can recall various forms of the grapheme *A* (**A, a,** *a*) without necessarily recalling any of the phonemes typically associated with them (e.g., long sound, short sound, schwa, r-controlled, l-controlled). Likewise, we can recall phonemes without recalling any of the graphemes that can be associated with them. That is, representational separateness allows us to associate various graphemes and phonemes in flexible and irregular ways consistent with a language like English.

In contrast, one need not be literate, or even know how to speak, to develop a large store of imagens. Nonverbal representations in all modalities are a part of memory that is not necessarily connected to language, although language commonly evokes imagery, and vice versa, in speakers, signers, and literates. Presumably, infants rapidly accumulate large stores of nonverbal representations to which language is later meaningfully associated. As with logogens, imagens are assumed to derive from sensory experience in various modalities.

Intra-Unit Organization and Processing Constraints

DCT not only assumes that the internal structure of logogens and imagens differs due to the experiences that gave rise to them, but further, that those differences in structure determine how logogens and imagens are processed. Both forms of within-unit organization are generally hierarchical, consisting of smaller components within larger ones, but the hierarchies are qualitatively different. Logogens have a more sequential hierarchy, and imagens have a more synchronous hierarchy.

Logogens. The internal sequences of logogens derive from the serial nature of verbal language. Speech utterances vibrate the air in a continuous, nonarbitrary sequence. Phonemes in certain sequences combine into spoken syllables, syllables in certain sequences combine into spoken words, words in certain sequences into spoken phrases, and so on. Some phonemes are sequential combinations within themselves, such as diphthongs where one vowel sound glides into another (e.g., /oi/ in *boy*). We must articulate our vocal apparatus in particular sequences to produce phonemes and longer utterances. We must manipulate our fingers in particular motor sequences to write. Likewise, because alphabetic writing maps onto speech, letters are arranged one after another in certain sequences into printed words, sentences, and texts. The familiar sequences in which language units are perceived and learned result in strong sequential constraints in their representation in memory.

The sequential constraints on the processing of logogens can be seen in everyday experience. For example, it is typically easier to spell a long word forward than backward from memory. This is because a left to right sequence is far more familiar in our experience, and the structure of the logogen derives from that experience. (The principle is reversed in languages that are read and written right to left.) And it is easier to complete the familiar syntactic sequences "Once upon a . . . " or "Two and two is . . . " than to complete "It befell to . . . " or "Fourteen times fourteen is . . . ". The former two sequences have a familiar syntactic unity that prompts immediate closure. The latter two sequences are not usually familiar enough to be considered unitary; their completion calls for activation of more logogens and more extended processing.

Imagens. Imagens have a different internal organization that derives from the nature of nonverbal experience. This organization is more synchronous, at least in the case of visual imagens. Synchronous means that all the information is available at one time: When we see a familiar room, much information is available synchronously, and our imagens retain this overall organization including the location of windows and doors, pieces of furniture, and so on. Similarly, an imagen of a familiar face represents the arrangement of the eyes, nose, mouth, and other facial features.

Mentally, these organizations take the form of nested sets. Each nested part can be separately imaged as a set, and the whole set may be nested in a still larger imaginal set, as a face as part of a head, and a head as part of a body. However, the simultaneous *availability* of this information does not imply that all this information can be *accessed* and *processed* simultaneously. That is, we can visualize many features of a well-known face all at once, but we cannot image both profiles at the same time, nor a room from each end at the same time. Visual perspective is a limitation in real life experience that seems to be retained in mental representations.

Unlike verbal structures, the processing of information in synchronous nonverbal structures (both perceptual and imaginal) is free from sequential constraints. We can mentally scan across a familiar face or room with equal dexterity from one side to the other, or from top to bottom or around about. When asked to describe a familiar scene, people often describe it from left to right, but this may be a habit learned through literacy. Asking people to describe the scene from right to left produces the same results with none of the difficulty experienced in spelling their own name backwards.

We have discussed the nature of logogens and imagens in DCT in some detail. Their structure and processing imply each other: structure derives from perceptual processing and behavioral usage, and, as it develops, structure constrains processing. We now turn to the way these units are arranged into separate systems and the connections between the systems.

THE ORGANIZATION AND INTERCONNECTIONS OF THE VERBAL AND IMAGERY SYSTEMS

Figure 3.1 presents a general model of DCT including the internal organizations of the two systems, connections within and between the systems, and their input and output structures. Three levels of processing are implied in the model including representational processing, referential processing, and associative processing. These organizations and processes are introduced and defined here and then discussed in more detail in following sections of the chapter.

The top of the model indicates verbal and nonverbal stimuli in the environment that are detected by our sensory systems. The representational connections between sensory detection and the activation of logogens or imagens indicate representational processing, or the direct activation of logogens or imagens complete with their internal processing constraints.

The verbal system is modeled as a network of logogens organized in sequential, hierarchical arrangements. By comparison, the nonverbal system is modeled as sets of imagens organized in overlapping and nested (hierarchical) arrangements.

Activity between systems (logogens to imagens or imagens to logogens) is carried out through referential connections and is called referential processing. Activity within a system (connections between logogens and logogens, or between imagens and imagens) is carried out through associative connections and is called associative processing.

The systems are theorized as separate and capable of operating independently (activity in one but not the other), in parallel (separate activity in both at the same time), or in a connected way. Finally, the model shows that the two systems are connected to sensory output systems that produce verbal and nonverbal responses.

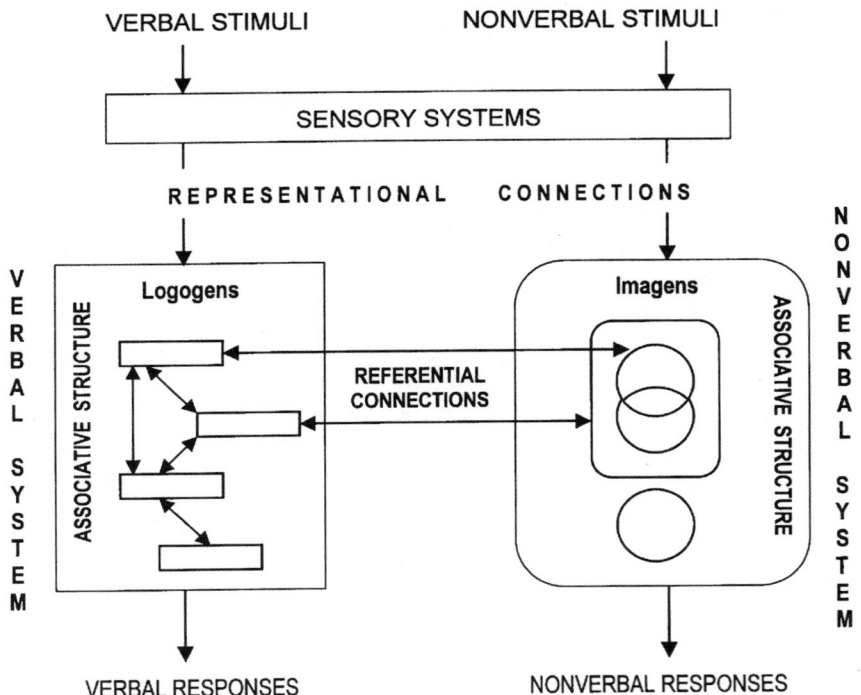

FIG. 3.1. *General model of DCT showing the verbal and nonverbal systems including representational units and their referential (between system) and associative (within system) interconnections as well as connections to input and output systems. From Paivio (1986, p. 67). Reprinted by permission of Oxford University Press.*

The independent or interconnected operations of the systems can be seen in everyday experience. That is, we can have mental images without reading, or we can read without experiencing mental images, but imaginal activity as part of reading is common and a matter of degree. We can even "read" and experience unrelated mental images at the same time, in parallel. Certainly, any of us who have been students can remember reading a textbook only to find that at the end of a page we could remember verbalizing the language but our minds had wandered elsewhere, experiencing completely unrelated images!

The points of contact for the interconnections between the systems (referential connections in Fig. 3.1) are logogens and imagens. Imaging to words or naming objects or pictures are simple examples. However, the theory implies that an activated logogen might not activate any imagen, or an activated imagen might not activate any logogen. Units with no referential connections in Fig. 3.1 represent logogens of highly abstract language and "nameless" imagens, respectively. For example, many words do not bring any referent image to mind. This is the case with function words such as *the* or *of,* or with highly abstract content words. Likewise, some images are difficult to express in language and remain "nameless."

The connections within the systems form the associative structures in Fig. 3.1. Networks of organized vocabulary items or scenes of associated objects are simple examples. The organization of the units within each system is characteristically different in ways analogous to the respective internal organizations of logogens and imagens as discussed previously, and can be seen as an extension of that organization. Associative processing can be viewed as spreading activation within a system and referential processing as spreading activation between the systems, respectively. This spreading activation fans out along connecting pathways as determined by the personal history of the individual and contextual factors. The frequency and recency of prior activation and the number and strength of competing connections (i.e., prior knowledge) affect the outcomes of the spreading activation through excitation and inhibition. Because all mental representations in DCT are specific to a sense modality, spreading activation may be across modes as well as across codes.

We next discuss the organization of logogens in the verbal system and the organization of imagens in the nonverbal system. This is followed by discussion of the three basic processing operations defined and some higher order processing operations.

The Organization of the Verbal System

We previously described how, theoretically, logogens are arranged in sequential, hierarchical structures so that logogens of smaller language units can be synthesized into larger language units or larger units can be analyzed into smaller units. Recall also that the logogens are theoretically unitary entities, so that a word can be recognized as a whole without us necessarily having to analyze every grapheme or phoneme that comprises it. Likewise, familiar phrases such as *rock 'n' roll, french fries,* or *once upon a time* may have a phrasal unity that can be recognized holistically, and so on. Although these units could be mentally synthesized from, or analyzed into, their separate parts, logogens at all levels of the hierarchy retain some degree of discrete unity.

This discrete unity is important in the verbal system to account for the great variety of associations with other units in the system necessary for literacy. For example, the digraph *ea* is associated with various phonemes in *hear, heart, head, heard, bear, each, great, create, react, theater,* and so on. Conversely, the phoneme /sh/ is associated with numerous graphemes as in *shirt, sugar, chute, action, issue, special, conscious, mansion, schwa, anxious,* or *ocean.* Lexicographers estimate that letter and letter combinations express an average of five sounds apiece in English (Bryant, 1993).

On the lexical level, associations between words form our familiar networks of associated vocabulary as reflected in free-association tests (e.g., black–white; arm–leg; table–chair). However, knowledge of a word or phrase does not imply that its family of derivations is necessarily known or associated. It may take considerable linguistic sophistication to realize that *health* derives from *heal* or *vicious* derives from *vice,* for example. We can have linguistically incorrect associations as when we mispronounce a spelling, misspell a pronunciation, or mistake a word or phrase meaning. Logogens and their associations derive from all kinds of formal and informal experience with language, and while this allows for error, it also allows for flexibility and creativity.

Such flexibility and creativity is reflected in the development of an extensive verbal-associative network, labeled the associative structure in Fig. 3.1. Logogens are associated with each other largely as a consequence of how often they are experienced or used together, and, to some extent independently, by their similarity to each other. Examples relevant to reading include familiar grapheme-phoneme combinations of the rime-onset kind (*-at, bat, cat, fat, hat, mat, pat*), familiar combinations of free and bound morphemes (*safe, unsafe, safety, safeguard*), synonyms and antonyms (*over, under; above, below*), subordinates (*container, cup*), superordinates (*dog, animal*), coordinates (*dog, cat*), prepositional phrase sets (e.g., *out of sight, out of mind*), convergent productions (e.g., *female-theater-actress*), and myriad other forms of verbal association.

Syntactic productivity includes a substantial component based on associative verbal connections. Habitual phrases and idiomatic expressions are common examples. Syntactic sequences characterize languages, such as the subject-verb-object sequence in English. Associative connections may also exert an influence as in generalizing by analogy from known syntactic constructions to new ones, as in adding modifiers. Although associative connections may not explain all syntactic behavior, they are implicated (Brazil, 1995).

These verbal associations go far beyond learning graphemephoneme generalizations and vocabulary or sentence building. Verbal associations are probabilistic and form the basis of linguistic usage, prediction, and inference. Redundancy in language involves probabilistic associations built from experience; the occurrence of one letter or letter combination may alter the probable set of letters likely to follow in our reading and writing experience just as the occurrence of a word or phrase alters the probability of words or phrases to follow.

The Organization of the Nonverbal System

The continuous nature of our nonverbal experiences with the world is retained in the organization of imagens in the imagery system. Imagens tend to be nested within other imagens in a hierarchical arrangement of associations, labeled the associative structure in Fig. 3. 1. We tend to generate mental images as part of a hierarchical environment, or context. We can imagine a cup as part of a place setting, as part of a table set for a meal, as part of a dining room, and so on. Eyes are continuous with faces, which are continuous with bodies, which move in continuous surroundings.

However, imagens can be discontinuous and discrete as well. We can shift from one scene to a completely different one immediately, as from home to work or from the earth to the moon. And some images tend to remain static, especially if our experiences with them come from static pictures. For example, those who have never seen the Taj Mahal in person tend to have a static, frontal image of it, probably derived from photographs. It is difficult to image detailed views of it from above, the sides, or the rear in this case. But more familiar scenes yield more readily to imagery from different perspectives. When asked the number of windows in their home, people often report taking a mental tour, a procedure reminiscent of the ancient loci method. Those who have never seen the Great Pyramid of Giza can still mentally adjust perspectives to any side or above because of experiences with other pyramid shapes and familiarity with their symmetry. The more perspectives we have for a given figure or scene, the more readily we can infer or interpolate those we have not.

The experience of imagery can take the form of a sequence. That is, imagery can be sequential as in scanning a static image; imagining a dynamic sequence of events such as entering a building, walking down a corridor, and going into a room; or imagining a continuous event such as a fireworks burst. The difference between verbal sequences and imaginal sequences is that verbal sequences are more constrained whereas imaginal sequences are less constrained. With images, it is as easy to imagine leaving a room, walking down a corridor, and exiting a building as the reverse sequence. It is much harder to say a familiar proverb backwards; we must work hard against the grain of the language.

We can also have organized, associated imagens in other modalities than the visual. As we have an "inner eye," so we have an "inner ear." We can imagine the clinking of coffee cups, or the sound of waves breaking on the shore, or the horns of taxis on city streets. These sounds can be associated in contextual hierarchies as in imagining the combined sound of a full orchestra opening Beethoven's Fifth Symphony or imagining the voice of a sports announcer over the background of a cheering crowd. Likewise, we can imagine the warmth, aroma, and flavor of a good cup of coffee; the touch of sandpaper contrasted with the touch of silk; the smell of perfume; the taste of chocolate. However, these images are typically less clear and vivid than visual imagery for most people.

In some cases our imagistic associations blend across modalities into a holistic, multimodal experience that reflects physical reality. Imagery in response to text descriptions can take such a multimodal, elaborate form, although it is perhaps seldom this intense for most people. However, such imagery is often reported by poets and novelists as the basis for composing.

The flexible, associative organization of imagens in the nonverbal system allows for great force and creativity. An important qualification is that we creatively imagine what we have never experienced in terms of what we have experienced either actually or vicariously. In reading science fiction, we may be able to imagine slime creatures in the caves of Planet Xenon, but only in terms of slimy things we have experienced, caves we have experienced, and so on. The imaginal associations produced in response to text, or as the basis for composing a text, are important aspects of reading and writing.

PROCESSING OPERATIONS

The basic units and organizational structures of DCT have now been discussed with reference to reading and literacy. Processing in DCT has been defined as the activation of those mental representations and the connections between them. Three levels of processing were defined: representational, referential, and associative. We next discuss each in turn.

Representational Processing

In reading, representational processing involves the direct activation of mental representations by text features. The probability of a representation being activated is a combined effect of the stimulus situation and individual differences. The stimulus situation is in turn comprised of the characteristics of the stimuli and the contexts in which they occur. Individual differences are differences in background experience interacting with innate characteristics. Characteristic or preferred modes of thinking (i.e., cognitive styles) may orient an individual to be more of a "verbalizer" or a "visualizer," that is, to use relatively more or less language or imagery in cognition (Richardson, 1994).

Direct examples of the representational processing of visual logogens in reading can be seen in tachistoscopic studies. Even without contextual support, familiar letters, words, and phrases can be recognized immediately. Another common example is found in anagrams. Scrambled letters are perceived as individual units until a sequential rearrangement activates a known word. In the haptic modality, representational processing in reading can be seen in recognizing the raised dots of Braille, or in touching signing fingers for those with both hearing and sight impairment.

However, which perceptual features activate which logogens is at least partially dependent on the context in which the features appear. In the absence of differences in font, the interpretation of a circle as either a geometric form, the letter *o,* or the numeral zero is completely a matter of context. Linguistic contexts activate certain logogens by increasing the probability of their activation beyond some threshold. We can read some illegible, incomplete, or even missing writing by using context to supply a degree of probability adequate to activate appropriate logogens. Completing incomplete words, doing crosswords, reading the highly abbreviated language of classified ads, or deciphering hastily scribbled shopping lists are common examples.

Referential Processing

Referential processing is necessarily indirect because it entails the activation of representations in one system by previously activated representations in the other system. For example, seeing the visual word *cup* or hearing the auditory word */kup/* would activate their respective logogens and in turn activate an image of the referent object, a cup. Conversely, the object cup or a picture of a cup would activate their respective imagens and in turn activate referentially related logogens, so that we might say /kup/ or write *cup* in response.

Referential connections are not theorized as one-to-one, but one-to-many in both directions. This accounts for how a thing can be called by many names or a name can have many referents. The word *cup* may evoke a variety of images of cups including dainty china teacups, rugged ceramic mugs, chalices, trophies, or tin cups in golf greens. And mental images of those various cups may evoke various word labels such as *cup, teacup, mug, chalice, trophy, hole,* and so on. Which word evokes which image or which image evokes which word depends probabilistically on both verbal and situational contexts and our own life experiences with things and events and their various vocabulary labels.

Concreteness is a key stimulus factor in referential processing in reading. Mental imagery is more likely to be evoked by concrete language than abstract language, and still more by pictures than by concrete language. The concrete phrase *cup of coffee* is more likely to evoke imagery than the abstract phrase *theory of mind,* although the latter could do so given an appropriate context and individual experiences with concrete circumstances in which such terms are used. For example, *theory of mind* might evoke an associated image of Freud the way the phrase *theory of relativity* might evoke an image of Einstein. Other abstract words can evoke concrete cultural symbols such as *religion* evoking images of churches. However, the comprehension of such abstract terms cannot rely heavily on referential imagery and must be accounted for in ways not necessarily dependent on referential processing.

Associative Processing

Associative processing is also necessarily indirect, with activated representations within either system in turn activating representations within the same system. This spreading activation can be between modalities within a system. For example, reading the written form *cup* activates a logogen in the visual modality of the verbal system, and it in turn ordinarily activates the logogens for the pronunciation /kup/ in the auditory and motor modalities of the verbal system. Spreading activation can also take place within modalities within a system. For example, the activation of the visual logogens for *cup* might activate associated visual logogens such as *coffee, saucer, spoon,* and so on. In reading, this has the effect of "priming" associates so that they might be visually expected in surrounding text. Theoretically, these verbal associations would occur probabilistically, according to context and individual differences (e.g., cloze passages). Associations are not necessarily logically related; associations among language units can be a product of idiosyncratic experience.

Nonverbal associations occur synchronously, as mental sets. An image of a cup might be an integrated image of a cup of steaming coffee on a saucer, possibly with associated images of a spoon and other items in a table setting. As noted previously, nonverbal associations can also occur in a continuous, imaginative stream (e.g., pouring coffee into a cup) or as separate events (e.g., pouring coffee, drinking coffee, removing the dishes). Likewise, these associations may be logical or idiosyncratic and are probable based on contexts and individual differences.

Organizational and Transformational Processing

Higher order processing such as organizing incoming information or manipulating and transforming information into new forms is an extension of the organizational characteristics of the verbal and nonverbal systems. Verbal organizations and transformations are carried out within a sequential framework of constraints, whereas nonverbal organizations and transformations are carried out in a nonsequential (e.g., spatial) framework.

These processing constraints raise the theoretical question of the relationship between intra-unit and inter-unit associations, that is, the difference between an integrated representation and closely associated representations. The DCT assumption is that representational and associative structures all entail associative learning. Repeated and invariant associative experience results in integrated higher order structures (logogens and imagens). Repeated but variable associative experience results in probabilistic connections between representations (both referential and associative). For example, the phrase *rock 'n' roll,* repeatedly experienced as an invariant sequence, becomes an integrated higher order logogen. Other familiar but more variable phrase sequences remain as separate logogens with highly probable associations, as in *down the (line, hatch, drain).* Imagens may be similarly integrated or associated. Referential connections between the systems are assumed to be one-to-many rather than one-to-one and varying in probability. Highly probable connections, both verbal and nonverbal, form higher order mental structures referred to as concepts, episodes, domains, and so on.

Verbal Organization and Transformation. All organization in the verbal system reflects the structuring of lower order representational units into higher order representational units in sequentially constrained ways. For example, sequential associative constraints on grammatical aspects of language at all levels affect its organized comprehension and production. Morphemes occur in sequential patterns (e.g., prefix + root + suffix), phrases occur in sequential patterns (e.g., determiner + noun; auxiliary + verb), sentences follow larger sequential patterns (e.g., noun phrase + verb phrase), and texts follow still larger sequential patterns (e.g., story grammars, expository outlines). Textual cohesion (Halliday & Hasan, 1976) is a set of familiar verbal cues that signal the organization of a text through associations between text units.

In producing language, we use articulatory and conventional constraints in organizing and transforming language. For example, only certain phonemes can be effectively articulated after other phonemes by the speech apparatus. Likewise, the spelling *s-u-n-g* is an allowable combination of letters in the conventions of English as are *s-n-u-g* and *g-u-n-s* and *g-n-u-s* but not *s-n-g-u*. The allowability comes much from the difficulty of supplying a pronunciation to the letter string, a problem of articulation. Sequential constraints learned from speech, reading, and writing affect language production at all levels including syntactic productivity and the writing of texts.

Nonverbal Organization and Transformations. Nonverbal processing operates within a synchronous framework where much information is manipulated in parallel. We can organize events into compound images that represent episodes holistically, as in a continuous, multimodal image of *We awoke to the smell of coffee and heard it being poured as we stumbled to the kitchen and saw our steaming cups.* Such organized imagery structures are useful in working memory and long-term memory in text comprehension and composition.

Imagery transformation has been extensively studied. For example, we can shift perspectives on a scene in a number of typical ways. In the visual modality, we can mentally "rotate" or "revolve" objects in two- or three-dimensional mental space to observe them from different orientations (Shepard & Cooper, 1982). We "pan" across a scene, "zoom" in or out of a scene, or "dissolve" or "cut" to other portions of the scene or to other scenes (Kosslyn, 1980, 1994). If we "zoom" in on a detail of a scene, the rest of the scene "overflows" from an area that is roughly eye-shaped. For example, imagine a field of flowers and slowly move in on one flower. Alternatively, we can "jump" or "cut" to the individual flower, or even a detail of it, in a mental "blink" analogous to the physical blink often employed to refocus the eyes quickly. We can "dissolve" or dissociate images into each other, a frequently surrealistic experience often associated with dreams. In this case the transformation is continuous but any hierarchy will not necessarily be logical. Nonverbal transformations can occur in other modalities also, as in imagining changes in pitch in speech or music.

FUNCTIONS

What do these structures and processes do? As we have pointed out repeatedly, the basis of literacy lies in these mental representations and their activation in various ways. On a larger scale, however, they serve important mediating roles in the performance of literacy tasks and the guidance of literacy behaviors. We will briefly address some functions here and deal with them more extensively in following chapters. (For a more extensive theoretical explanation of functions served by the representational systems, see Paivio, 1986, pp. 74–81.)

Mnemonic Functions

A direct mnemonic implication of DCT is that memory is served by the encoding of information in both a verbal and nonverbal form. DCT assumes that the codes are independent and additive; therefore, information encoded both verbally and nonverbally should be remembered better than information encoded only one way. Considerable research has shown that concrete language units of all sizes—words, phrases, sentences, paragraphs—are recalled better than abstract language units matched for familiarity, meaningfulness, readability, and other relevant variables (e.g., Cornoldi & Paivio, 1982; Sadoski, Goetz, & Fritz, 1993b). Recall for concrete material is typically twice that of abstract material even if imagery is not reported as consciously experienced.

Mnemonic strategies are often intentionally employed in literacy. Both verbal and nonverbal memory devices have been known and used since antiquity, as chapter 2 chronicled. A single word or image can serve as a retrieval device for large amounts of related information that has been read or is to be composed into a text. Both key words and symbolic images are well-known study and memory aids for students (e.g., the key word HOMES for the Great Lakes—Huron, Ontario, Michigan, Erie, Superior; or remembering Italy as shaped like a boot). A mnemonic aspect of DCT is the conceptual peg hypothesis, which states that imagery, in particular, serves as a mental peg on which related information is mentally hung.

Evaluative and Monitoring Functions

The use of verbal cues in monitoring ongoing performance in literacy tasks is a common experience. We spontaneously verbally evaluate and monitor our comprehension with inner speech statements such as "I see" or "I don't get this." The rereading of difficult passages is often subvocalized or even fully vocalized. Think-aloud research in both reading and composing suggests the ongoing use of verbal strategies to monitor and adjust performance. Intense study prompts verbal action such as making notes in the margins of textbooks and underscoring important sentences. Further, reading-study strategies such as SQ3R use verbalizations to guide comprehension behavior. Theoretically, the activation of such verbal mechanisms is not necessarily conscious; in well-learned situations, verbal cues might help to keep us "on track" without conscious utterance.

We frequently solve problems using images ("Where did I leave that coffee cup? The last time I had it was . . . "). Imagery is likewise used in evaluating and monitoring activity prompted by verbal material. Imagery is commonly experienced in evaluating simple, verbally presented problems such as: "If Louise is taller than Ann, and Chris is shorter than Ann, who is tallest?" or "Which is darker red, a candy apple or a fire hydrant?" Spatial reasoning is a component in mathematics performances such as visualizing and evaluating geometric spaces. In complex text-monitoring acts, imagery is used to keep track of ongoing events in described locations and to predict visualized outcomes. In composing, the effects of word choice or longer text units are often evaluated and adjusted in terms of an imagined audience, the proverbial reader over your shoulder.

Emotional and Motivational Functions

A considerable research literature has developed indicating that the experience of mental imagery while reading is related to emotional response and interest (e.g., Goetz & Sadoski, 1996; Wade, Buxton, & Kelly, 1999). The imagery and emotions evoked by romance novels or horror stories are obvious examples, but the relationship pertains to a variety of text types including history, biography, science, feature journalism, and news articles. In DCT, such affective reactions are theoretically identified with the nonverbal system because they are nonverbal by definition and therefore would be expected to accompany imagery to some degree.

However, affective and motivational responses are related to the verbal system as well. Abstract terms such as *beauty* or *honesty* are low in concreteness but high in emotional value. A vocabulary of primarily abstract critical terms is used in describing judgments of writing quality, literary value, and so on (e.g., *coherent, artistic, significant*). Verbal instructions and cues serve motivational and monitoring functions, as in assignments and self-regulating statements to read to memorize versus skim to get the general idea or in writing to achieve specific purposes.

Creative Functions

Both imagery and verbal processes are theoretically and empirically implicated in cognitive creativity (Intons-Peterson, 1993; Paivio, 1986; Shepard, 1978). Creativity is often seen as imagination expressed in language or some other medium. For example, in a remarkable historical work, Miller (1984) showed how the entire progress of 20th-century physics was a creative interplay between mental imagery and language.

Verbal creativity can be seen in the process of creating novel arrangements of units within the framework of sequential constraints in the verbal system. Common examples of creative expressions within this framework are the coining of new terms consistent with lexical conventions (e.g., compounding), new lexical usages within syntactic conventions (e.g., "verbing" nouns, novel metaphors), new sentences within syntactic conventions, and new texts within some general text structure conventions. Creativity is implied in all theories of language where a relatively few syntactic patterns and a larger but limited store of words are used to produce new sentences indefinitely.

Imagery is highly useful as a mental strategy for "trying out" alternative scenarios. Thus, we often conduct small theaters of the mind in which we assume various roles and rehearse future or past events. A key feature of human imagination is the ability to rearrange our world or to create new worlds, whether this takes the form of imagining how furniture would go in an empty room or conceiving of black holes. Imagery organization, transformation, and manipulation are common experiences in reading comprehension and in composing text. The elaborate imagery of literary absorption can go far beyond what was described in the text or intended by the author. The creative situations imagined by poets and novelists, often captured in creative uses of language, form our literary heritage.

Summary

This chapter presented a basic outline of a general theory of cognition (DCT) with reference to reading and literacy. Mental representations are derived from sensory experience and encoded as verbal and nonverbal units of various size. They are organized into two separate coding systems with qualitatively different hierarchical characteristics that can operate independently, in parallel, or through interconnections. Three basic levels of processing were theorized that account for the initial activation of representations and spreading activation within and between systems. Higher order organizational and transformational processing is accomplished within the qualitative constraints imposed by the two systems. The units and representations in the theory serve mnemonic, evaluative/monitoring, emotional/motivational, and creative functions. DCT does not include abstract, amodal forms of mental representation that are qualitatively different from the structures and processes of the concrete, modality-specific representations in the two codes. In DCT, all cognition including perception, memory, meaning, and knowledge must be accounted for by the operations of the representations within and between the two codes, and such an accounting can explain a great variety of literacy activities.

CHAPTER 4

Meaning
and
Comprehension

This chapter expands the discussion of cognition in literacy to the enduring and controversial problem of meaning and comprehension. DCT principles can be directly applied to the analysis of meaning and comprehension. The presentation of the theory in the previous chapter forms the basis of our approach, and this chapter may be seen as a continuation and application of that presentation.

Theoretical analyses of meaning and comprehension can be found in philosophy, linguistics, and psychology and are characterized by several key themes. One theme involves the verbal–nonverbal distinction, the distinction between language and the nonlinguistic world experience to which language refers. Another key theme is the distinction between features and contexts. If meaning is an arrangement of abstract semantic features, then comprehension is a matter of abstracting those features and combining them; but if meaning varies depending on context, then comprehension is a matter of narrowing down an interpretation by ruling out alternatives. Another common theme is that meaning or comprehension occurs in gradations from superficial impressions to deeper, more complete understandings. As we shall see, DCT implicates elements of all these themes in its explanation of meaning.

Current views of meaning and comprehension in literacy have evolved away from extracting meaning from stimuli and toward the view of an active comprehender who operates continually in both internal and external, verbal and nonverbal situational contexts. This active meaning-maker regularly infers, models, distorts, and reads more into a message than was presented. Meaning and comprehension are seen both as building up and narrowing down information at various levels that involve everything from print information to memories of which we are no longer consciously aware. The complexity of current views of meaning and comprehension is daunting for scientific theorizing, and few such theories have undertaken an in-depth analysis of meaning and comprehension. This chapter will explain the dual coding approach to these issues.

THE MEANING OF MEANING

Meaning is a central theme in DCT. Without the activation of mental representations, no meaning can be present; the potential in the cognitive system lies dormant. The activation of a mental representation initiates processing activity in the cognitive system that may or may not be very meaningful; meaning occurs in degrees. Let us illustrate with a series of examples.

If a stimulus, say, several clusters of printed characters, activates no familiar mental representations such as letters, words, pronunciations, verbal associates, or referent images, it would be considered "meaningless" (e.g., @~~/ #x+ ~| #~| |&&). But if we substitute familiar letters for the characters in the same pattern, logogens would be triggered, recognition would occur, further connections could be activated, and the character string would be considered more "meaningful" (e.g., *good cup of coffee*).

As a second example, take the character string *ABP99S-C*. Its units are familiar and the names of the characters can be pronounced, but it is neither pronounceable as a whole nor is it likely to directly evoke any familiar verbal or nonverbal connections beyond the names of the characters. We can name the characters in order, and we may undertake a memory search for similar known encodings such as serial numbers, but as a whole it is likely to remain meaningless. But to an auto parts supply clerk checking stock codes, *ABP99S-C* might be read "air bag, passenger, 1999 S model (sedan), compatible with C model (coupe)." Although still not pronounceable, the character string can now be directly recoded into other language units that form a context and have direct reference to nonverbal representations, in this case images of a specific make and year of automobile in two models.

As another example, take the letter string *bipled*. This sequence is comprised of familiar letters and can be quickly associated with several conventional pronunciations (e.g., *bi pled, bi pld, bipld*). It has at least two potentially meaning-producing parts, the morphemes *bi-* and *-ed*. An overall coherent meaning does not occur, however, because the character string as a whole is unfamiliar and its parts are ambiguous. If *bi-* is recognized as the morpheme meaning two, the remaining letters are likely to be taken as a noun (*pled*, perhaps by association with *biped*). But if the *-ed* is taken as a past tense verb marker, the foregoing letters are likely to be taken as a verb (*biple*).

Context could serve to resolve the issue of syntactic function and probable pronunciation, as in *The sneek bipled the snork*. Context could further specify meaning by increasing the probability of verbal and/or imagery associates, as in *The chef lightly bipled the roast duck with sauce*. In this sense, the word *bipled* seems synonymous with *basted* or *seasoned*. These meanings would be consistent with typical activities of chefs with roast ducks, although other meanings are possible in the absence of further contextual constraints.

These examples suggest that, in its broadest sense, the psychological meaning of any linguistic unit is the set of reactions evoked by it directly or brought to bear on it by the vehicles of reference and association from our linguistic and nonlinguistic knowledge. The richer the elaboration of activated mental representations and their defining interconnections, the richer the meaning. The meaning potential of written language is determined by internal, individual differences and by external contexts both on and off the page. The nature and degree of that potential is variable over people and situations.

Contextual influences are critical to meaning; situations determine the degree of meaning and shades of meaning to a large extent. Common experiences account for shared meanings in a community, and some reactions are highly probable within individuals and groups. This gives a degree of stability to meanings of common words and phrases and allows for extensive, rapid communication in shared communities and contexts. This stability allows lexicographers, for example, to write dictionary definitions covering a variety of different typical usages of words and phrases.

Mental imagery forms an important aspect of context by representing knowledge of the world. The mental connections between language and the nonverbal experience to which it refers serve to provide concrete referents for the language and also to restrict the set of images that are aroused in any given situation. Context serves to progressively narrow and focus the comprehension of a message. Imagery provides an inner context that contributes to meaning.

Meaning is activated in degrees rather than all-or-none, and several everyday metaphors are commonly invoked to illustrate this. The alimentary metaphor, common in medieval times, treated the text as something to be savored, consumed, ruminated, and absorbed. The clarity metaphor suggests that the meaning of something can be more or less "clear," just as vision or other senses can be more or less vivid or obscured; we see as through a glass darkly. The grasping metaphor suggests getting a grip on something or the process of pulling things together; *comprehend* literally means a grasping together (Latin *com-,* together, and *prehendere,* to grasp; the monkey has a prehensile tail). The construction metaphor suggests the arrangement of parts into a whole with a connotation of planned bottom-up activity; a builder arranges units in a plan to overcome chaotic forces such as gravity. The related "levels" metaphor is architectural and is commonly used in theories of cognition and reading as levels of processing or levels of meaning.

LEVELS OF PROCESSING AND MEANING

Cognition does not literally occur in levels; degree of elaboration is perhaps a more accurate description. However, it is a theoretically useful metaphor in psychology and a practically useful distinction in describing reading behavior, as in the distinction between the literal comprehension of stated information and the inferential comprehension of implied information. However, these conceptualizations of levels are not the same, and we will next discuss psychological levels of meaning as defined in DCT.

Recall from chapter 3 that DCT theorizes three levels of processing involving the verbal and nonverbal systems: the *representational* level, the initial activation of one or both systems; the *referential* level, the activation of connections between systems; and the *associative* level, the activation of connections within a system. These levels of processing activity can be applied directly to meaning. At each level, there is an underlying, or dormant, mental structure in memory that is often referred to as semantic memory (also episodic memory, see chap. 5). We experience different aspects of comprehension as these semantic memory structures are activated, or processed.

An important point here is that the structural base at each level is not static. As words are encountered in various contexts and as our cognitive system (both language and imagery) develops, the underlying meaning base changes, perhaps ever so slightly: Old representations and their connections are strengthened or weakened, new representations and connections are formed, and so on. Thus, experience constantly modifies dual coding structure and processing potential. We next discuss each of the three levels in turn.

The Representational Level of Meaning

The most elementary level of meaning is the representational level. The underlying, dormant structure at this level can be simply described as the availability in memory of modality-specific logogens or imagens (neuronal structures). Comprehension at this level refers to the relatively direct activation of logogens by linguistic stimuli and imagens by nonlinguistic stimuli.

The qualifier "relatively" is needed because of the nature of perceiving language in different modalities. For example, it takes slightly longer to name written words than to repeat spoken words, suggesting that recoding print to speech requires additional processing. This is consistent with the DCT view that intermodal recoding between visual logogens and articulatory logogens occurs in the naming of written words. But this connection is often rapid and highly probable in literate persons without congenital hearing impairment, and it takes less time than either referential processing tasks (e.g., imaging to words) or associative processing tasks (e.g., providing synonyms or antonyms). That is, recoding a visual word to speech implies indirect associative processing that follows direct representational processing, but it is often included as part of the representational level of meaning. In some cases, recoding to speech is determined by meaning at other levels; we will return to this point shortly.

Processing at the representational level corresponds intuitively to familiarity in that being familiar with, or "knowing," something that is sensed is a simple kind of meaning. Familiarity may only imply the beginning of recognition and does not imply an extensive set of responses as indicated by the ability to define, paraphrase, or give examples. Familiarity implies that a representation is available, but if other connections are lacking, no elaboration to other levels of meaning will occur.

Recalling examples from earlier in this chapter, the familiar written phrase *good cup of coffee* is readily recognized at the representational level, but the isolated "word" *bipled* is not, except possibly through the fragmented verbal associations to "two of" or "past tense." Even recoding *bipled* to speech depends on the relative familiarity of the morphemes *bi-* and *-ed* and on similarity to other, more familiar words such as *tripled* or *biped*. (A short *i* association to *tripled* may be more likely because *triple* is a more frequently occurring word than *biped* and because the morpheme *tri-* means three as the morpheme *bi-* means two, an association to a familiar numerical sequence.) This similarity to two familiar associates with different pronunciations sets up a pronunciation ambiguity. As noted earlier, context effects can resolve some if not all of this ambiguity so that top-down effects on representational processing are implicated.

This example also illustrates that meaning is not always dependent on recoding to speech; in fact, context often determines pronunciation (e.g., homographs such as *read, bow, wind, minute, desert,* and so on). In actuality, representational meaning without the influence of meaning at other levels is largely an idealized simplification because the levels merge continuously in bottom-up, top-down fashion. However, the representational level can be experimentally demonstrated to a degree with restricted reading times or tachistoscopic exposures (e.g., Gernsbacher, 1984; Paivio & O'Neill, 1970; Strain, Patterson, & Seidenberg, 1995).

A common generalization in cognitive psychology is that the meaningful is always familiar, but the familiar is not always meaningful. The example *ABP99S-C* illustrates this generalization. It is comprised of familiar characters, but its meaning is "unclear" until a context of associations is provided whereupon its meaning is "grasped." Similarly, the familiar formula $E = mc^2$ is meaningfully comprehended (as opposed to recognized), only insofar as the reader has a knowledge of physics, relativity, Einstein, and so on. A sense of felt familiarity based on representational processing may be all that is necessary in many situations. But a higher level, more meaningful comprehension of the physics involved in the equation would entail a highly organized structure of mental representations involving advanced mathematics and science.

An interesting aspect of the representational level is the strategies typically used to encode unfamiliar verbal stimuli. Clark and Paivio (1987) reviewed decades of studies of learning nonsense words and foreign words and determined that they are often encoded as known words (i.e., they look like or sound like known words), that such encoding involves the similarity of their perceptual features at the representational level, and that memory is largely determined by the ease with which these connections are made. Reading teachers administering decoding tests that involve nonsense syllables often notice the tendency of children to read a nonsense syllable as a similar, familiar, known word (e.g., pronouncing *grouch* for *gouch*). Such meaningful associations can override the application of pronunciation rules, for better or for worse.

The Referential Level of Meaning

Referential connections are between-system connections that run back and forth between logogens in the verbal system and imagens in the nonverbal system. The underlying structure here is the set of connections between the language units known to someone and the mental images that have come to be associated with them through world experience; in DCT this is part of semantic memory. These connections have a neurological base so that referential processing potential is ultimately in the form of neural pathways that become activated with high probability under certain conditions.

These connections are not necessarily symmetrical or obligatory; language units can evoke a variety of images or no images, and images can evoke a variety of language units or no language units. In reading, the progression would typically go from logogens to imagens, although evoked images could introduce a strong anticipation set for upcoming language, thereby facilitating its recognition and comprehension. Imagery can form a strong internal context that becomes not just a companion to verbal context, but integral with it.

For example, take the sentence *Adrift on the life raft, the survivors saw dark shapes circling around them in the water*. The image evoked is probably one of sharks, and a reader might form an immediate prediction that what will follow will be language describing sharks and a possible encounter with sharks. The image evoked could serve as a context so powerfully that a skillful author might not need to literally use the word *sharks* to establish their presence, allowing readers to engage themselves more deeply in the evocation of the story through their own imaginal inferences. But the internal imagery evoked by the sentence could prime referential language to such a degree that readers might later report actually having read the word *sharks*, or might miscue the word *sharks* in oral reading.

Referential imagery evoked by language is a form of elaboration that adds an additional level of meaning. This can occur either literally, through images evoked by direct description, or inferentially. It is central to *making sense* of text where that phrase is taken literally. We invest a text with meaning by making it a quasi-sensory event; the referential evocation of images gives form, shape, and substance to meaning. Imagery may not be consciously experienced while reading some texts, and, strictly speaking, it is not theoretically necessary to a meaningful reading of at least some texts. But it is experienced by virtually all readers in some situations and by some readers in virtually all situations. Thus, it is a phenomenon of reading behavior that must be theoretically accounted for, and no theory of reading can be complete without it.

DCT is especially suited to explaining the difference in the effects of concrete language that is relatively high in the evocation of imagery and abstract language that is relatively low in the evocation of imagery. The major theoretical difference between concrete and abstract language is that logogens for concrete language have more direct referential connections to imagens than do logogens for abstract language. This implies that the main semantic difference between concrete and abstract language is in the degree of referential connections.

For example, the phrase *royal wedding* is relatively concrete, evoking images of a newlywed couple and regal ceremony. The DCT explanation of the evocation of such imagery is that this phrase would be processed at the representational level in the verbal system and then at the referential level in the nonverbal system. The written phrase "royal wedding" is detected by the visual sensory system and corresponding logogens are activated, resulting in initial recognition of the phrase at the representational level. Referential connections in turn activate imagens for a royal couple, perhaps formally dressed and located at a cathedral. These imagens may then referentially activate associated logogens such as *king* and *queen* (or *prince* and *princess* or *duke* and *duchess* depending on the situation), *bride* and *groom, husband* and *wife, cathedral,* and so on. The rapidly spreading cross-activation of connections forms an internal verbal–nonverbal context for the comprehension of the phrase.

This example serves only to illustrate referential processing and is an incomplete picture of comprehension because no associative connections in the verbal or nonverbal systems are mentioned. We return to this example, but we must first explain the associative level.

The Associative Level of Meaning

Associative connections are within-system connections that run between logogens within the verbal system and between imagens within the nonverbal system. As described in chapter 3, the structural organization of each system is qualitatively different. Associations between logogens are sequential whereas associations between imagens are synchronous.

Because logogens vary in size, their sequential connections may be between letters, morphemes, words, or larger units. A familiar interletter association is the letter q being associated with a following u and one or more other vowels. Intra-word associations include free morphemes modified by bound morphemes or connected to form compound words. A compound word may have a separate logogen from each of its components so that it is comprehended differently from its parts; *makeshift* means something beyond *make* and *shift*. Interword, interphrase, interclause, and intersentence associations form various syntactic and semantic contexts that are integral to meaning.

Associations between imagens form imaginal contexts that are often overlapping and nested sets. Like logogens, imagens are not theorized to be of any particular size, so that what the whole is and what the parts are becomes somewhat fluid. Foregrounds merge with backgrounds into environmental surroundings that change with imagined time, space, and motion so that we can adjust perspective in a variety of ways. These inner environments form inner situational contexts that are also integral to meaning.

The associative level of meaning can be illustrated using the phrase *royal wedding* as a continuing example. Logogens for *royal wedding* are directly activated by the printed stimuli and in turn activate other logogens in a spreading activation within the verbal system. These logogens might include *king* and *queen* (or *prince* and *princess,* etc.) as well as *bride, groom, husband, wife* and other nuptial terms.

Organization and hierarchy among the evoked logogens can be seen in the relationship between the phrase elements *royal* and *wedding,* which apply to both parties separately (i.e., both parties are wed equally, but one party may become royal only after the wedding). The wedding can be between a *king* and *queen* (or a *prince* and *princess* or *duke* and *duchess,* etc.), but not more than one pair in a single union. These terms plus *bride* and *groom* and *husband* and *wife* are gender-specific terms associated with the respective parties.

The verbal semantic organization also could be represented in other ways. The terms *husband* and *wife* could be seen as superordinate to all the other terms above (i.e., all the other cases are special cases of a husband–wife relationship). Or all the terms could be seen to have a coordinate, lateral organization (i.e., all are equally applicable but in different contexts). That is, the organization of these terms might vary between individuals or within an individual in different situations. The activation of associative connections has considerable flexibility.

The logogens for *cathedral* and *castle* also might be activated in the context of a royal wedding, with *cathedral* more associated with *wedding* and *castle* more associated with *royal*. Finally, these terms might also be associated with each other in a broader organizational set, as both fall in the domain of large buildings often associated with royalty and high position.

In the nonverbal system, the spread of associative connections can occur on its own once nonverbal connections have been made referentially. For example, the phrase *royal wedding* may evoke images of the royal couple in a cathedral; that is, the royal couple may be nested inside a larger imaginal setting, a cathedral. This image may then referentially activate the logogen for *cathedral* separately from any association between logogens within the verbal system. Nonverbal associative connections between an image of a cathedral and an image of a castle may also be activated, with or without any referential activation. Referential activation is highly probable with concrete language, but the systems can operate independently.

Even in the case of abstract language, imagery may have more effect on comprehension than is often acknowledged. It is difficult to find abstract language to which people cannot experience a degree of imagery (e.g., *nuptial*). When such abstract language units are composed together in text, an imaginal substrate may develop and form a part of the larger context. This is discussed further in a later section. However, we will probably be more aware of the verbal context effects at the associative level, at least for abstract text.

Keep in mind that the different levels of processing and meaning do not ordinarily occur in isolation. In everyday reading situations, these levels blend continuously. Keep in mind also that individual differences and external instructions can affect the degree and kind of processing experienced. That is, the complexity of the process must ultimately be understood in terms of all the internal and external factors that affect it. Finally, imagery can be dynamic and transformational rather than static; thus, the highly elaborated comprehension of a phrase like *royal wedding* may involve dynamic sequences and transformational images.

Figure 4.1 presents an illustration of the combined representational, referential, and associative levels of meaning for the phrase *royal wedding* using the general model of DCT presented in chapter 3. The logogens for words and phrases used as examples in the foregoing sections are shown in frames. Accordingly, these words and phrases could be recognized as individual words and possibly as whole phrases for those familiar enough with them. Imagens are represented in circles. The arrows indicate referential connections between the systems or associative connections within each system. The web of activated connections constitutes the meaning of the phrase to a reader in a relatively elaborate way. We further discuss this illustration in the next section.

MENTAL MODELS AND MEANING

The terms *mental models, situation models,* or *semantic models* are commonly used to refer to internal simulations of a real or imag-

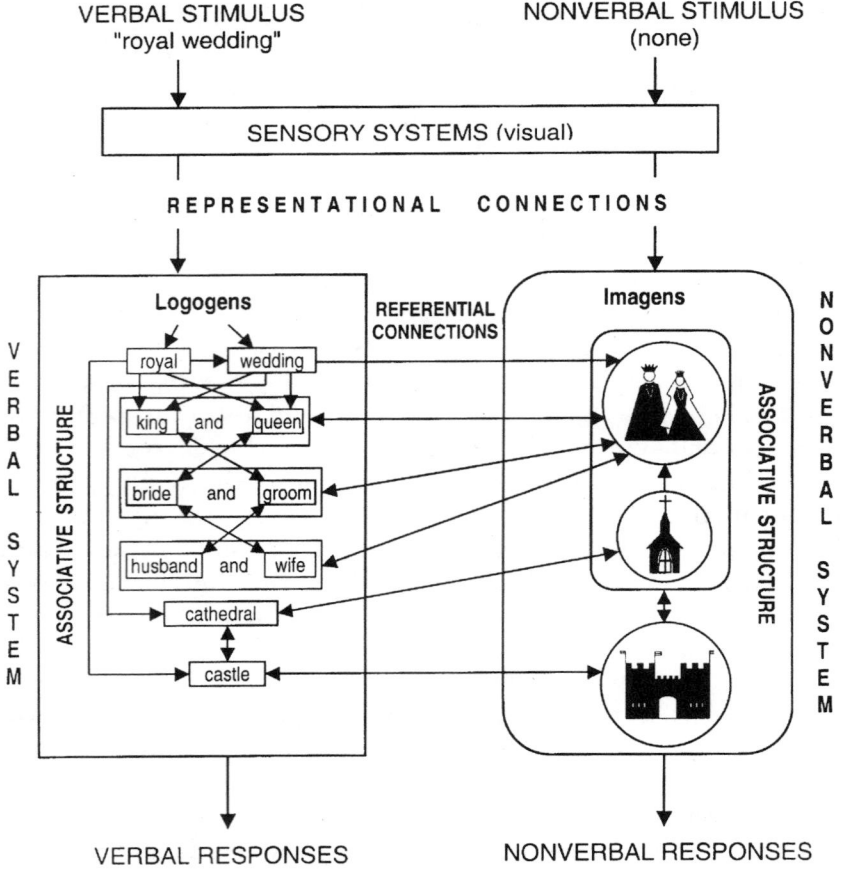

FIG. 4.1. *Example of representational, referential, and associative connections for the concrete phrase "royal wedding." This is one possible mental model of the phrase as theorized by DCT.*

ined situation (e.g., Johnson-Laird, 1983; McKellar, 1957; Miller, 1979; van Dijk & Kintsch, 1983). The more inclusive term *mental model* is most common, although the theoretical specificity of the terms varies with users. In DCT, this term simply refers to an activated set of logogens and/or imagens and the referential and/or associative connections between them. The activation of such a set follows directly from the discussion of levels of meaning and comprehension.

That is, the use of the term *mental model* does not imply any theoretical construct that has not already been introduced; the term does not explain anything additional and is simply used as a shorthand way of referring to an activated set of logogens and imagens as described. In DCT, mental models can take the form of mental language, mental images, or a combination of mental language and mental images together. In reading comprehension, mental models would necessarily involve language, but they also would involve imagery to varying degrees.

Figure 4.1 is therefore a graphic illustration of one possible mental model of the concrete phrase *royal wedding* as theorized in DCT. It is necessarily a schematic depiction, lacking any dynamic or multimodal imagery, color, or affective responses that might be evoked. It is not the only possible mental model of this phrase; as noted previously, context could substantially alter the activation of referential and associative connections and the resulting model. For example, if the phrase *Royal Wedding* was encountered by a film buff consulting the television listings for old movies, it might evoke images of the 1951 film with Fred Astaire dancing on the walls and ceiling!

In contrast to concrete language such as *royal wedding,* abstract language must rely more exclusively on associative processing for the formation of mental models because of the relative absence of referential connections. Figure 4.2 graphically illustrates a possible mental model for the phrase *official union,* here used as an abstract counterpart of *royal wedding*.

The printed stimulus is detected by the visual sense and logogens are activated at the representational level. These logogens in turn activate associated logogens such as *regulated, authorized, formal* for *official* and *uniting, joining, merging* for *union*. Associative interconnections within the respective sets are also activated. Taken as a phrase, *official union* may activate contextually related words or phrases such as the more concrete *royal wedding*.

Note here that *royal wedding* activates a referential connection, indirectly implicating imagery (the nonverbal system is not illustrated in Fig. 4. 2). As we have noted previously, the comprehension of abstract language comes largely from verbal-associative processing with imagery assisting as available. Note also that in another context *official union* might mean something quite different, such as a labor organization.

In either the more concrete or more abstract case, the formulation of the mental model follows from the general principles of the theory. The representational level of activation corresponds to initial recognition, and the spreading activation of referential and associative connections corresponds to deeper, more complete com-

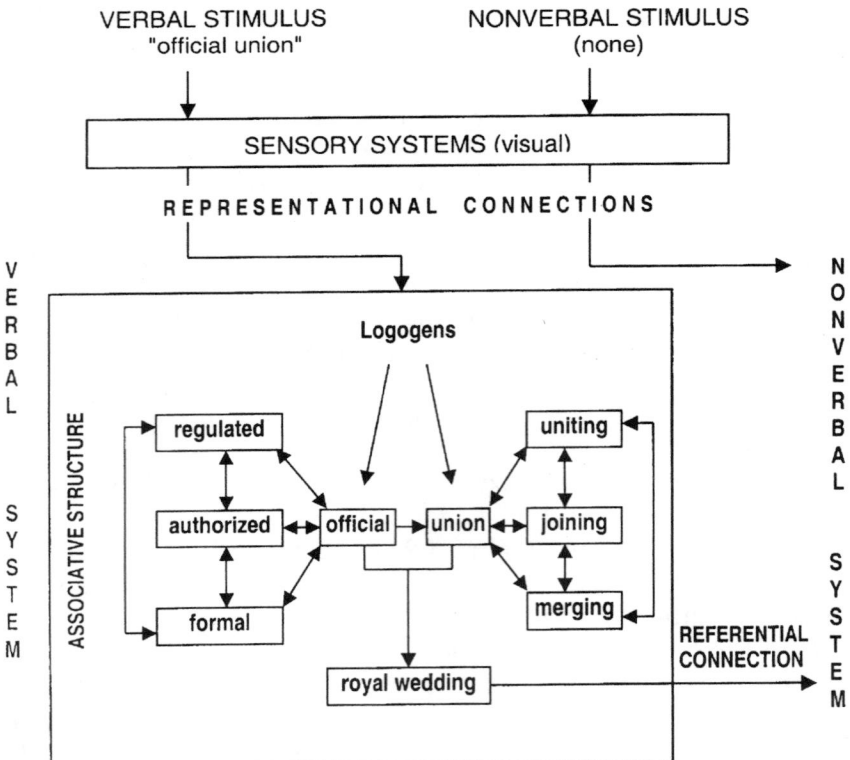

FIG. 4.2. *Example of representational and associative connections for the abstract phrase "official union." This would be one possible mental model for the phrase as theorized by DCT.*

prehension. Once activation begins, associative and referential connections could continue to build a model as long as such processing continued or until the reader moved on.

This implies that mental models are formed and revised continuously during reading. DCT does not assume that mental models or situation models are formed only after a text base of abstract propositions is established (Kintsch, 1998; van Dijk & Kintsch, 1983). Rather, the formation of the model is implicated at all levels of processing. In fact, individual words and their grammatical relations effect the ongoing formation and modification of such models.

GRAMMAR, MEANING, AND MENTAL MODELS

The idea that grammar and meaning (i.e., syntax and semantics) are both related to nonverbal aspects of comprehension is now generally accepted. For example, Fillmore (1977) revised his case grammar theory by putting special emphasis on the perceptual, or imagined, scenes to which linguistic units refer. He proposed that meanings are related to scenes in the sense that our perspective can vary depending on the saliency of such cases as agent, instrument, or object (cf. Fillmore, 1984; Fillmore & Kay, 1983). These differences in perspective are implied in the cases and grammatical structures of sentences. Lakoff (1977, 1993), Chafe (1977, 1994), and others (see Tomasello, 1998) have similarly proposed that linguistic elements and structures derive from concrete situations and actions and are dependent on them for meaning.

The DCT view is consistent with these views regarding the construction of integrated scenes from sentences and texts. Grammatical classes of words alone are important initiators of different kinds of processing. For example, imperative verbs such as *push, pull, stop,* or *sit* can alone evoke nonverbal motor images or even actions. Even slight changes in relational words such as prepositions can make significant changes in the model evoked. For example, the sentence *The fish swam under the turtles on the log* is understood differently than *The fish swam under the turtles by the log* (cf. Bransford, Barclay, & Franks, 1972). In the first sentence, the turtles would be imagined to be on the log with the fish swimming under the log. In the second sentence, the turtles would be imagined to be in the water near the log with fish swimming under the turtles but not necessarily under the log. The difference in the mental model or the arrangement of image parts within the larger image is signaled simply by the change in the preposition from *on* to *by*.

Likewise, the sentence *Terry finished working in the yard and went into the house* is comprehended differently from the sentence *Terry finished working in the yard and came into the house.* The former has a consistent vantage point (outside the house), while the latter calls for a change in vantage point (from outside the house to inside the house). Sentences that call for a change in vantage point take longer to comprehend, are rated harder to understand, and are likely to be recalled from a single vantage point (Black, Turner, & Bower, 1979).

Modeling some complex syntactic constructions can also be explained this way, without recourse to abstract transformational rules. For example, take the sentence *The girl with red hair won the race.* The traditional transformational grammar view of this sentence is that the embedded construction *with red hair* is derived from an underlying sentence of the form *The girl has red hair* and then embedded in the sentence *The girl won the race* following complex transformational rules. However, the subject of the sentence could also be seen to be an extended nominal holistically captured in an image of a girl with red hair. The verbal-associative hierarchical sequence *girl (hair[red])* referentially evokes an image of such a person, perhaps elaborated to include light skin and freckles. In fact, the predicate of the sentence, *won the race,* might be seen as a further extension or modifier of the nominal, which places the person in an imagined environment, possibly dressed in racing gear and crossing a finish line ahead of others. Such a view of grammar may help to explain syntactic anomalies such as why *a good cup of coffee* and *a cup of good coffee* mean the same thing.

The grammar of more abstract language such as *Urban real estate investment increased last quarter* could be explained with relatively more emphasis on sequential and hierarchical verbal associations and relatively less on imagery. Cumulative verbal elaborations such as *urban* (city, not rural) + *real estate* (buildings, lots) + *investment* (buying, selling) could be parsed into the verbal-associative hierarchical sequence *investment (real estate [urban])* as the sentence's subject. Alternatively, the phrase *urban real estate* may be holistically captured in an image of city buildings and lots, thereby recoding the language into imagery and reducing the number of hierarchical parsing operations necessary. Likewise, the phrase *last quarter* may be verbally elaborated into *three months* or the names of the previous three months, or, because a quarter is often associated with a season, an image of a cityscape during that particular season. Such imagery may be only vaguely experienced or not consciously experienced at all, but verbal associations such those between *urban* and *city* or between *quarter* and *three months* may not be consciously experienced either.

Grammatical relations occur between sentences as well. Textual cohesion (Halliday & Hasan, 1976) describes the grammatical and lexical relations between sentences that help establish textual coherence beyond what is contributed by the constituent sentences themselves (i.e., the whole is more than the sum of the parts). Cohesive ties form textual connections in the verbal system and can referentially evoke textual connections in the nonverbal system.

The overall point regarding grammar, meaning, and mental models is that clusters of associations in the verbal system and clusters of associations in the nonverbal system can combine to form meaningful contexts, including syntactic contexts, that are inherent aspects of mental models of text situations. Concatenations of verbal associations in the verbal system can referentially evoke images in the nonverbal system, which can be embedded in larger imaginal contexts and transformed dynamically. These in turn can evoke referent language that may be grammatically and textually organized. The ongoing activation within and between codes elaborates and specifies meaning, including priming anticipated language and images that may never be expressed in the text. This last point further implies that mental models are not necessarily the end product of some already comprehended text. Some of their form may already be in memory preceding the reading of the text.

Both verbal and nonverbal representations can be primed when the text we are set to encounter is familiar and predictable (i.e., top-down processing). For example, if we were to pick up a book of fairy tales and encounter a fairy tale entitled *The Royal Wedding,* we might strongly expect it to begin with the phrase *Once upon a time.* We would likewise be primed to encounter words like *king, queen, prince, princess, castle, dragon, magic,* or similar words typical of fairy tales. Likewise, images corresponding to these terms might be primed. Abstract fairy-tale language without direct imaginal referent could be primed (e.g., *enchantment*), as could images without direct verbal referents (e.g., how would one describe in words the noise made by a dragon when it breathes fire?). On the other hand, we would not anticipate language or imagery dealing with modern locations or objects.

In the case of encountering language that is unfamiliar and unpredictable, the activation of mental representations will be relatively more dependent on the graphic stimuli and contexts present on the printed page (i.e, bottom-up processing). This implies greater attention to the verbal code and the cues provided by orthography and grammar, but it does not eliminate the role of the nonverbal code, which is implicated in grammar.

The comprehension of familiar but abstract language also theoretically calls for more attention to the verbal code, but inner verbal contexts (as opposed to nonverbal ones) would provide a higher degree of predictability for familiar text. This analysis implies that unfamiliar, abstract language is very difficult to comprehend, a common phenomenon. Without concrete referents or familiar verbal connections the reader has little to go on. We next elaborate on the role of direct experience in meaning, particularly in understanding abstract language.

MEANING AND DIRECT EXPERIENCE

A useful analogy for understanding the DCT view of language and meaning is that proposed by Saussure (1974) in which he compared language to currency (Paivio & Begg, 1981). The value of money can be expressed in two different ways. On one hand, money has a formal, within-system syntactic value, such that a $5 bill can be exchanged for any specific combination of other bills or coins that total $5. On the other hand, money has value in terms of the goods and services for which it can be exchanged. Analogously, DCT holds that logogens can be interpreted in terms of other logogens (e.g., synonyms, antonyms, paraphrases, syntactic alternatives) or in relation to nonverbal imagens of the objects, events, or situations for which they stand (both static and dynamic images). To continue the analogy, we can trade goods and services for other goods and services, or for money. In DCT, images can evoke other images associatively within the nonverbal system or images can evoke language referentially in the verbal system.

We employ this extended semiotic analogy to make the point that all meaning may ultimately lie on a foundation of direct, nonverbal experience. Exchanging some forms of money for other forms of money may facilitate spending, but such exchanges do not buy bread. Likewise, the meaning of concrete language may rely heavily on its evocation of imagery, and abstract language may be understood more in terms of its verbal associates, but somewhere among the verbal-associative links abstract language must find outside reference to something that is not language. This is the DCT view of "deep structure."

For example, we may understand the abstract word *justice* in terms of verbal associates such as *law, precedent, jury system, fairness,* and so on. However, these are abstractions themselves which in turn must be explained. To say that they are explained by verbal association with *justice* is circular. Perhaps the verbal associate *fairness* evokes memories of concrete situations experienced earlier when the word was used to refer to concrete objects and acts (e.g., fairness is when there are no favorites; fairness is when everyone is treated equally). The original experiences may be unavailable for conscious recall, but the basis of understanding words like *fairness* and *justice* may ultimately rely on them, or some key exemplar experience appropriate to the context. Our understanding of abstractions may be no more than the sum total of the actual life experiences we have had where such language was used or to which such language might apply in our memories or imaginations.

Literally speaking, this is what the word *abstract* means. It derives from the Latin morphemes *ab-,* out of or away from, and *tract,* to pull or draw. Hence, abstractions are drawn out of something: in the case of language, the life objects and events to which they refer and in the presence of which they have been used in our experience. In this way, even abstract function words such as *and, but, very, with,* and so on, come to have a residuum of meaning derived from experience. Such words might be seen to lack any unique meaning in isolation and only take meaning from the contexts in which they have appeared. However, people do report having spatial or haptic images of prepositions such as *under, inside,* or *with,* as in looking for or placing objects in spatial relation to one another.

Meaning as action can be seen more directly in the use of imperatives, as noted previously. Imperatives such as *push, pull, stop, go, sit,* or *stand* can be understood as direct action in a particular context. Such action tendencies are explained in DCT by logogens for imperative words or phrases, referentially activated and contextually appropriate dynamic images, and possibly physical action as nonverbal output. Recipes or instructions for assembling gadgets are common examples; advertising and propaganda are more subtle.

In sum, the relationships between language and imagery may eventually define meaning in virtually all its cognitive senses. Meaningful reading comprehension and the formation and modification of mental models for all kinds of text is theoretically carried out in this way.

There is considerable precedent for such a view. Pragmatist philosophy centered on the act; meaning was seen as the imagined completion of an act and its consequences (Mead, 1934). Evolutionary philosophers speculate that all natural language originally had a concrete referent, and that language evolved in the service of mental imagery (Bronowski, 1977; Langer, 1962). Further, English etymology suggests that words that are today taken as abstractions originally had direct concrete referents, as the word *abstract,* analyzed above. *Concrete* originally meant to grow together in a mass (construction concrete is a single mass of sand, gravel, cement, etc.). Qualities were seen to grow together with their things: a redheaded bird as opposed to redness; redness withdrawn from the concrete head becomes an abstraction. The word *comprehend,* analyzed earlier, literally means to take or grasp together, and so on. Most lexical items prove to be "dead" metaphors (e.g., *fall* in love, *leg* of a table, *head* of lettuce) that were once meant literally (Sadock, 1993). That is, all language may have the element of *metaphor*—literally, to bear or carry over—carrying meaning from the linguistic symbol to the real-world referent.

METAPHOR, FIGURATIVE LANGUAGE, AND MEANING

The comprehension of metaphors in and of itself poses interesting complexities for the study of meaning. The application of dual coding principles to metaphor and idiom has been theoretically and empirically investigated (for a review, see Paivio & Walsh, 1993).

Both verbal-associative and imaginal processes were found to be implicated.

In a metaphorical statement such as "Douglas firs are the skyscrapers of the western forests," three components can be identified: the *topic* (Douglas firs), the *vehicle* (skyscrapers), and the *ground,* or whatever they have in common that permits a comparison (height, narrowness, etc.). Controlled studies have indicated that the topic must be understood before the relevant meanings of the vehicle can be applied, but once the topic is known, the vehicle dominates the meaning (Paivio & Clark, 1986). In the present case, Douglas firs need to be known as tall trees, but then skyscrapers dominate the scene through reference to their extraordinary height. Verbal associations keep the relations between the topic and vehicle categorical and constrained, whereas images provides a meaningful, memorable base for one or both. Novel metaphors in particular appear to need imagery for interpretation, especially vehicle imagery (Marschark, Katz, & Paivio, 1983).

Metaphors and idioms, interpreted both verbally and imaginally, may serve a mental modeling function that is basic to our everyday thought and expression. Lakoff and Johnson (1980) proposed that we live by metaphors, seen in such extended metaphors as the journey of love (milestone in a relationship), argument as war (defend a position), communications as conduit (pour out ideas), and so on. Lakoff (1993) furthered that view by proposing that image-based reasoning is fundamental and that abstract reasoning is a special case of image-based reasoning using metaphor. He applied this principle to such basic abstract concepts as time (motion in space), causation (physical force), purpose (travel to a destination), and category (container), proposing that as thought moves away from the concrete toward the abstract or the emotional, metaphorical comprehension becomes the norm. Lakoff and Johnson (1999) have expanded this basis into a complete philosophy. We finally turn to the DCT interpretation of the role of affect in meaning.

AFFECTIVE ASPECTS OF MEANING

No theory of meaning could be complete without reference to the affective aspects of meaning. Affective reactions account for differences in our usage of terms describing meaningful responses. Cognitive processing alone may be sufficient for the use of terms such as *understand* or *comprehend,* but affective responses are implied when we use terms such as *interesting, engaging, moving,* or *profound.* Affective responses are even more implicated in the use of terms such as *inspiring, offensive, awesome,* and a host of other terms from our critical vocabularies.

In reading, cognition would theoretically precede affect, at least in its early phases. That is, while we may have a prior preference for the general subject of a text at hand, it would be difficult to have much affective response to the content of a text that we found completely obscure. In DCT terms, some degree of representational meaning would have to occur before specific affective reactions to it could follow. This implies that while affective reactions could be primed, they would occur mainly at the referential and associative levels of meaning and therefore would involve both the nonverbal and verbal systems.

Since affective and emotional reactions are nonverbal by definition, they must be theoretically identified with the nonverbal system and would be expected to accompany such nonverbal cognitive reactions as imagery. This is evident in the everyday experience of pleasant and unpleasant memories, fantasies, and dreams. However, while they may be associated, emotions are not theorized as imagens or components of them, nor does DCT specify a separate cognitive code for representing emotions. Emotional aspects of meaning are either (a) the dormant connotations of language, objects, and events, or (b) actual emotional reactions evoked by language or images of particular objects or events. Emotions are not abstract nodes in a knowledge network, but somatic, corporeal responses associated with language and situations that may be felt or expressed through language labels or ratings.

Although affect and imagery are not theoretically the same, we can experience them both in the absence of any direct, external stimuli. For example, in reading we can experience an emotion vicariously, in the absence of real events that we might otherwise wish to avoid. The tingling suspense of mystery stories, the physical danger of adventure stories, the heartbreak of romance, or the catharsis of the great tragedies accompany the imaginings of characters and events. Such vicarious experiences often satisfy emotional interests while avoiding the first-hand arousal associated with actual life events. That is, we experience the feelings in a controlled way so as to make them only as strong as we prefer.

In the case of reading, the DCT interpretation would be that imagery and affect are referentially activated by the language of the text after it has been verbally processed at the representational level. However, once an emotion is engaged, it may set a mood for the rest of the reading, priming upcoming language and images consistent with the mood. Emotionally predictable texts, such as Greek tragedies constructed to provide a sustained encounter with one emotion, are classic examples. Modern texts, such as black comedies, provide interesting, often surprising, juxtapositions of imageable situations and emotions that are both intellectually and emotionally novel and challenging.

However, affect is also related to the verbal system in a fairly direct way. For example, the use of certain phonemes produces consistent changes in brain blood temperature that influence subjective feelings (e.g., soft vowels like *calm* versus long vowels like *muse;* Zajonc, Murphy, & McIntosh, 1993). Rhetoricians have long known that language carries connotation, that words and phrases can directly elicit moods (e.g., *allure, seduce, bait*). The DCT explanation of this effect is similar to referential processing, but the reference in this case is directly to emotions, although the effect could be mediated by images. Either case presumably results from the association of language to life experiences that had memorable emotional content.

The relationship between affect and cognition is presently controversial in psychology, and much more needs to be learned. This subject has gained increasing attention as the link between cognition and affect becomes important in eliciting students' interest in learning from text (Renninger, Hidi, & Krapp, 1992). We discuss the important relationship between imagery and affect more in subsequent chapters.

Summary

This chapter has presented a comprehensive account of meaning that draws from the general theory presented in chapter 3. The cognitive system is dormant until mental representations and their interconnections are activated. Meaning is built up through spreading activation in bottom-up fashion, but it is also restricted in top-down fashion as verbal and nonverbal contexts limit the likely alternatives for activation. Examples based on the general theoretical model and its levels of meaning or processing were presented, including the representational level, the referential level, and the associative level. The DCT view of mental models derives from the general principles of the theory. Mental models in reading inherently involve language but also mental imagery to varying degrees as language variables such as concreteness and context vary and individual differences dispose. The foundation of all meaning in direct experience was postulated. The comprehension of figurative language follows from the general cognitive theory, with the activation of verbal and nonverbal representations in sometimes novel ways. Affective and emotional responses were also presented in this view of meaning.

CHAPTER 5

Memory
and
Remembering

Chapter 4 introduced the DCT view of meaning, mental modeling, and the structure of semantic memory. According to that view, memory is infused throughout all aspects of comprehension, and therefore our discussion of memory in this chapter is inherently intertwined with the discussion of meaning and comprehension in chapter 4. There can be no meaning or comprehension without memory—either short-term memory for wordings or long-term, semantic and episodic memory for interpretations. We first summarize some current approaches to memory and then elaborate on the traditional memory categories of semantic memory and episodic memory from a dual coding perspective as they relate to literacy. This discussion is particularly relevant to a fuller understanding of theoretical models of reading, the subject of the next chapter.

MEMORY

Memory and remembering are extraordinarily rich and diverse subjects. Memory has been categorized in various ways including the stages of sensory register, short-term memory, working memory, long-term memory, and even long-term working memory. Long-term memory has been subcategorized as semantic memory, episodic memory, and even permanent memory. Similarly, semantic memory has been further subdivided into declarative and procedural memory, and so on. All these distinctions are controversial because they are seen to interact and overlap considerably, although some neuropsychological evidence suggests that the brain areas that subserve at least some aspects of semantic and episodic memory performance are anatomically different (e.g., Ley, 1983; Paivio & te Linde, 1982; West et al., 1998; Wilkins & Moscovitch, 1978). Further complications involve the formation and use of concepts, the way retrieval cues affect remembering, and memory illusions such as imagination inflation (remembering an actual event as you imagined it happened, e.g., Goff & Roediger, 1998).

The important general distinction for our purposes here is that literacy entails memory from two sources: the text itself and what the text evokes in the form of verbal associations, imagery, and emotions. Some of our memories of text are literal in the form of the names of people, places, things, and other specific wordings. More of what we remember is in the form of the verbal and nonverbal mental evocations from text wordings that are themselves rapidly forgotten. Those remembered evocations rather than the specific wordings that gave rise to them are the focus of our discussion here. While recognizing the problems with memory distinctions, we discuss memory for text in terms of semantic and episodic memory, one of the better supported memory distinctions.

SEMANTIC MEMORY

DCT and Other Theories of Semantic Memory

The DCT view of semantic memory can be understood by contrast to other cognitive theories. As we have noted previously, many contemporary theories of cognition hold that all knowledge is abstract and amodal, derived from experience but with no retention of the contextual information of the particular episodes from which the knowledge was abstracted. In that view, knowledge and memory are seen as different because knowledge is general whereas memory involves specific events.

This difference is often expressed in the distinction between semantic memory for abstract, general knowledge and episodic memory for concrete, specific events. The distinction is not a perfect one: In reading, the verbal associations, images, and emotions evoked by a text (i.e., its semantic content) become a part of the reading episode and are remembered in the same manner as events that actually happened, although they can usually be distinguished.

Other theories take an exemplar view. This view is that knowledge is not abstract but derives from specific past experiences. Hence, DCT is more of an exemplar theory because it holds that all mental representations are modality-specific and retain some of their original perceptual information.

However, it is not enough to say that DCT is an exemplar theory because DCT also accounts for abstractions that apply to a variety of episodes without applying to any one in particular. Abstractions can exist as verbal generalizations in the form of mental word labels and statements that can refer to various instances either real or imagined (e.g., *peace* and *justice*), and imagery can serve symbolic or semiotic functions by concretizing abstract concepts (e.g., the dove as a symbol of peace; the blindfolded goddess Themis with weighing scale as a symbol of justice).

Verbal language adapts particularly well to symbolizing the abstract because it is arbitrary and needs bear no actual resemblance to that for which it stands. For example, the printed word *cup* bears no visual resemblance to a cup the way a picture of a cup does. Likewise, the pronunciation /kup/ and its individual phonemes are auditory representations abstracted from the stream of speech and bear no auditory resemblance to any sounds associated with real cups. This feature of symbolic language (as opposed to pictographic language or onomatopoeia, for example) allows it to symbolize the abstract and the general as easily as the concrete and the specific.

Hence the word *cup* can stand for all cups in the abstract without referring to any particular one, and *justice* can refer to the ideal of justice without referring to any instance of its occurrence. The important theoretical point here is that while these verbal representations function as abstract symbols, they are themselves concrete in some modality such as visual or auditory. Thus, language performs an abstract function without being abstract itself.

The DCT View of Semantic Memory

The DCT view of semantic memory organization comes straight from the general theory. Mental representations are organized in both the verbal and nonverbal codes. Referential connections between the codes provide for a variety of semantic alternatives and elaborations. The verbal system can be seen to have vertical, superordinate organizations ranging from the general to the specific (e.g., *objects, dishes, cups*) and horizontal, coordinate organizations among members of a class (e.g., *cups, mugs, steins, tankards*). The nonverbal system provides imagery exemplars for these terms at varying levels of inclusiveness. For example, the phrase *wash the dishes* may evoke images of dishes, silverware, pots and pans, whereas *use the good dishes* usually refers more specifically to table settings.

Concepts and concept formation are explained this way in DCT. A traditional definition of a concept is a category that belongs to one or more superordinate categories, has defining characteristics, and has examples and possibly nonexamples available (Klausmeier, Ghatala, & Frayer, 1974; Smith & Medin, 1981). For concrete concepts, all of these may be represented verbally, and the characteristics, examples, and nonexamples may be represented by imagery as well. The verbal abstraction *cup* symbolizes a certain set of cylindrical vessels of generally small size made for holding liquids for drinking, often having a handle, and so on. A favorite coffee cup may serve as a familiar example; bowls or pitchers may serve as nonexamples. The basis of the concept is language units (e.g., *cup, vessel, dish, bowl, handle, coffee cup*) and the mental images of objects to which those language units refer in our experience. The concept in its fullest sense would also include affective properties, functions, connections to other concepts, and so on, that further extend and define it.

Note that the exemplar(s) evoked may be different in different situational contexts and are not fixed. For example, a cup at a picnic is likely to be understood as paper or styrofoam whereas a cup at a formal dinner is likely to be understood as china. A cup does not always have to hold a liquid, as a cup in a golf green or using a cup to hold pencils on a desk. Hence meaning and function are experiential but probabilistic and not necessarily fixed to one particular time and situation. The indefiniteness here is deliberate: All encoding, memory, and meaning is probabilistic to some degree in DCT.

Concepts for more abstract ideas are handled in the same way but with relatively more emphasis on verbal associations. Chapter 4 introduced the analogy between meaning and currency. Language units can be exchanged for other language units the way currency can be exchanged for other currency, or language can be exchanged for images and feelings the way money can be exchanged for goods and services. Thus, the concrete synonyms *cup* and *mug* are parts of a larger verbal-associative network and also converge on a common image or set of images, but abstract language synonyms must rely more on the verbal associations (Clark, 1983). This analogy applies well to explaining the formation of abstract concepts.

Elaborating on an example from chapter 4, the abstract concept labeled *justice* delimits a condition in which behavior to oneself or to another is consistent with cultural ethics or laws. The defining characteristics of *justice* in most contemporary cultures include the abstractions *fairness, impartiality, legal precedent,* and so on. The meanings of these terms derive primarily from their close network of verbal associations to each other. However, these abstract terms are also associated with more concrete terms such as *judge, jury, court,* and so on. These concrete terms are somewhat more likely to evoke mental images that provide concrete examples and/or nonexamples such as particular legal cases. Even an abstract term like *fairness* can mentally refer to familiar concrete situations where the term applies, such as when laws apply the same to the rich and the poor.

Other abstract concepts have even less dependence on referential imagery. An example is grammar concepts. Terms such as *noun, verb, subject, predicate, phrase, clause,* or *sentence* refer primarily to other language abstractions and are understood intraverbally. Another example is the use of word labels to refer to mathematical concepts such as *number, square root, polygon,* and so on. Here words are used to refer to mathematical abstractions that form another language and the concepts are understood interlinguistically, between the two languages. Concrete operations are clearly involved in understanding mathematical concepts and their functions (Skemp, 1987), and are involved in learning grammar concepts as well (Moeser & Bregman, 1972, 1973), but language and linguistic associations are prominent in their definition and classification.

Likewise, the theory also allows for conceptual knowledge in the nonverbal realm alone, with no reference to language. For example, one might mentally classify different tempos of music by different mood states (slow and mournful, fast and sprightly) or motor acts (walking, trotting, running) without applying any musical terminology or other language, although such language may be later applied.

Newer views of concepts and their functions are likewise highly consistent with DCT. For example, Soloman, Medin, and Lynch (1999) define concepts as mental representations that serve multiple interacting functions and can only be understood in context (e.g., the concept *tree* differs according to verbal plant taxonomy, but also according to shape, as landscapers can "tree" shrubs by pruning). This view holds that concepts serve other functions besides categorization such as reasoning and conceptual integration, all of which interact with, and are determined by, the experiential history of the individual in comparing and differentiating words and things in different contexts including cultural contexts. This view is compatible with the dual coding view of mental representations (i.e., logogens and imagens as concepts), their processes, and functions as discussed here and in previous chapters.

In sum, both traditional and current views of semantic memory and conceptual knowledge can be accounted for by the verbal and nonverbal systems of DCT, including their referential and associative connections. The verbal system has a salience in this regard, particularly in the representation of abstract concepts.

EPISODIC MEMORY

The DCT View of Episodic Memory

Episodic memory has been of particular interest to researchers in reading comprehension. In DCT, a memory episode is a composite of modality-specific, verbal and nonverbal representations derived from externally experienced events and the internal verbal and nonverbal representations that are evoked by those events. Episodic memories can be detailed and accurate but are often incomplete and altered. They are incomplete because of limitations on encoding; some detail is always lost. They are altered because internal representations are associatively added to the episode. The imperfect encoding of original information and the importation of associated information account for the common recall phenomena of elaboration and distortion.

Among other functions, episodic memories serve an important "chunking" function during text processing. Pieces of a text such as individual story events, points in an exposition or argument, or even individual sentences are temporarily held in memory as represented by key language and/or key images. These key language units and images serve convenient unifying and symbolizing functions and can be integrated into larger episodes. These episodes may be linked or merged with others into still larger episodic structures as a reading progresses. Whole texts and their constituent episodes may later be represented or symbolized in memory by language and images and can be retrieved via them.

Verbal cohesion of various kinds including lexical, grammatical, causal, and thematic connections provide verbal links between text units that help to structure separate constituents into coherent episodes (Halliday & Hasan, 1976; Trabasso & van den Broek, 1985; Zholkovsky, 1984). However, verbal cohesive devices have been shown to be neither a necessary nor a sufficient condition for textual coherence (Enkvist, 1978). The only necessary and sufficient condition for text coherence appears to be that the text's language elicits an envisioned world in the experience or imagination of the reader (Enkvist, 1978; Fillmore, 1977; Fillmore & Kay, 1983).

Therefore, both language and imagery have important roles in the memory of coherent text episodes. We next discuss their roles in several widely cited episodic memory studies in reading. We review selected studies, provide a dual coding interpretation of each, and then report on critical reviews of this literature.

DCT Interpretations of Episodic Memory Studies in Reading

"The War of the Ghosts." In a classic episodic memory study, Bartlett (1932) had British students read a story from Native

American culture called "The War of the Ghosts." The story concerns a young Kathlamet, who is invited to go on a war party one night by warriors in canoes. During the battle, he is wounded but feels no pain. Realizing that the warriors are ghosts, he returns home, relates his tale, and dies at sunup. As he dies, something black comes out of his mouth. The story is related as a brief, disconnected series of events with little elaboration such as causal explanations typical of Western stories.

Students' recollections of the story over an extended period of time were often elaborated to include causal language beyond what was stated in the original text. Some distortions also occurred, usually involving making the story more familiar. For example, some of the British students remembered the canoes as rowboats. Bartlett used this study as an example of the constructive nature of memory; that is, people integrate new information with existing, familiar knowledge to establish coherence.

The dual coding interpretation of the "War of the Ghosts" study is that the narrative may have been partially remembered as a sequence of images of the events of the story. Those images could be distorted by the importation of more familiar objects, such as remembering canoes as rowboats (or simply replacing a less familiar term with a more familiar term on the verbal side in recall). Because verbal-associative connections between events were not strongly stated, causal language connections between the events may have been added in the recalls to elaborate logical causal connections more familiar to Western stories.

One of the longest remembered events in the story was that something black came out of the young man's mouth as he died, a vivid image. But even in this case, some students remembered the "something black" as his dying breath, a distortion to an image more familiar to them than the mythical symbols of the Kathlamets. While Bartlett attributed his findings to abstract knowledge schemata, dual coding theoretical concepts could explain the results equally well and more parsimoniously. It is noteworthy that whereas he employed the term *schema,* Bartlett expressed strong dislike for it as seeming at once too definite and too vague.

Sentence Integration Studies. Many studies have investigated the way information is integrated across related sentences. In a widely cited example, Bransford and Franks (1971) presented participants with sentences that contained a series of simple ideas, then presented a set of recognition test sentences that included both the original simple ideas and combinations of them that had not been presented together originally. For example, the four-idea unit sentence *The ants in the kitchen ate the sweet jelly that was on the table* was not itself presented, but subsets of it were such as *The ants ate the jelly* (one idea unit) or *The ants in the kitchen ate the jelly* (two idea units). The test sentences included the old ones as well as new combinations including the four-idea unit sentence.

Results indicated that participants correctly recognized previously presented sentences that contained more idea units better than those that contained fewer idea units. Moreover, the participants in the study were most confident that they recognized the four-idea unit sentences although they had never actually been presented with them. Also, participants incorrectly "recognized" many new-but-consistent sentences that were never actually presented while rejecting some new-but-inconsistent sentences.

The researchers concluded that the participants acquired an integrated and elaborated representation of the combined meaning of the sentences, not just an accumulation of individual word or sentence meanings. Furthermore, inconsistent information was consistently rejected, suggesting considerable precision in the integrated episode.

The DCT interpretation here is that the episodes may have been encoded as integrated images with details elaborated beyond those specified by the words in any one sentence. Hence, a short sentence such as *The ants ate the jelly* could be elaborated by combining it with information from other sentences such as *on the table, in the kitchen,* and *sweet jelly* into an integrated image of the overall episode. Recognition of longer descriptions of this episode would be more consistent with such a holistic image than shorter versions containing subsets of information. A complex, integrated image containing visual and possibly gustatory elements might also draw in familiar associated images and referential language, accounting for the finding that new-but-consistent sentences were "recognized" better than new-but-inconsistent sentences. In short, language and mental imagery processes can completely account for the recollections.

Perspective Studies. A set of memory studies assigned readers to read from a particular point of view, or perspective, to see how this affected recall. Several of these studies used a passage in which two boys play hooky from school and visit the home of one of the boys (e.g., Pichert & Anderson, 1977). They encounter such objects as 10-speed bikes, a coin collection, a new fireplace, and a leaky roof.

Readers assigned to read from the perspective of a burglar tended to recall objects more important to a burglar such the 10-speed bikes and coin collection, whereas readers assigned to read from the perspective of a homebuyer tended to recall objects more important to a homebuyer such as the new fireplace and the leaky roof. When the readers were later asked to recall the episode from the opposite perspective, they tended to better recall information important to that perspective. Thus, the perspective studies indicated that readers store rich, integrated representations of episodes in memory but may recall them differently depending on task instructions and prior knowledge.

In the Pichert and Anderson (1977) and related studies, the DCT interpretation is that verbal instructions and the passage together activated different patterns of verbal and imaginal encoding. The verbal cue *burglar* would prime encoding of the 10-speed bikes and coin collection, whereas the cue *homebuyer* would prime encoding of the new fireplace and leaky roof. The different patterns of verbal activation would referentially evoke different patterns of imagery.

However, complex images of the rooms and their contents would allow for the additional encoding of other information not salient to the assigned point of view. For example, if the passage described a room with a new fireplace and a coin collection, this information might be encoded in an complex image of the room that would simultaneously provide information important to both perspectives. This would explain the later recall of information important to the other, previously unassigned, perspective. This finding poses a difficulty for schema theory: Information not fitting the assigned schema should not have been encoded for later recall, which occurred up to weeks later in some of the perspective studies.

Critical Reviews of Episodic Memory Studies. In reviewing many years of these and other episodic memory studies, Alba and Hasher (1983) concluded that a rich and detailed representation of a complex event is stored in memory, and what people tell of what they have stored depends on a variety of circumstances such as encoding and/or recall instructions, context effects, and the characteristics of the materials. Among the findings of the review were (a) recall for sensory, lexical, and syntactic detail of verbal passages was above chance; (b) separate integrated units of a complex episode were stored rather than an overall schematic representation in which many details are lost; (c) people were frequently aware of the difference between externally derived and internally generated parts of the episode; and (d) episodic integration does not exclude the memory of other information; unintegrated or uninterpreted information can still be recalled under various conditions.

The results of this review are consistent with the DCT view of episodic memory, a view that can provide a quite explicit account of the representations and processes involved in episodic memory research in reading. Such an account was provided by Sadoski, et al. (1991) in a general critique of schema theory in reading and a dual coding interpretation of schema studies. Rather than invoking schemata or other abstract forms of memory, the results of all these studies were consistently and parsimoniously explained using language and imagery in particular as integrating media. This analysis was extended to still other influential studies of memory for text including passages with more abstract language. However, the integration of abstract text poses special problems that implicate the verbal system in particular ways. We next turn to that issue.

The Integration of Abstract Text

Questions about the DCT view of imagery effects in the integration and recall of abstract text were originally raised by Marschark and Paivio (1977). In a study of cued recall of concrete and abstract sentences they found, as expected, that recall was higher for concrete than for abstract sentences. But they unexpectedly found that the two types of sentences did not differ in the extent to which recall was integrated as measured by the retrieval effectiveness of verbal cues that were related to the meaning of the whole sentence as compared to cues that related only to one of the content words in the sentence. The higher recall for concrete sentences was consistent with the dual coding hypothesis that dually encoded information is more memorable, but the equal integration effect was inconsistent with the hypothesis that imagery is a superior integrating medium.

The researchers concluded that dual coding accounted for the higher recall of concrete sentences, but some other explanation was needed to explain the equivalent integration effects. Verbal associative processes are a likely DCT candidate because they apply equally to concrete and abstract language. An alternative theoretical interpretation involved an interaction between relational and distinctive processing (Marschark & Hunt, 1989). This theory assumes that distinctiveness and relatedness are partners in affecting memory; that is, concreteness-induced imagery increases the contrast of concrete language units to abstract language units rather than providing a separate memory code, but this distinctiveness effect is dependent on an established relationship between the language units.

A DCT resolution to the issue was obtained by Paivio, Walsh, and Bons (1994). Their results demonstrated that strong verbal associations are *necessary* to produce integration of abstract word pairs, whereas imagery is *sufficient* to produce integration of concrete word pairs even when verbal associations are weak. The results were not consistent with the relational-distinctiveness view because integration still occurred for concrete word pairs in which the pair members were unrelated. These findings provided a DCT explanation for the integration of abstract language, but they further explain the integration of even weakly related concrete language.

For example, the abstract sentence *When ideals clash contrary standards emerge* might be integrated through the verbal associations between *ideals* and *standards, clash* and *contrary,* and the modification of the main clause *contrary standards emerge* by the relative clause *when ideals clash.* However, the concrete sentence *The fire glowed warmly; a storm lashed the shutters* lacks the same degree of verbal association; the two parts are separate with less unifying lexical or grammatical association. However, this sentence can be holistically integrated as an image of a cozy fireplace with a storm raging outside. Hence, both concrete and abstract sentences might be recalled as integrated units but for theoretically different reasons.

Another alternative proposal for integration of abstract text comes from context availability theory (Kieras, 1978). According to this theory, concrete language is easier to remember because it more readily finds a context in the knowledge network; the content of high-imagery sentences has more connections with permanent memory information. But that advantage is theoretically removed when abstract language deals with highly familiar information and/or when it is presented in a supportive sentence context. In that case, the theory predicts that abstract language and concrete language should be recalled equally.

Accordingly, DCT and context availability theory make contradictory predictions where familiar language in a supportive context is concerned: Dual coding predicts that concrete language should be recalled better than abstract language due to the additional integrating force provided by imagery, whereas context availability predicts that they should be recalled equally. A test of these competing predictions was performed by Sadoski, Goetz, and Avila (1995).

They used four factual paragraphs about historical figures (Michelangelo and James Madison) that were matched for number of sentences, words, and syllables, sentence length, information density, cohesion, and rated comprehensibility. In one set, two paragraphs were rated equal in familiarity but one paragraph was rated more concrete than the other. In the other set, the paragraphs differed in both familiarity and concreteness, with the abstract paragraph being more familiar.

In the case where the concrete and abstract paragraphs were equally familiar, the concrete paragraph was recalled significantly better. In the case where the abstract paragraph was more familiar, the paragraphs were recalled equally well. These results were consistent with DCT and inconsistent with context availability theory (cf. Holcomb et al., 1999; Kounios & Holcomb, 1994; Nelson & Schreiber, 1992; Sadoski et al., 1993b).

In sum, DCT can account for the integration of both concrete and abstract text in a theoretically consistent and parsimonious manner across the memory research in reading. The specifics of the processing mechanisms involved were detailed in the previous chapters on referential and associative processing, which introduced the principle of code additivity to explain differences in the way concrete and abstract text episodes are encoded and recalled. Another principle, called the conceptual peg hypothesis, is also important to understanding the DCT account of episodic memory. We will next discuss code additivity and then the conceptual peg hypothesis.

Code Additivity in Text Memory

In DCT, the verbal and nonverbal codes are theoretically independent of each other, each capable of operating in isolation or in parallel (chap. 3). A functional implication of this independence is that the effects of encoding a stimulus as both imagery and language should be statistically additive rather than interactive. The principle of code additivity offers several general implications for text memory.

The principle assumes a descending degree of memorability for common literacy materials. Pictures are directly encoded as images and are especially likely to be accompanied by language labels or text explanations in literacy situations, giving them a high probability of being encoded both nonverbally and verbally by readers. Concrete language directly evokes verbal representations in a reader and is also likely to evoke mental images in that reader, although the imagery is indirect as opposed to direct in the case of pictures. Abstract language also directly evokes the verbal code, but it is less likely to evoke internal images and it is generally harder to illustrate; it tends to be encoded mainly verbally. These assumptions generally imply that pictures with labels and/or associated (concrete) text are remembered better than concrete text alone and that concrete text alone is remembered better than abstract text alone, other things being equal. The qualifier is theoretically necessary because differences such as context effects, familiarity, instructions, or individual differences can alter the general pattern. These assumptions have been specified and well supported in research, and we review several such studies next. (See Paivio, 1975a, 1986, 1991b, 1996, for extensive reviews; we also review some educational implications in chap. 8.)

A program of experiments has empirically demonstrated the statistical additivity of the two codes at approximately the 2:1 ratio, with the imagery code contributing more to the total than the verbal code in most situations. Suggestive evidence for such an effect was first obtained by Paivio (1965). He tested recall for 32 nouns in 16 paired combinations of concrete-concrete (e.g., *coffee-pencil*), concrete-abstract (e.g., *coffee-fact*), abstract-concrete (e.g., *fact-pencil*), and abstract-abstract (e.g., *virtue-fact*). The first word was used as a cue to recall the second word in the pair. The results were consistent with the idea that the concrete words evoked imagery that greatly aided their recall: Cued recall declined in the order just given, with recall for the concrete-concrete combinations about twice that of the abstract-abstract combinations (71% vs. 38%).

This experiment was controlled, and later replicated with further controls, to ensure that concreteness was the operative factor and not another quality that was correlated with concreteness (e.g., distinctiveness, comprehensibility). The subsequent experiments in the program used various procedures including picture-word combinations and imagery and verbal coding instructions to demonstrate directly that imagery and verbal codes had statistically additive effects on concrete words, as anticipated by the 1965 experiment (see Paivio, 1975a, for a specific review of these studies).

In an effort to extend the Paivio (1965) findings to longer texts, Sadoski et al. (1993b) conducted a similar study. They prepared four factual sentences, two concrete and two abstract, about each of 10 historical figures. The concrete and abstract sentence sets were matched for familiarity, readability, number of syllables, length in words, repetition of content words, and number of idea units. An example of an abstract sentence was *Georgia O'Keeffe's career covers most of the history of modern art in America, and she shares the inner world of reflection with the earliest of the modernists.* An example of a matched concrete sentence was *Georgia O'Keeffe perceived art everywhere—she once purchased a house because she admired the way a black double door was placed in a long, low adobe wall.* Similar to the Paivio (1965) study, the four concrete and abstract sentences about each historical figure were presented to participants in sets of all possible combinations.

The results were strikingly similar to those of Paivio (1965). That is, the concrete-concrete pairs were recalled more than twice as well as the abstract-abstract pairs both immediately and after five days. These results can be seen in the columns for the totals in Table 5.1. Similar results were found in a second experiment with matched concrete and abstract paragraphs about historical figures that varied from 110 words to 265 words in length. These results were further replicated by Sadoski, Goetz, and Rodriguez (2000) with persuasive, literary, expository, and narrative text passages of about 56 words.

In sum, across experiments involving word pairs, sentences, and paragraphs of varying lengths and genres, the recall of concrete text units was much greater than abstract text units with other variables controlled. This is entirely consistent with the additivity of the verbal and nonverbal codes as specified in DCT.

TABLE 5.1. *Mean percentage of gist recall for concrete and abstract sentence pairs. From Sadoski et al. (1993b). Copyright © 1993 by the American Psychological Association. Adapted with permission.*

		Immediate recall			Five-day recall	
Pairs	Total	First Sentence	Second Sentence	Total	First Sentence	Second Sentence
CC	40	40	41	27	27	26
CA	37	47	27	24	30	17
AC	34	22	47	23	13	32
AA	18	18	17	10	11	9

Note: C = concrete sentence, A = abstract sentence.

The Conceptual Peg Hypothesis

The conceptual peg hypothesis states that mental images play a central role in organization and retrieval from memory by serving as mental "pegs" to which at least some of the other parts of the episode are "hooked." That is, mental imagery plays a central role in chunking information in memory. The ancient method of loci, discussed in chapter 2, used images as mental reference points for the organization of oratory and was an intuitive early application of this principle. In experimental studies of the recall of concrete and abstract phrases, sentences, and longer text units, results have consistently shown an advantage for concrete language units when one member of the pair was used as a cue for the recall of the other member (reviewed in Paivio, 1986, 1991b).

For example, in the Paivio (1965) study discussed above, the items in the concrete-concrete combination *coffee-pencil* are not closely associated as individual words, but they can be readily integrated or "chunked" into an image of a pencil next to (or in) a cup of coffee. By comparison, the words in the abstract-abstract combination *virtue-fact* are not closely associated either, but they cannot be as easily chunked into a memorable unit.

But the effect goes further. Concrete-abstract combinations like *coffee-fact* prove easier to recall than abstract-abstract combinations like *virtue-fact,* especially when the concrete member is used as a recall cue. That is, *fact* would be easier to recall given *coffee* as a cue than *fact* would be given *virtue* as a cue. Imagery seems to serve as a peg for recalling abstract information as well. Moreover, *coffee-fact* is better recalled than *fact-coffee,* suggesting the importance of establishing the peg before the attachments.

The effect also occurs with larger text units. In the Sadoski et al. (1993b) study discussed above, participants were presented concrete and abstract sentences about historical figures. Findings indicated that placing a concrete sentence before an abstract sentence about the same historical figure increased the recall of the abstract sentence by about 70% over placing another abstract sentence before the abstract sentence. Table 5.1 shows the recall of each sentence by its position in the presented pair (first or second) for both time periods. Again, a concrete sentence in the first position appears to have provided a stable peg to which the related abstract sentence in the second position could attach.

This result is even more striking than in the case of word pairs because the recall cue was not the entire first sentence, but only the name of the historical figure, a name that began all the sentences about that historical figure whether concrete or abstract (note the examples about Georgia O'Keeffe). That is, the preceding concrete sentence presumably gave concrete form to the historical figure in the subsequent abstract sentence, so the improved recall of the abstract sentence must have come from the integrative power of the concrete sentence as well as the peg effect of the concrete cue.

The conceptual peg effect also has been found with other sized text units. A concrete noun phrase in a sentence has been found to assist recall of the verb phrase of the same sentence (Anderson, Goetz, Pichert, & Halff, 1977). For example, concrete noun phrases in sentences like *The tribal marriage customs fascinated the tourists* were later better recognized as having been read than abstract noun phrases in sentences like *The traditional customs fascinated the tourists.* In addition, once the concrete noun phrases were recognized, their predicates were recalled more easily than in the abstract sentences. The researchers concluded that a concrete noun phrase formed a stable conceptual peg for a unified, integrated memory of the whole sentence.

Concrete advance organizers assist recall of related abstract passages as extensive as textbook chapters (Corkill, Glover, & Bruning, 1988). Reading a concrete paragraph even assists recall of a following abstract paragraph of differing content (Royer & Cable,

1975, 1976). In composition, writing definitions of concrete terms affects the way the definitions of abstract terms are written immediately afterwards (Sadoski, Kealy, Goetz, & Paivio, 1997), and using a concrete verb is associated with the increased use of modifiers later in the same sentence (Sadoski & Goetz, 1998). These studies are discussed in more detail in chapters 7 and 8.

A key episode such as the climax of the story may serve naturally as a mental peg for the recollection of the rest of the story. Common examples may be seen in being asked to recall a familiar story. In recalling *Cinderella,* for example, people often report recalling an image of the glass slipper, the royal ball, or a similarly salient episode and then reconstructing the story's details from that starting point. This effect has been found even with young children (Sadoski, 1983, 1985).

For example, Sadoski (1985) had third and fourth graders read an unillustrated basal reader story aloud and then perform a series of comprehension tasks including a free verbal recall (story retelling) and a report of any images recalled from the story. The story was about a pet canary in a space station, who, at the climax, saves the lives of all by passing out and thereby alerting the crew to an oxygen leak much the way coal miners once used canaries. Half of the students were asked to do the retelling before the imagery reports, and the other half performed the tasks in the reverse order. In both orders, about half the students reported an image of the climax of the story (i.e., the canary passing out and being revived with oxygen). However, the effect of having a climax image to report dramatically interacted with recall for the two groups.

Figure 5.1 illustrates this interaction. Mean retelling scores (out of a possible 100) are shown for the groups that reported a climax image either before or after their retelling and those who did not. Where the retelling was done first, there was no statistically significant difference in the retelling scores for the climax imagery groups. But where the retelling was done after the imagery reports, those who reported an image of the story's climax performed significantly better. That is, those students who had a climax image in memory and reported it before their retelling recalled the story better, but those that had no climax image to report lost recall rapidly while reporting their images first. The key image apparently served as a conceptual peg that dramatically enhanced story recall.

Besides serving as a mnemonic device, imagery may serve to capture or symbolize the essential ideas of a text. Yuille and Paivio (1969) varied the imagery level and the organization level of passages and found that recall was better for the thematically organized passages that were high in imagery value but not for those that were medium or low in imagery value. They suggested that the essential idea of thematically organized material may be in the form of organized imagery.

Consistent with this suggestion, reporting an image of the climax of a story was found to be moderately correlated with grasping deeper levels of story meaning as demonstrated by the ability to summarize its plot or state its unifying theme (Sadoski, 1983,

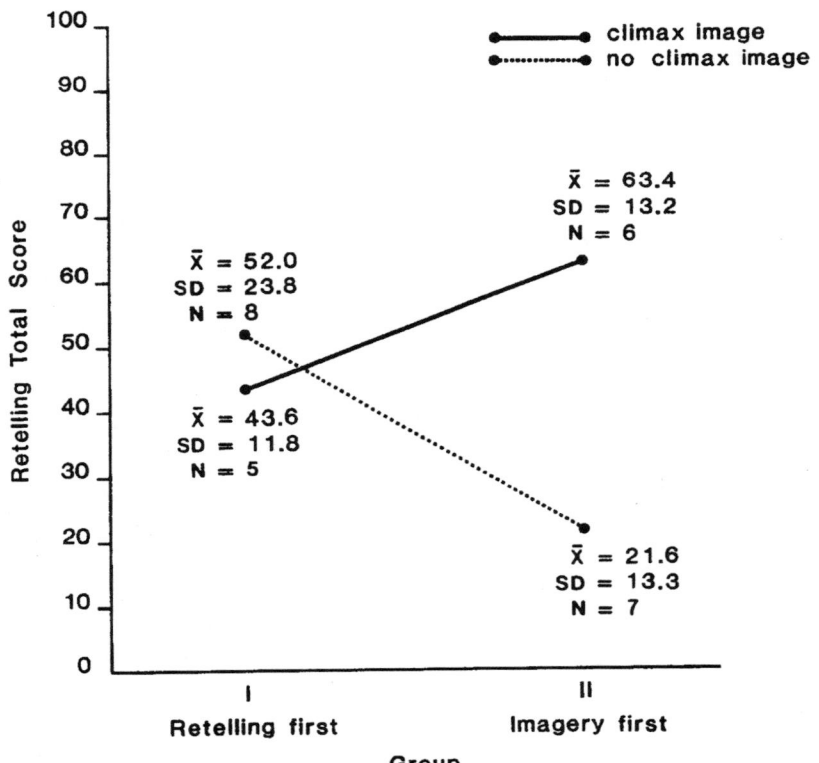

FIG. 5.1. *Retelling scores as a function of reporting an image of the climax of the story and performing a retelling first or reporting imagery first. From Sadoski (1985). Copyright by the International Reading Association. All rights reserved.*

1985). Comprehension of story structure as defined by story grammar analysis was found to be moderately correlated with reported story imagery (Sadoski, Goetz, Olivarez, Lee, & Roberts, 1990). Moderate positive correlations also have been found between text-constrained imagery and main idea comprehension in expository text passages (McCallum & Moore, 1999).

In sum, mental images play an important role in episodic memory by providing conceptual pegs that link, integrate, and unify memories. They can serve symbolic functions that capture the essential meaning of a text. Although language can also serve this function, imagery seems to be particularly salient in chunking or integrating memories for text material.

Summary

Semantic and episodic memory are often differentiated: semantic memory for general, conceptual knowledge and episodic memory for events situated in a particular place and time. DCT can explain much of both semantic and episodic memory within its framework of assumptions. Semantic memory and concept formation derive from connections between verbal and nonverbal representations with an emphasis on the quality of verbal representations to serve as abstract symbols.

Episodic memory studies of "chunking" have been of special interest to text comprehension researchers. Widely cited episodic memory studies can be reinterpreted in DCT terms in a consistent and parsimonious way. The episodic integration of abstract text can be explained through strong verbal-associative (contextual) relationships, whereas concrete text can be integrated even where verbal-associative relationships are weaker.

Memory of text episodes of varying length has been shown to be an additive effect of verbal and nonverbal coding. Imagery plays an important role in episodic memory by acting as a conceptual peg that links and integrates text material and serves to symbolize its essential meanings.

CHAPTER 6

The Reading Process

DCT is a general theory of cognition that provides a specific explanation of the reading process in its own terms. This chapter presents that explanation. Deriving a specific theory of the reading process from a general theory of cognition has obvious advantages. Ultimately, all theories of reading and writing need to accommodate larger, general theories of cognition. The goal of scientific explanation in any field is for individual observations and local theories to fuse with larger, general theories to consistently and parsimoniously explain the widest range of phenomena.

Previous chapters have given detailed accounts of meaning and memory in reading as explained by DCT. We begin this chapter with a brief overview of the reading process in dual coding terms, followed by an illustrative example of a reading episode from a dual coding perspective. Then we provide more extensive dual coding explanations of bottom-up and top-down phenomena in the reading process. Finally, we give a brief comparison of DCT to certain other theories of the reading process.

DUAL CODING IN THE READING PROCESS

Explanations of the reading process typically begin with the sensory detection of printed language through purposeful attention to a text. Sensory activation is visual in reading (except Braille), and visual logogens are activated at the representational level. In some situations, visual logogens could be primed prior to detecting printed words, as in rereading a well-known verse or looking up a word in the dictionary. In other situations some of the words encountered will be completely unfamiliar and logogens for letters and letter combinations will be activated, as in a first reading of *Jabberwocky* (*"'Twas brillig, and the slithy toves . . . "*).

Spreading activation begins next, initially in the form of the activation of auditory-motor logogens through their neural connections (recoding at the representational level). Spreading activation between representations can also occur on the basis of pattern similarity (e.g., *brillig* is similar to *broiling* or *brilliant* and *slithy* is similar to *lithe* and *slimy*). Top-down effects can influence activation at this level as in the phonological recoding of homographs such as *dove* as determined by context.

As spreading activation continues, referential connections to imagens and/or associative connections to still other logogens are activated rapidly. These connections are probabilistic and may be direct or indirect. This does not imply a linear, connect-the-dots activity; spreading activation fans out in parallel in the verbal and nonverbal systems and through connections between the two systems. Referential and associative activity produces comprehension in varying degrees.

Context both constrains the spread of this activity and has a cumulative integrating effect as the reading progresses; reading proceeds in bottom-up, top-down cycles. Familiarity, grammar, verbal-associative contexts, and nonverbal contexts all serve to shape and elaborate the emerging interpretation. Readers hold verbal and nonverbal textual "chunks" in short-term memory in parallel forms such as inner speech and visual imagery and integrate them into tentative interpretations or mental models in episodic memory. Further language and imagery are then primed and/or activated as the reading progresses and the interpretation or model is elaborated and constrained.

Memory for text information and the retrieval of that information are facilitated by verbal–nonverbal dual coding. The mechanisms for these processes have been detailed in previous chapters. We next illustrate the dual coding view of the reading process through an extended example.

A DCT VIEW OF A READING EPISODE

Consider this sentence: *The diver did a one-and-a-half into the pool.* Let's assume that a skilled reader, reading for full comprehension and recall, visually focuses on a span of the first nine characters (an estimate from eye movement studies) encompassing the phrase *The diver.* The fixation will likely center on *diver* because content words tend to receive more processing in reading; besides, the word *The* is highly familiar and often begins a sentence as a nominal marker.

Lacking any priming from prior context in this simplified instance, the reader needs to process considerable print information from *diver* to establish its meaning as a base. Perception activates letter-level and word-level visual logogens (remember that logogens are a shorthand way of expressing the neurological activity associated with language units of all sizes). For example, the loop on the *d* distinguishes it from *l* and hence *diver* from *liver;* the diagonal lines and the opening at the top of *v* distinguish it from the vertical lines and the opening at the bottom of *n* and hence *diver* from *diner.* The letter sequence *d-i-v-e-r* distinguishes *diver* from *drive,* which includes exactly the same features and letters but in a different sequence. That is, the visual pattern of the word provides cues for its recognition and discrimination from close alternatives. Auditory-motor logogens may also be activated for phonological recoding to elaborate the recognition of the words, to help retain the phrase in short-term memory, and to facilitate additional connections. The phrase has now achieved the representational level of meaning. This will have occurred in perhaps a quarter of a second (also an estimate from eye movement and neuropsychological studies).

The activated phrase *The diver* may then evoke a variety of associations, both verbal and nonverbal (i.e., spreading activation).

Recall that in DCT, spreading activation within the verbal code is called associative processing, and spreading activation to the nonverbal code is called referential processing. The phrase *The diver* could activate common verbal associates such as *swimmer* or *skin diver*. Depending on specialized individual experiences, it might also evoke associates such as *dive bomber* or *grebe*. The phrase *The diver* could also referentially activate imagens (shorthand for the neurological activity associated with mental imagery). These mental images might be, respectively, someone diving into water, a scuba diver under water, a military aircraft, or a fish-eating bird. The phrase might remain momentarily ambiguous, but readers typically adopt one interpretation based probabilistically on their own experience and any context. The referential and associative levels of meaning have now been tentatively achieved. All this will have occurred in perhaps half a second or less (an estimate from neuropsychological studies), with little or no conscious awareness of the spreading activation.

Let's say that the next perceptual span encompasses *did a one-and-a-half*. This would involve several eye fixations, but they would be rapidly blended together. Prior knowledge and context now come more centrally into play. Verbal-associative and syntactic knowledge suggests that verb phrases have a high probability of following noun phrases. *Did* is a high-frequency verb with a distinct configuration perhaps already perceived in the parafovea of the first fixation. That is, its logogen might already be primed so its activation occurs with little more analysis. Direct objects or modifiers tend to follow action verbs, and the phrase *a one-and-a-half* occupies this predictable syntactic position.

Now the phrase *did a one-and-a-half* enters the verbal and imaginal semantic network activated by *The diver*. In isolation, the possible verbal and nonverbal associates of *one-an-a-half* might include the multiplication procedure, an increase in amount, and so on. But in this context, the probability is rapidly constrained to an acrobatic maneuver.

More specifically, the phrase *did a one-and-a-half* might activate logogens consistent with this context such as *somersault, flip, gainer,* and so on. It might also evoke dynamic images of divers launching themselves from diving boards or platforms, rotating in the air, and splashing into the water. A slight haptic or affective arousal might also be associated with the imagery, a moment of action. Meanwhile, the verbal system might be recoding the phrase into the auditory representation of the sentence thus far.

However, this is not the only possible interpretation of the sentence so far. If the *diver* was imagined to be a military aircraft, the phrase *did a one-and-a-half* could activate words such as *roll, spin* or *loop,* and images of aerobatics. Still other interpretations are possible. However, the upcoming text, often previewed in the visual parafovea, may serve to reduce these alternative interpretations.

The final fixation(s) encompass the phrase *into the pool.* Its syntactic function as a modifying phrase is announced by the familiar preposition *into* and the phrase's position and length. The word *pool* has a distinctive configuration, and, given any peripheral preview and prior context effects, its phrase- or word-level logogens may already have been primed and are now activated with little more analysis (neuropsychological studies indicate an increasing context effect across a coherent sentence). Images of swimming pools may be referentially activated, if they have not already been. Both linguistically and imaginally, the meaning of the sentence is now constrained with high probability to an acrobatic swimming act, and the referential and associative levels of meaning have been fully achieved. Approximately 2.5 seconds will have expired at a typical reading rate of between 250 and 300 words a minute.

But from the DCT perspective, the story does not end here. Many inferences will probably have occurred to the reader during this process. For example, a diver may be imagined to be either male or female, although the sentence does not specify which. The dive will have to be either a forward or backward dive, but the sentence does not specify which. The pool will be imagined to be indoor or outdoor, but the sentence does not specify which. The dive will have been done from a springboard or platform of some height above the water, but the sentence does not specify any of this. Whether consciously or unconsciously experienced, imagery inferentially elaborates the episode in ways central to its meaning, and without it the sentence cannot claim to have a meaning fully realized at all levels. That is, imagery is an inherent part of the meaningful mental model of the episode.

Note that abstract schema theories cannot easily explain such inferences because where information is not specified, default information is theoretically provided by the schema. But there is no default reason why divers should be either male or female, why dives should be forward or backward, why pools should be indoor or outdoor, and so on. These options are about equally likely by default, so the reader is left with no clear instantiation of gender, direction, and location. But readers are often clear in these interpretations. Note also that the entire episode can be accounted for by evoked language and imagery, without recourse to abstract mental propositions or the construction of a propositional text base that in turn generates a situation model. We return to this point later in the chapter.

We should finally point out that, as noted in chapter 4, comprehension is a matter of degree that can be affected by a variety of factors. For example, reading situations vary in the extent to which they call for elaboration, inference, and recall. Readers vary in linguistic and world knowledge and in their tendency to use language or imagery in thought. While the scenario above is consistent with much reading research, it might vary according to such factors.

How would DCT explain the reading of a more abstract sentence? As explained in previous chapters, the answer is that the sentence would be processed and its meaning determined more through verbal associations, with imagery supplying support as available.

For example, take the highly abstract sentence: *Support elements maximize evolving systems*. There is little concreteness in this sentence, and any meaning must therefore come primarily from verbal associations. Familiar verbal-associative syntax can be detected and the sentence parsed. The noun phrase *Support elements* may associatively activate word-level logogens such as *helpful, assisting; units, parts*. The verb phrase *maximize evolving systems* might activate the verbal associates *augment; developing; integrated parts*, and so on. Beyond such mental paraphrasing, the reader may speculatively infer a concrete, imaginal example of, say, advertising executives planning a coordinated product campaign. But without any such concrete referents, the sentence is largely a verbalism without a clear meaning.

More specifics of the mechanisms underlying the processing in these scenarios can be found in chapters 3 and 4. We will go into more depth on issues raised in these and other scenarios in the remainder of the chapter as they come up in discussions of particular processes involved in reading.

DCT AND CONTEMPORARY THEORIES OF THE READING PROCESS

DCT is an overall theory of cognition that encompasses all the phenomena covered by theories designed more specifically for the reading process. Contemporary theories of the reading process are interactive. Although articles and textbooks in the field often categorize theories as bottom-up, top-down, and interactive, such a categorization derives from the type of processing emphasized by a theory and can be misleading.

Purely bottom-up theories of the reading process have been proposed (e.g., Gough, 1972; LaBerge & Samuels, 1974), but have been subsequently discounted (e.g., Gough, 1985) or modified to render them interactive (e.g., Samuels, 1977). These bottom-up theories held reading to be a serial process beginning with graphic input from the page, visual encoding, and phonological recoding of the visual encoding, before any higher order processes such as syntactic and semantic interpretations occurred. Considerable evidence from eye movement research (e.g., Just & Carpenter, 1980; Paulson & Goodman, 1999; Rayner, 1997; Rayner & Pollatsek, 1989), neurophysiological studies of reading (e.g., Holcomb et al., 1999; Kounios & Holcomb, 1994; Kutas, 1993; Van Petten, 1993; West et al., 1998), as well as behavioral studies (e.g., Rumelhart, 1977), has rendered such an approach untenable, primarily because higher—order processes have been shown to affect lower order processes.

Interactive theories maintain that processing at one level of analysis can affect processing at another level, so that top-down processes can affect bottom-up processes and vice versa. Thus, how we respond to print is influenced by prior knowledge of language, prior knowledge of the content of the text, situational contexts associated with the reading, and the context arising from previously interpreted parts of the text, as well as the print itself. In the following sections, we will show how DCT explains bottom-up and top-down phenomena in the reading process.

BOTTOM-UP ASPECTS OF THE READING PROCESS

Simply put, bottom-up processing consists of the perception of the print and the use of that information in interpreting the meaning of a text. The bottom-up flow of information in reading begins with graphic information sensed by visual feature detectors. Evidence of visual feature detectors in animals (e.g., Hubel & Wiesel, 1962) indicated that different types of neurons are specialized for responding selectively to different elementary geometric forms. Print features include lines, angles, intersections, curvature, openness, and so on, as well as the spatial orientation of features such as left, right, up, or down (e.g., *d, b, p, q*). These print distinctions are typically learned through access and attention to printed language in emergent literacy (Harste, Woodward, & Burke, 1984; Sulzby & Teale, 1991).

Through neurological connections, activated visual feature detectors activate visual logogens of letters, common spelling patterns (e.g., onsets, rimes, affixes), words, or even short phrases learned as visual units. The size of the unit activated varies situationally depending on familiarity, context, and individual factors.

Referential and associative connections follow in turn through spreading activation. Referential connections to imagens may occur directly from visual logogens but often occur indirectly through auditory-motor logogens because many of these pathways are formed through speech before reading the printed form was learned. The indirect route appears more common for younger children and immature readers; large-scale developmental studies show an initial importance for word recoding as a predictor of both reading comprehension and reading rate that declines as children mature (Rupley, Willson, & Nichols, 1998). In DCT, logogens can be primed prior to the presentation of the graphic stimulus without conscious attention, so that what we expect to see can affect our responses (e.g., the "proofreading effect" where typos are missed because of what the reader expects to see).

DCT assumes that mental representations are not abstract but modality-specific (e.g., visual), can be associated with representations in other sensory modalities (e.g., auditory), can be activated by top-down effects, and can differ in size so that some logogens are activated by a simple feature such as a straight line whereas others are activated by a more complex pattern such as the configuration of a word. Such specification is necessary to account for the variety of behaviors that reflect the bottom-up aspects of reading at the level of the perception of features, letters, and words. We discuss these in turn.

Feature and Letter Perception

Even in formal printed fonts such as what you are now reading, few or no graphemes are made up of unique features that are not found in other graphemes. In handwriting, letter formation is even more variable, often necessitating top-down reduction of uncertainty (e.g., the notorious handwriting of physicians that is easily read by pharmacists, cf. Nash-Webber, 1975). A quick stop at a greeting card shop exposes a reader to a vast array of fonts and script styles that display considerable variation in what stands for any single grapheme or feature. DCT assumes that different types of visual logogens develop to accommodate different writing patterns and that similarity to known writing patterns helps to identify new ones through interpolation and extrapolation.

DCT also assumes that visual features are interpreted as linguistic or nonlinguistic depending on context. For example, circles and lines are perceived either as letters, numbers, or geometric shapes depending on their context. A circular life preserver may look like the letter *o* or the numeral zero but is normally not interpreted as a letter or numeral because of its nonlinguistic context. However, the letter *o* or numeral zero in printed words or numbers on the life preserver would be. Since logogens are language units, they are probabilistically activated in linguistic contexts.

DCT also assumes that the activation of a logogen in the visual modality can activate a logogen in another modality via associative connections. Few graphemes or grapheme combinations are associated with only one phoneme in English, especially when "silent" letters and variations in dialect are considered, and few phonemes are represented by only one grapheme or grapheme combination. Acoustical and articulatory phonemes, syllables, words, and larger speech units are theoretically arranged in a hierarchical system analogous to visual graphemes, spelling patterns, words, and larger written units. Connections between these units are multiple and asymmetrical (e.g., *c* in *cup, city, chin* or /k/ in *cup, chasm, key*, see chap. 3). Grapheme-and phoneme-level logogens are separate in visual and auditory modalities and not inherently connected, although they may be closely assocaited through linguistic consistencies.

This separateness or modularity allows for using the visual modality without the auditory modality, as in comprehending graphic symbols or foreign spellings to which we cannot readily assign a pronunciation, or in the case of readers who are congenitally deaf. Separateness also allows for modalities other than the visual modality to be associated with the auditory modality, as in the case of blind readers using Braille. It also allows for reading in a primary modality other than the visual modality without access to the auditory modality, as with readers born both blind and deaf who have learned to read haptically, by active touch.

While grapheme-phoneme correspondences are an important aspect of reading for those without sensory impairments, DCT does not specify that visual and auditory logogens must automatically be co-activated in reading. Graphemic information can possibly be decoded to meaning with or without phonological recoding. For example, many punctuation marks (e.g., apostrophe, quotation marks, ampersand, slash, question mark) and printed logograms (e.g., $, @, #, %) are meaningful but do not have grapheme-phoneme correspondence (Waller, 1991). They can be named (e.g., "and" for &) or may affect prosodic or extralinguistic responses such as pauses and pitch changes, but many such responses are not automatic or even typical (e.g., we don't say "quotation marks" when we encounter them in text such as you did just now). Of course, some scripts are completely logographic (e.g., Japanese kanji). The auditory and articulatory phonological processes that accompany visual processes in reading are neither simple nor completely automatic (Smith, Reisberg, & Wilson, 1992).

A critical theoretical point from the DCT perspective is that visual and auditory-motor logogens are separate and modality-specific, not parts of a unitary, abstract code. This point is important in explaining the perceptual behaviors in reading seen above, and it applies to the recognition of words as well.

Word Recognition

The recognition of words in reading is a subject of ongoing controversy (e.g., Samuels, 1994; Stanovich, 1991). DCT assumes that the activation of meaning is central to the processing of language and that recognition of word units is part of a larger continuum of processing that includes letters, syllables, morphemes, words, and larger units (i.e., logogens of various sizes). Whatever unit appears to be privileged at a given moment is largely determined by the reader's shifting position on the continuum. Different theories of reading may emphasize different units because they stress different parts of the continuum; such an interpretation of the controversies surrounding word recognition is discussed at length by Samuels (1994). The concept of a processing continuum on which features, letters, words, and larger units serve only as conventionally labeled benchmarks offers a useful vehicle for understanding bottom-up processing in reading.

For example, at one end of the continuum letter features can be critical in differentiating words and meanings. (Recall the distinction between *diver* and *liver* or *diner* earlier in the chapter.) The sentences *Look for it in the news* and *Look for it on the news* differ by only one letter but evoke different images of different media. Likewise, the sentences *Change the battery* and *Charge the battery* are differentiated by only one letter, but the difference in outcome is significant. Both sets of sentences fit the same situational contexts to the point that context might offer little assistance in either case, and the interpretation of a single letter therefore may be critical. Skilled readers must, and do, notice such small differences.

In situations such as these, processing the words *in/on* or *change/charge* is primarily bottom-up. But whether the letter, word, or available context takes perceptual or cognitive precedence even in these limited cases becomes an interesting theoretical question.

In the *change/charge* example, are letter features carefully discriminated and the detailed visual representation recoded to phonological form and used to access semantic memory, with context used to resolve the question of which of the possible meanings best fits? Or is only the general configuration shared by *change* and *charge* and some other words perceived and left ambiguous until context checks quickly limit the alternatives? Or does the reader use whatever situational and linguistic context is available to predict a set of potential meanings and then sample the print to the depth necessary to confirm one of the alternatives? All of these possibilities have been suggested by various theories of the reading process. Still other explanations are possible.

Theoretically, any of these alternatives could account for the reading of the above example or other examples that could be presented. While logically they may not all be true *at once,* each may occur in different situations. The concept of a moment-to-moment shift along a processing continuum that stretches between bottom-up feature detection and top-down contextual priming and/or constraint allows for changes in the "look" of the processing that could include all these theoretical perspectives but at different moments for different readers. Considerable flexibility is needed in a general theoretical accounting of the phenomena possible in the bottom-up processing of words.

The DCT assumption of logogens of various sizes and context effects from both verbal and nonverbal sources provides such flexibility. The DCT approach accounts for the first explanation above in that logogens of various size, such as letters and words, could be activated directly by print with phonological recoding involved in various ways (discussed later); semantic and episodic memory are then activated through referential and associative processing. Further, the DCT approach accounts for the second explanation in that multiple logogens activated on the basis of similarity can generate a network of associates that is tested against context as the interpretation evolves (e.g., the *brillig* and *slithy* examples from early in the chapter). Finally, the DCT approach accounts for the third explanation through including the priming effects of context and emphasizing the centrality of the search for meaning in all cognition.

But DCT exceeds each of these explanations by including imagery as an aspect of word meaning. The sentences *Look for it in the news* and *Look for it on the news* or *Charge the battery* and *Change the battery* referentially evoke different images of incompatible acts, and a specific analysis of certain letter features is critical in choosing between the two acts. Imagery therefore helps explain in a specific way why a reader must process some letters and words extensively. Other theories propose abstract explanations such as semantic word codes or propositional nodes to account for meaning in word recognition. Rather than *in* or *on* or *charge* or *change* activating abstract semantic memory codes or propositional nodes, dual coding assumes that a contextually appropriate imagen could be activated.

DCT also helps us to understand the role of phonological recoding and verbal rehearsal in the bottom-up aspects of the reading process. While phonological recoding may not be necessary for the comprehension of all print, visually processing print is regularly associated with auditory and articulatory activity in readers with hearing. Obviously, visual information from print is important in its own right (or its haptic counterpart to readers without sight). If visual print information was simply converted to phonemic form and the phonemic form used to determine meaning while the visual form was extinguished, we might be unable to distinguish the meanings of some homophones even in context (e.g., *born, borne; raise, raze; some others, some mothers*). Theoretically, we could go from the visual form directly to meaning, but inner speech performs important functions as well. One function already noted is that hearing people have first learned to go from speech to meaning so that recoding to inner speech is vital as reading ability matures. Inner speech may also serve a mnemonic function by holding information in short-term memory while further visual processing is conducted.

This implicates the DCT principle of modality-specific interference—the difficulty of attending to too much at once in the same sensory modality (chap. 3). Recoding the visual to the auditory-motor may serve the additional purpose of holding a word or phrase in auditory-motor short-term memory to free up some capacity in the visual modality to process more print and/or to experience visual images that contribute to meaning. If the visual representation of the print bore the burden of short-term memory alone, additional visual processing could overtax the visual pathways in the brain and exceed limited short-term capacity in the visual modality (Brooks, 1967, 1968).

For example, in the scenario earlier in the chapter, the words *The dive . . .* may be phonetically recoded in order to free capacity in the visual modality to visually process the upcoming, featurally-dense text segment *did a one-and-a-half . . . .* Likewise, rehearsing *The diver did a one-and-a half . . .* as inner speech retains that information in auditory memory while the visual modality is freed to process the remaining print in the sentence and form an image of a diver in action without overtaxing visual capacity.

This assumption is abundantly supported by evidence for modality-specific memory codes and modality-specific interference in reading (e.g., Brooks, 1967, 1968; Eddy & Glass, 1981; Paivio, 1986; Sadoski, 1983, 1985), separate auditory and visual working memory capacities (Baddeley, 1986), evidence that images can be activated before sentence comprehension is completed (Paivio & Begg, 1971), evidence that readers interpret syntax before a sentence is completed (Just & Carpenter, 1987), evidence for the use of inner speech in working memory in reading (Daneman, 1991; Patterson & Coltheart, 1987; Pollatsek, Lesch, Morris, & Rayner, 1992), and the greater effect of vocalization on short-term than long-term memory and the greater effect of imagery on long-term memory than short-term memory (Murray, Leung, & McVie, 1974). This interpretation of the role of verbal recoding and rehearsal is generally consistent with interpretations of Adams (1990) and Perfetti (1985) with the important difference that mental imagery explains part of the reason for this phenomenon; that is, auditory-motor rehearsal is used partly to prevent modality-specific visual overload.

In sum, the principles of DCT provide an explanatory framework for bottom-up phenomena in reading including the visual and phonological processing of letters and words and its role in the process of interpreting meaning. The assumption of mental representations of various sizes in separate modalities provides the flexibility and specificity to account for a wide variety of phenomena that encompasses many other theoretical accounts.

TOP-DOWN ASPECTS OF THE READING PROCESS

Simply put, top-down processing in reading involves the use of information from the reader's memory to interpret the meaning of a text. Consistent with an interactive view of reading, DCT assumes that the processing of information at lower levels of analysis is partially determined by higher levels of analysis, and that this phenomenon can be observed in language units of all sizes: Letter features behave differently in letters than they do in isolation (e.g., the ascender in *b, d, h, k,* or *l*). Letters behave differently in words than they do in isolation (e.g., the phonological recoding of *a* in *at, ate, are, all, about,* or *aisle*). Words behave differently in sentences than they do in isolation (e.g, the meanings of *ship* and *sinks* in *The ship sinks* and *Ship the sinks*). Sentences behave differently in discourse than they do in isolation (e.g., *Use the powder carefully* in discussions of cooking, makeup, medicine, or explosives). Finally, discourses differ according to situational pragmatics (e.g., a *bargain* to a buyer or a seller).

Many letter strings cannot be phonologically recoded appropriately or assigned a syntactic or semantic interpretation without consideration of the context in which they appear. For example, homographs take different pronunciations depending on their intended meanings and their syntax (e.g., *row, sow, tear, wind, wound, dove, lead, live, close, house, bass, desert, minute, refuse, buffet, content, project, estimate, sewer*). In discourse, the pronunciation of *read* is rarely in doubt because of other tense markers in sentences (in the present sentence the pronunciation is moot).

But even sentence contexts can be insufficient to signal meaning and pronunciation. A sentence such as *The bow was stiff* does not signal either the meaning or pronunciation of *bow*; in different contexts it could variously describe a knot of starched fabric, a bending forward that was ungraceful, a weapon for launching arrows that was not supple, or the prow of an icebreaker. Thus, both the meaning and the pronunciation would have to be inferred from information beyond the sentence. DCT assumes that such information is imagistic as well as linguistic when language is relatively concrete.

With abstract language, the use of context is further necessary to specify the particular shade of meaning. Skilled readers must, and do, make subtle distinctions in the connotative uses of inherently ambiguous terms such as *important, relevant, condition, circumstance,* and so on. These terms are so subject to shadings that denotative, lexical meaning is virtually inapplicable. Whether any useful discourse meaning for such general terms is available from bottom-up decoding processes and lexical access prior to contextual interpretation (i.e., the activation of more meaningful verbal associates and imagery) is questionable from a semantic point of view (Anderson & Nagy, 1991). This point applies particularly to our abstract sentence from earlier in the chapter, *Support elements maximize evolving systems*. Even in a sentence context, the word meanings remain elusively vague.

Coherence

Beyond its mediating role in the interpretation of specific print information, top-down processing provides text coherence, the subjective interpretation by the reader of the extent to which the mental representations evoked by a text form a comprehensible, unified pattern. However, language that enjoys rich context in the form of familiar verbal associations, straightforward syntax, and textual cohesion still may not be coherent to readers.

For example, in his famous sentence *Colorless green ideas sleep furiously,* Chomsky (1965) demonstrated that familiar words in familiar syntactical arrangements are not necessarily coherent. Allowable syntax and semantics can be difficult to interpret coherently in ambiguous "garden path" sentences such as *The horse raced past the barn fell down* (the horse that had been run rapidly past the barn suddenly tripped and fell). More commonplace examples involve awkward phrasings such as the disreputable dangling participle: *Singing in the shower, the shampoo ran into my mouth* or the mischievous mixed metaphor: *I hear the distant rumbling of the handwriting on the wall.*

The difficulty with these sentences is not in linguistic parsing but in their ambiguous or incongruous imagery, their evocation of worlds that are distracting to imagine or that cannot be imagined. As noted in previous chapters, the only necessary and sufficient condition for textual coherence appears to be that the sentences in a text conform to an image of a possible world in the experience or imagination of the reader, and that this pragmatic unity is adequately signalled on the textual surface (Enkvist, 1978; Fillmore & Kay, 1983; Lakoff, 1993). The abstract example *Support elements maximize evolving systems* is likewise difficult to imagine; without some concrete referent that escapes the web of language, a coherent theme is equivocal.

The DCT view of mental models of text and the role of imagery in mental modeling was discussed in chapter 4. Mental modelling is an inherent aspect of text processing that affects all levels including the lexical and grammatical; it occurs in memory and provides a coherent structure and a testing ground or hypothesis for print information. In the swimming episode, the beginning phrase *The diver* may initially have a degree of ambiguity (e.g., swimmer, aircraft, fishing bird) which is reduced by *did a one-and-a-half* and further reduced by *into the pool* (incompatible with all but swimmers in common experience). Note that the mental model of a swimmer is not the only possible model—airplanes or birds could literally dive into pools—but it is the most probable hypothesis in terms of conventional experience and the language of the text.

Unconventional experience is by definition less likely and more apt to be signaled by an author.

But unconventional language situations can still be interpreted coherently, sometimes charmingly or profoundly so. The *Jabberwocky* example from the beginning of the chapter is a famous instance of the use of familiar-sounding but novel words, conventional syntax, and conventional poetic meter and rhyme that produces an unconventional interpretation of a fantastic but coherent world. The unconventional is not limited to the fantastic; some of James Joyce's *Ulysses* and much of *Finnegan's Wake* use similarly unconventional and creative language to make profound statements about modern life.

Inferencing

Top-down processing is involved in inference by definition, and virtually any statement written or spoken invites inferences. Inferences can be broadly classified as *logical* or *pragmatic*.

Logical inferences take the form of verbal reasoning that may not involve imagery (e.g., if A equals B and B equals C, A must equal C) or may involve imagery (e.g., if Louise is taller than Ann, and Chris is shorter than Ann, who is tallest?). Logical inferences are conclusions that follow from given statements and are often heavily implied by the language of the text.

Pragmatic or "commonsense" inferences, which are more common, do not have to follow deductively from statements; instead, they are probabilistically allowable based on a coherent situation in memory. These situations frequently involve imagery.

Consider the logical and pragmatic inferences derived from the example *The diver did a one-and-a-half into the pool*. Based on the information in the sentence and the reader's mental model of the situation, the diver may be inferred to be either male or female, the dive forward or backward, the pool indoors or outdoors, and the diving surface a springboard or platform of some imagined height. The expression *one-and-a-half* is inferred to be an elliptical form of *one-and-a-half somersault*. These inferences may be seen to follow logically as consequences of the given information, although they do not necessarily involve the conscious application of deductive reasoning rules. In any case, other inferences that are more pragmatic can also be drawn, such as the inference that the diver wore a swimsuit rather than street clothes, the pool was filled with water, the dive was performed with some skill, and so on. These are pragmatic suppositions based on world knowledge, but they are less directly implied by the language of the sentence.

DCT provides a direct explanation for the formation of pragmatic inferences. Images of events or objects theoretically occur in the context of imagined environments with unspecified details elaborated from memory to varying degrees. Imagery only weakly aroused might include little detail so that matters such as whether the pool was enclosed or not may not be inferred. Even the gender of the diver may not be realized, just as in actual perception a fleeting, obscured, or distant glimpse may leave the matter unsure. Such sketchy or "generic" images may even be advantageous pending further text information or when task demands preclude detail. For example, in evaluating the relative tallness of Louise and Ann and Chris in the previous paragraph, gender is insignificant— Chris could be male or female—and stick figures could serve the purpose as well as fully realized persons. Likewise, little detail might be imaged where the comprehension task calls only for spatial reasoning such as the relative locations of rooms in a house or dots in a grid. Such spatial imagery can be highly schematic, abstracted, and devoid of detail.

Where full comprehension and recall are required, a more elaborate and detailed image of the diver diving into the pool would likely instantiate a male or female diver, a board or a platform, and a front or back somersault. A still more elaborate image might provide additional inferred information such as the diver's physical attributes, the cut and shade of the swimsuit, the skill of the dive, the size and sound of the splash, and so on. Backgrounds could also be inferred including the indoor or outdoor location of the pool and the presence of spectators. The integrated mental scene that is evoked brings with it an array of inferred, pragmatically consistent, coherent information. The scene serves as a hypothetical model of the text situation and the testing ground for subsequent information. That is, a mental model is itself an evolving inference.

Language cues are involved in inferencing as well. Cohesive ties provide for interpretive links between text units and between the text and its situational context. Even simple pronoun reference implies a degree of inference. In the simple text: *The early inhabitants built stone structures. They provided shelter and protection for them,* we infer that *they* refers to the stone structures and *them* to the early inhabitants. The language allows for the inference that the inhabitants provided shelter and protection for their stone structures, but such an inference violates "common sense," that is, our quasi-sensory, pragmatic imagining of the situation. Text language is replete with such subtle inferential cues (Halliday & Hasan, 1976).

Verbal cues are often used to establish text structure. Cues such as *because, consequently,* or *as a result* can signal causation; *before, then,* or *finally* can signal sequences; *similarly, but,* or *however* can signal comparison and contrast, and so on. Theoretically, such verbal cues could be internally inferred without explicit text language, but this appears to depend on verbal ability and other variables such as the amount of detail in the text and the reader's content knowledge. Highly verbal young adults appear to need few such structural cues to form inferences even in the presence of highly detailed expository texts, whereas highly verbal older adults and average verbal young adults have difficulty unless text detail is reduced (Meyer & Rice, 1989). The combined processing demands of structural inference and extensive verbal description are apparently excessive for most readers, suggesting the use of verbal structural cues where text detail is complex.

Britton and Gulgoz (1991) similarly determined that high verbal demands may interfere with cohesive inferencing in expository text. They found that repeating the same word for a concept improves text integration between sentences and warned writers against elegant variation, the practice of using different terms for the same concept when it is mentioned again.

Causal inferences have been studied extensively in narrative text where readers continually infer causal connections between events. Verbally implied causal connections have been found to be strong predictors of story recall, but noncausal information such as settings, graphic descriptions, and overall theme statements are also recalled well (van den Broek, Rohleder, & Narvaez, 1996). Consistent with a dual coding view, the evolving imagery of the story situation as evoked by descriptions of the story's setting and events may provide the grounds on which causal inferences are made, and to which theme statements apply.

In sum, DCT can account for top-down phenomena in the reading process such as mediation in word recognition, text coherence, and inferencing. It does so within its theoretical framework of verbal and nonverbal mental representations and their connections without recourse to abstract propositions or schemata as assumed by some other theories. We next show how DCT compares favorably with theories designed specifically for the reading process.

DCT AND OTHER THEORIES OF THE READING PROCESS

Many detailed theories of text processing have been proposed during the last 30 years (Ruddell, Ruddell, & Singer, 1994). As noted earlier, the most influential contemporary theories are interactive theories. Theories in this class differ in important ways, particularly in their emphasis on bottom-up or top-down processes, but also in their assumptions about cognitive units and processes. In the remainder of this chapter, we will show how DCT explains the same phenomena covered by selected theories of the reading process while offering significant theoretical advantages. Our treatment of these selected theories does not constitute a critical evaluation of their validity or a rejection of other theories, only a demonstration of how DCT can accommodate this class of theories.

A DCT Comparison With Rumelhart (1977)

The flow of information in reading is theorized in detail in the parallel distributed processing model of Rumelhart (1977), a theory often cited as a principal example of interactive reading theories. This theory assumes that simultaneous, or parallel, input from various levels produces both perception and comprehension in reading. The central feature of the theory is a "message center" that can be visualized as a cube divided into horizontal layers. The width dimension is the visual print information derived from the reader's eye fixations and perceptions. The height dimension is the moment-to-moment interpretation of the text as determined by the reader's location in layers or levels of processing ranging from graphic features through letters, letter clusters, words, syntax, and semantic integration. Finally, the depth dimension includes the different possible interpretations (alternative hypotheses) available at each level.

The theory assumes that the hypotheses generated at each level are not independent; for instance, a hypothesis at the word level may be constrained by hypotheses at the letter, feature, syntactic, and semantic levels as well as alternative hypotheses at the word level. Therefore, any hypothesis is subject to a probability estimate based on the input from all relevant levels. A hypothesis can be generated at any level and processing can ebb and flow in any direction in the message center.

Rumelhart (1977) provides an extended example of the operation of the message center that is relevant to DCT. We slightly adapt that example here and then provide a DCT comparison. The example is an experimental procedure where a reader is first presented briefly with a picture of a Volkswagen Beetle passing through a small country village with a snow-capped mountain in the background. Experimental instructions inform the reader that a tachistoscopic presentation of a phrase referring to an object in the picture will be presented, and that the participant is to decide which object. The phrase to be presented is *THE VOLKSWAGEN.*

The instruction that the phrase will refer to an object in the picture initiates one or more hypotheses at various levels. Given the composition of the picture, several objects are salient enough to suggest themselves including the Volkswagen, the village, and the mountain. The participant's syntactic knowledge of common phrases denoting objects further suggests that the phrase will probably take the typical sequence: determiner + noun, or possibly: determiner + adjective(s) + noun. High frequency determiners include *A* or *THE*.

Meanwhile, the tachistoscopic exposure occurs and graphic input enters the message center. Feature detectors activate feature, letter, and/or word information and compel the acceptance of *THE* over *A* as the first word with such a high probability that further processing ceases. The short, two-word configuration of the phrase also sharply reduces the probability of the determiner + adjective(s) + noun syntactic hypothesis in favor of the shorter determiner + noun hypothesis. Thus, the alternatives *VOLKSWAGEN, VILLAGE,* and *MOUNTAIN* serve as rival hypotheses for the noun at the word level.

Several processing alternatives might occur here. Overall configuration might discriminate among the three alternatives by increasing the probability of *VOLKSWAGEN* over *VILLAGE* and

MOUNTAIN, which are 30% and 20% shorter, respectively. The detection of key beginning letters might increase the probabilities of both *VOLKSWAGEN* and *VILLAGE* over *MOUNTAIN* because they both begin with *V* whereas *MOUNTAIN* does not. The detection of the additional letters *O, L, K,* and *S* eliminates the possibility of *VILLAGE.* The rest of the word might be processed only peripherally (i.e., -*WAGEN* has a very high probability of following *VOLKS*-). The word *VOLKSWAGEN* is then integrated with the word *THE* at the syntactic level, and this phrase confirms the semantic level hypothesis that matches it.

The DCT version of this scenario entails somewhat similar verbal processing, but it introduces imagery as well. The brief presentation of the picture and the subsequent verbal instructions that the tachistoscopic phrase will refer to an object in the picture activate imagens of the whole picture and its nested parts. The imagens referentially prime logogens in the verbal code for probable noun phrase sequences such as *THE VOLKSWAGEN, A MOUNTAIN, THE VILLAGE.* Related adjective logogens primed either referentially from the imagens or associatively from the logogens might include a color for the Volkswagen (if the picture was in color), *COUNTRY* for the village, or *SNOW-CAPPED* for the mountain, among others.

The tachistoscopic exposure would provide the graphic stimulus and activate familiar letter and word logogens. The exposed phrase *THE VOLKSWAGEN* would activate those primed logogens over the alternatives. The use of overall length, word division, the features of initial letters, and so on, would be much as described above to accomplish this perception. Phonological recoding, not mentioned in Rumelhart's account, could also aid in elaborating the perception. Finally, the perceived verbal phrase would referentially reactivate the imagen for the Volkswagen in the nonverbal system, providing a meaningful interpretation (i.e., semantic integration).

The DCT scenario demonstrates how this episode can be accounted for by a theoretical framework of familiar verbal and nonverbal mental representations and their interconnections. It shows how the imagery inherent in this episode plays a key role in the top-down aspects of processing including the overall semantic interpretation of the episode.

Another advantage is the explanatory simplicity offered by using a small number of powerful, concrete knowledge structures in two codes and predictable connections between them to explain both top-down and bottom-up processes. These few structures and connections replace the metaphorical "message center" and its many discrete processing levels, a model that presents difficulties for empirical testing. In short, the DCT version accounts for more reading phenomena and is simpler and more testable because its theoretical concepts and assumptions are grounded more directly in variables that can be measured and manipulated (see chap. 3).

A DCT Comparison With Kintsch (1988, 1998)

A general comparison of DCT and the van Dijk and Kintsch (1983) theory of reading as elaborated by Perrig and Kintsch (1985) was presented in Sadoski et al. (1991). The van Dijk and Kintsch theory proposed a triple coding model that included verbatim text language, a propositional text base, and a situation model. A subsequent revision of the theory (Kintsch, 1988, 1998) proposed a two-stage construction-integration model that incorporated prior knowledge more directly.

In the revised theory, memory is seen as a loose associative network in which there are stronger and weaker positive and negative connections between a vast array of abstract mental propositions. As a word in a text is visually processed, its many associated propositions are activated in a bottom-up spreading fan according to their strengths and without any priming from context. This is the construction stage. This spread is rapidly limited by local context to one or more most likely candidates. This begins the integration stage, which continues through iterations of context checks until the mutual constraints among all the activated propositions in the text are satisfied. A stable interpretation emerges in the form of an integrated propositional text base that in turn generates a situation model that may take several forms.

The basis of the reading process in this theory is the construction and interconnection of a network of propositions. Although the theory distinguishes between linguistic and nonlinguistic mental representations, the workstation in the theory is the propositional network. The ultimate basis of all text representation is the "atomic proposition," a predicate-argument schema based on case grammar that exists in the abstract and becomes instantiated by perceiving the language of the text. A "script-proposition" is also theorized that exists in the abstract and acts as a general frame for an emergent script, which can organize the interpretation; prior knowledge schemata are not included in this version of the theory. During the two stages of the reading process, propositions are formed, linked into a textbase, and associated with prior knowledge to produce an episodic memory of the text. The episodic memory has components that may include the propositional text base alone, imagery, or an emergent script.

Consider how this model might account for the reading of *The diver did a one-and-a-half into the pool*. The words in the sentence would activate the atomic proposition schema and would ultimately be formed into an abstract proposition of the general form: [DID, AGENT: DIVER, OBJECT: DIVE [VARIETY: ONE-AND-A-HALF], GOAL: POOL]. During this process, the text word *diver* would activate all its mental associates in the form of other propositions such as SWIMMER, SCUBA, FISHING BIRD, and so on. As the words *did a one-and-a-half* are perceived, the SWIMMER proposition would be strengthened and the others weakened. At the same time *did* and *one-and-a-half* would activate their own bottom-up spread of associates such as PAST and ACTION for *did* and SOMERSAULT and MULTIPLICATION for *one-and-a-half*. Context checks would strengthen appropriate alternatives and weaken the others until mutual contextual constraints were satisfied and the atomic proposition schema was instantiated.

The propositions activated by each word or phrase are themselves abstract entities, defined within networks of other such entities. For example, the proposition SOMERSAULT might be defined by belonging to the superordinate category ACROBATICS, having properties such as BODY ROTATES VERTICALLY IN SPACE, and so on. These defining propositions are further defined by other propositions. The ultimate mental model of the text is propositional but may also take the form of imagery. The theory gives no guidelines for how a propositional text base generates imagery except that propositional spatial relations (e.g., INTO, UNDER, BETWEEN) may be involved. That is, imagery appears to be derived from propositions.

What is missing from this theory? The powerful influence of imagery as a part of the comprehension process at all levels. The theory is based on abstract propositional representations for word and phrase interpretation prior to the formation of images, if these are formed at all. The imagery of the situation model is not specifically implicated in word comprehension in the theory; it only occurs at a level at which the words themselves have lost their individuality and their content has become integrated into an abstract propositional form.

Compare this with the DCT interpretation provided throughout this chapter. A spreading activation among associates is assumed in both theories. However, the DCT view is that the network of activated associates is composed of modality-specific verbal and nonverbal representations (logogens and imagens) rather than amodal, abstract propositions. DCT invokes imagery as a part of word and phrase meaning and as an additional, nonverbal aspect of context that elaborates and constrains that meaning. The DCT view provides a direct explanation of how imagery can provide mental modelling during online interactive processing and does not require the nonparsimoniuos assumptions of atomic propositions, script propositions, or mechanisms for the generation of imagery situation models from propositions.

Accordingly, the dual coding view provides a direct explanation of the improved comprehensibility and memorability of concrete language over abstract language, an issue not resolved in Kintsch (1988, 1998) or other theories assuming a propositional code. Theories that assume that all text language is abstracted into a common, amodal, propositional form have difficulty explaining why this should be so. Where such theories recognize imagery at all, it is without any functional significance, a secondary epiphenomenon.

Furthermore, such theories seem to disregard the highly evolved graphophonemic, orthographic, syntactic, and semantic cuing systems of natural language. DCT assumes that natural language systems directly cue mental representations and processes without being first converted into a propositional form. This accounts more readily for such reading phenomena as phonological recoding and imagery experienced in reaction to concrete language.

The dual coding model differs from triple coding models in that it uses natural language as the basis of one code and nonverbal world experience in the form of imagery as the basis of the other code. Abstract entities such as propositions, scripts, and schemata are difficult to demonstrate empirically and are not theoretically necessary to explain reading phenomena. In sum, the DCT view explains all the reading phenomena addressed by triple coding theories and more, including neuropsychological evidence of processing differences for concrete and abstract text and the powerful, ubiquitous experience of imagery during the reading of a wide variety of text types (Sadoski, 1999a; Sadoski & Paivio, 1994; Sadoski et al., 1991).

This concludes our discussion of theories of the reading process from a DCT perspective. The discussion has been restricted to selected theories and limited examples. Other theories of reading could be addressed similarly. The main theoretical advance offered in this chapter is that DCT can explain the reading process within the framework of a general theory of cognition, an important scientific step. The DCT account of the interplay between verbal processes and imaginal processes during the act of reading offers a comprehensive and parsimonious explanation that covers more reading phenomena than other current theories of the reading process.

Summary

DCT is a general theory of cognition that applies directly to the reading process and can account for its various phenomena. For any theory of the reading process to be adequate, it ultimately must be compatible with larger theories that attempt to account for all cognition. Current theories of the reading process are interactive theories that invoke both bottom-up and top-down processes. In terms of bottom-up processes, DCT assumes an organization of language units derived from natural language that are mentally represented in various sensory modalities (logogens). Depending on familiarity and the effects of context, the reader may use these representations variously in perceiving grapheme-phoneme correspondences and the visual, auditory, and/or articulatory configurations of letters, words, or word sequences. In terms of top-down processes, DCT provides a broader and more specific account of the effects of varying degrees of meaning, coherence, and inference. In particular, verbal–nonverbal connections provide alternative, interconnected contexts for the generation of inferences and/or the integration of text. In DCT, readers are assumed to vary their position from moment to moment along a continuum from feature perception to inferential text modeling in activating verbal and nonverbal mental representations of text. This view compares favorably with other contemporary theories of the reading process with DCT adding specificity, parsimony, and broader application.

CHAPTER 7

Written Composition

In this chapter we apply the dual coding approach to written composition. Our aim is to show that the theory provides an effective, parsimonious, and far-reaching explanation of the process of composing. Specifically, we (a) briefly review DCT with an emphasis on aspects that are unique to writing, (b) give an example of the act of composing viewed from the perspective of the theory, (c) interpret another influential cognitive theory of composing in DCT terms, (d) review anecdotal evidence of dual coding processes in composing, and, (e) attempt an explanation of the key rhetorical concept of persona.

DCT PRINCIPLES APPLIED TO WRITTEN COMPOSITION

Recall that DCT assumes that mental representations are concrete, modality-specific analogs of sensory and motor events that are organized into two codes: a nonverbal code for dealing with environmental objects and events and a verbal code for language. The units in the two codes differ in character and vary hierarchically in inclusiveness such that the nonverbal code is organized into holistic, nested sets, and the verbal code is organized sequentially into longer representational units. The codes are activated directly by words and objects or indirectly through connections between the internal codes. Activation and processing can go on at any of three levels including the representational level (when a stimulus is recognized), the referential level (as in naming objects or imaging to words), and the associative level (activation spreads among language units or among images). No abstract entities such as schemata or propositions are assumed, nor is a separate executive device or monitor. These general principles have been elaborated in previous chapters.

Written composition differs from other forms of language production such as speech or conversation in several important ways that must be addressed by a cognitive theory of writing. Most composition is produced autonomously, often consuming considerable time for planning, drafting, revising, and editing before it is seen by an external audience. This involves elaborate mental processing that must be theoretically explained. Written composition involves the motivational and evaluative influence of an imagined audience, unlike speech or dialogue where the audience is usually present and providing feedback (speaking to a tape recorder is an exception). These motivational and evaluative (metacognitive) functions also must be explained. Further, a complete theory of written composition must include motor representations for the production of written language in addition to representations in the other sensory modalities of the verbal and imagery systems.

A word about motor activity in writing: We avoid a detailed explanation of motor acts due to our focus on mental rather than physical processes. However, DCT assumes that the motor representations used in writing language are part of the verbal code and the haptic modality. Therefore, they share the sequential processing constraints of the verbal system and can operate independently of other verbal modalities although associated with them. This independence of modalities explains how, for example, we can begin the physical act of writing a sentence while we are still mentally composing the sentence using inner speech and imagery, or why we can regularly produce written misspellings of a word whose letter sequence we can correctly say. Throughout the remainder of the chapter, we refer to *composing* and *writing* interchangeably except when specifically referring to the motor processes of writing.

A DCT VIEW OF AN EPISODE OF COMPOSING

Let us illustrate how DCT addresses the issues above through a sample episode of composing a brief text. This episode contains many of the elements of writing found in longer, more complex episodes and illustrates the way dual coding is involved in even the simplest writing situations. For theoretical purposes, we provide parallel explanations of each part of the episode in everyday, general terms and then in theoretical, more technical terms.

A written composition begins with the motivation to compose. This motivation may be external, such as a deadline, or internal, such as a felt need to communicate ideas or feelings in writing. A common example with both external and internal motivations is writing a personal thank-you note for a gift from, say, a kindly grandmother. Thank-you notes typically express affection, and social convention requires that they be sent in a timely manner. But let's make the situation a bit difficult. Let's say that the gift is an article of clothing, a scarf or necktie, that is ghastly. The problem is how to communicate affection for thoughtfulness without revealing disappointment with the gift. Let's further assume that social convention favors a brief, handwritten note.

Memories of informal thank-you notes could be verbal or nonverbal. Visualized examples of such notes, or verbally recalled rules learned through education, would include an opening, a body, and a closing. In some theories, this type of knowledge is variously referred to as formulaic knowledge, procedural knowledge, or metacognitive knowledge; in DCT terms, knowledge consists of logogens and imagens of various size.

Informal openings will include the familiar salutation *Dear . . .* to be followed in this situation by the addressee, *Grandma.* In DCT terms, these are visual and/or auditory-motor logogens activated in phrase sequence, which in turn activate associated motor representations for the physical act of penning the phrase.

The familiar phrase *Thank you* typically begins the body of a thank-you note, followed by *for the.* The intensifier *very much* might also be used with syntactic sequencing constraining its insertion between the two phrases above. The writer next pens the sentence *Thank you very much for the (scarf, tie)*. In DCT terms, the production of this sentence is explained by the contextually probabilistic activation of the phrase *Thank you,* which in turn produces a new context for other highly probable and sequentially constrained verbal associations, although images (e.g., the ghastly scarf or tie) may also be referentially evoked.

Considerable evidence suggests that writing occurs in phrases and clauses with pauses between them to consider the next phrase or clause and/or review text already produced. The writer next reviews *Thank you very much for the (scarf, tie)* and finds it bland ("Ugh . . . too dull . . . I can just see how Grandma will react to that"). In DCT terms, this takes the form of reading the sentence and finding that the language evokes mildly negative affect. It also referentially activates an image of the reader, Grandma, disappointed that so little effort was taken in writing such tired prose to her.

Note here that the writer has just assumed two separate points of view, or personae: one for the writer and one for the imagined audience. In the theory, these serve evaluative or monitoring (i.e., metacognitive) functions. The concept of persona is discussed in detail later in the chapter.

Accordingly, these images and feelings next serve as motivators to produce a more positive result. The affective verb *appreciate* and adjective *thoughtful* are searched from memory and arranged with the subject *I* and object *gift* into *I appreciate the thoughtful gift*. To evoke a still more personal tone, the pronoun *your* replaces *the*, and the second sentence is penned *I appreciate your thoughtful gift*. In DCT terms, a verbal search was motivated and constrained referentially by nonverbal images and affect. Verbal-associative processing then activated an initial syntactic sequence of logogens, with affect further motivating an alternative logogen.

But these two sentences are not enough; at least one more sentence seems to be needed. Besides, the bland, clichéd feeling still persists ("Need another sentence here . . . still dull . . . can't let on I didn't like the gift!) Let's say that the final phrase of the second sentence, *your thoughtful gift,* evoked an image of Grandma shopping. The phrases *picking out* and *spending time* occur in response and are combined into the unwritten mental sequence *You were thoughtful to spend your time picking out a gift for me.*

In DCT terms, visualized exemplars of the length of thank-you notes, the unpleasant affective state, and the dynamic image of Grandma and its referentially evoked phrases served as the motivation for this sentence. The unpenned sentence itself is a verbal-associative syntactic combination of activated auditory-motor logogens rehearsed in short-term memory.

But another pause and review of the previous text, *Thank you very much for the (scarf/tie). I appreciate your thoughtful gift,* followed by a rehearsal of the sentence in short-term memory ("You were thoughtful to spend your time picking out a gift for me"), reveals a problem. The words *thoughtful* and *gift* will have been used twice in close proximity, something the writer remembers being taught to avoid ("Careless repetition—too close").

Several options exist, including (a) pen the sentence anyway and be done, (b) revise for unrepetitive wording, or (c) start over in an effort to be less clichéd and more sensitive to Grandma. Let's end this episode by assuming that the writer notices that the word *appreciate* was misspelled, calling for the note to be rewritten in any case, and decides to start over.

This episode probably would be experienced more rapidly and less consciously than this extensive explanation implies, but it illustrates much of the writing process as it would be explained by DCT. Written composition is characterized by verbal and nonverbal mental representations and processes and is replete with recursive, hierarchical operations. External and internal motivations and evaluations in the form of verbal prescriptions and nonverbal images and affects are inherent. Imagined audiences are implicated. In all cases, verbal or nonverbal representations are activated at the representational level; further processed associatively, referentially, or both; and verbal output is produced through motor action (e.g., writing as well as talking to ourselves silently or aloud). That is, the theory accounts for the elaborate verbal and nonverbal thinking, motivation, and evaluation involved in the writing process without recourse to abstract theoretical mechanisms that are difficult to explain in terms of our everyday experience.

This explanation further invites scientific testability. This simple episode involved concrete objects, events, and people, and much of the motivation to write came from nonverbal imagery and affect that in turn referentially activated organized language. This implies that writing about concrete events and objects might motivate quicker starts, more writing per unit of time, and more self-reports of mental imagery, among other predictions. As we shall see later, these predictions are well supported in research.

As with reading, specific theories of the writing process have been proposed and have become influential during the last several decades. These theories often rely heavily on mental abstractions such as schemata, propositions, and executive devices. We next examine one such theory from a DCT perspective with an eye toward the theoretical difficulties that these explanatory devices introduce and how DCT can reinterpret that theory.

THEORIES OF COGNITION SPECIFIC TO WRITTEN COMPOSITION

An influential cognitive theory of the composing process was proposed by Flower and Hayes (1981; Hayes & Flower, 1980). Like the interactive theories of the reading process that emerged about the same time, this theory is an interactive theory proposed as a response to linear stage models of composing (e.g., Britton et al., 1975; Garrett, 1975).

Linear stage theories suggest that composing proceeds through the stages of prewriting, writing, and rewriting, or, at the sentence level, deciding on a message, then a syntactic outline, then content words, then function words, affixes, and so on. The Flower and Hayes (1981) interactive theory is a more flexible approach in which processing activity is assumed to occur at many levels at once. Flower and Hayes (1984) elaborated the theory to include an analysis of meaning and its role in the writing process.

We first review this theory and its approach to meaning, using it as an example of cognitive views of composing during the past two decades, and then provide a DCT reinterpretation with relevant research evidence. Our purpose is to examine the many assumptions in the theory and show that DCT can explain the process of written composition in a simpler way that lends itself to operationalization and scientific test.

The Flower and Hayes Theory of Composition

This theory rests on four basic assumptions about writing behavior. The assumptions, discussed here, are that (a) writing consists of distinct cognitive processes, (b) those processes are hierarchically embedded, (c) writing is goal-directed, and (d) writing stimulates the discovery of new goals as it progresses.

The first assumption includes three sets of distinct processes that interact continuously in a nonlinear fashion: (a) the task environment, including everything outside the writer such as any external purpose for writing, the audience, and the text produced so far; (b) the writer's long-term memory, including knowledge of the current topic, the imagined audience, and writing conventions; and (c) the thought processes that writers use while composing, including planning, translating, and reviewing, all under the direction of a monitor. Planning involves generating and organizing content and setting goals. Translating is expressing the content in written language. Reviewing involves evaluating what has been planned or translated, often leading to revision. The monitor is a set of executive routines that controls switches between processes.

The second assumption in this theory is that the processes of writing are hierarchically embedded in recursive fashion. Unlike those in a linear organization, any process can be called up at any time and embedded within another process or within another instance of itself.

The third assumption is that writing is goal-directed. Goals may be global or local and may be content goals or process goals. Global goals may have local subgoals embedded in them. Content goals specify topic and intended effects on the audience. Process goals are instructions writers give themselves.

The fourth assumption is that writing stimulates the discovery of new goals through insights triggered by the act of writing. This takes the form of creating a changing network of subgoals or regenerating original goals.

Flower and Hayes (1984) elaborated their theory to explain the representation of meaning in writing. They proposed a "multiple representation thesis" covering a variety of general and specific theoretical alternatives in four categories based on an increase in the amount of linguistic information in the category: nonverbal imagery, abstract knowledge networks, the text base, and the written text. The category of nonverbal imagery includes images in various modalities. The remaining three categories cover a variety of theoretical concepts, including, respectively: abstract schemata, the text base (e.g., abstract propositions and auditory images of words and phrases), and actual written text (e.g., outlines, drafts). These categories are given equal conceptual status in the theory.

For example, Flower and Hayes (1984) elaborated on the nature of plans, stating that they were *not* like a Kintschean text base consisting of information in a uniform propositional representation. Rather, plans variously take the form of names or cues used to retrieve information stored as schemata, episodes, or images; auditory images of language; and goals (e.g., influencing an audience). Flower and Hayes additionally indicated that the declarative knowledge used in plans was represented in the form of semantic networks, abstract propositions, and gists that differ from both nonverbal imagery and procedural knowledge.

A DCT Reinterpretation of the Flower and Hayes Theory

This theory and DCT have much in common. The commonalities include the assumptions that cognition consists of distinct representations and processes, that these representations and processes can be hierarchically organized and embedded, that cognitive processing can be interactive rather than linear, and that cognitive representations are multiple rather than of a common code. However, the particulars of these assumptions differ in two important ways.

The first difference is that Flower and Hayes (1984) provide little specification on the nature of mental representations. Thus, equal status is given to specific representations (e.g., mental images and words), more general representations (e.g., plans and goals), and completely abstract representations (e.g, propositions and schemata).

DCT specifies the nature of our knowledge of the task environment, the writer's long-term memory, and the thought processes of composing including planning, translating, and reviewing: In all instances, internal memory representations and processing operations are either nonverbal (i.e., imagery, affect) or verbal (i.e., mental language). The DCT assumption provides a more parsimonious account of generalizations such as ideas, goals, and plans, which appear to be experienced as imagery or inner speech anyway, as illustrative examples in Flower and Hayes (1981) suggest.

Thus, in DCT terms, the rhetorical problem posed by the task environment could take the form of a verbal assignment (e.g., instructions from others or self-regulatory instructions such as "must write a thank-you note to Grandma") or the imagined effect of the writing on an audience (e.g., Grandma's reaction at reading the note and being appreciated). Any text produced so far would be verbal in its external form, but it could produce further verbal and nonverbal responses internally. For example, responses could take the form of verbal associations useful in continuing or editing a sentence (e.g., replacing *the gift* with *your gift),* or images of the impact of the writing on the audience (e.g., Grandma's disappointment with a dull thank-you note). Such responses might also associatively evoke motor output responses as specified in DCT, as when our fingers rush to record the just-right word as it comes to mind.

The DCT view of long-term memory has been detailed in previous chapters and was summarized earlier in this chapter. Memory representations of writing formats, topics, audiences, and the conventions of written language are either verbal or nonverbal in various modalities. For example, format knowledge can be characterized as a network of closely associated mental language units that can serve as a plan for a letter or note (e.g., *opening, body, closing*). That knowledge can exist in parallel in the form of images of the spatial arrangement of letters or notes. Those representations can referentially and associatively evoke related language or images (e.g., the opening of a thank-you note is placed at the top and includes the salutation *Dear . . .*). Knowledge of topics and conventions in DCT is likewise represented both verbally and nonverbally and processed representationally, referentially, or associatively. Audiences may be mentally represented as images of individuals or groups that provide motivation and an evaluative criterion for writing.

The Flower and Hayes (1984) account of meaning, plans, and goals is partly consistent with the DCT view of cognition, but DCT reduces the multiplicity of representational alternatives to two: nonverbal imagery and language. Thus, plans take the form of verbal networks of associated words and phrases possibly ordered sequentially and/or hierarchically; nonverbal images of objects, events, or episodes to be described; regulatory inner speech (e.g., "Need another sentence here"); or verbal and nonverbal cues such as keywords or peg images (e.g., a verbal cue such as "thank-you note" or an image of Grandma shopping). Declarative and procedural knowledge would likewise be either verbal or imaginal in form. In short, DCT accounts for these various forms of writing plans—schemata, episodes, gists, sequences, cues, and so on—using the rich possibilities provided by nonverbal and verbal representations and connections between them.

The second important difference between DCT and the Flower and Hayes theory involves their assumption of a monitor. The cognitive nature of the monitor is not discussed, except that it functions as a strategist that determines when to shift from one writing process to another. This differs from DCT, which does not include any executive external to the verbal and nonverbal systems.

There is no need to postulate a separate monitor in DCT because its basic processes can account for monitoring functions as described above. In DCT, evaluative and monitoring functions are verbal and nonverbal in nature and occur within and between the two codes. Thus, monitoring could take the form of self-regulatory covert or overt speech (e.g., "Too dull," "That spelling doesn't look right"), or nonverbal images such as the imagined effect of the writing on Grandma. Such evaluative activity in turn could trigger changes in processing at all levels.

The metacognitive processes used in reviewing, evaluating, and revising verbal material have been of interest to linguists and psychologists for some time. For example, Hockett (1963) proposed reflexiveness (using language to talk about language) as a universal quality of language, and Guilford and Hoepfner (1971) empirically demonstrated separate perceptual and linguistic factors of judgment concerning meaning. Carroll's (1993) review of factor-analytic studies of cognitive abilities describes several unique factors related to evaluating verbal material (e.g., sentence ambiguity, critical evaluation of reasoning, story titles, proofreading).

Paivio (1986, pp. 112–115) suggested that such evaluative tasks involve both verbal and nonverbal processing and that these functions are largely controlled by overt or covert verbal activity. In the DCT view of writing, such processing may occur at the overt surface level by producing physical text to try out syntax, spellings, and so on. Evaluation and revision also may occur at a deeper semantic level as when the writer "steps back" to reread a passage for its meaning and expressiveness or to test its organizational coherence. At this point, there may be subtle shifts from the persona of the writer to the persona of the audience.

In summary, critical aspects of the Flower and Hayes (1981, 1984) theory can be reinterpreted in DCT terms. This is an important scientific step because it explains a cognitive theory specific to the writing process in terms of a larger, general theory of cognition that provides a simpler, more direct, and more empirically testable account of the writing process.

Empirical Evidence Supporting a DCT Explanation of Composing

The Flower and Hayes (1981) theory was based on protocol analyses (i.e., writers' think-aloud reports while writing), and it has been subjected to little experimental test since its introduction. Butterfield, Hacker, and Albertson (1996) reported a considerable difference of opinion in the literature on whether the Flower and Hayes model was speculation or whether it stated testable hypotheses. They concluded that the model should be credited for its heuristic value, but few of its implications had been tested (but see Hayes, Flower, Schriver, Stratman, & Carey, 1987, for some empirical demonstration and a discussion of this issue; Hayes (1996) also proposed revisions in the model that included a number of testable hypotheses).

Although think-aloud reports provide a rich database for interpretation, experiments provide a more rigorous test of predictions and explanations. In a recent experimental study, DCT predictions regarding writing were tested and supported. Sadoski et al. (1997) asked college students to compose on word processors written definitions for concrete and abstract nouns that were matched for familiarity and meaningfulness. The aim was to investigate the roles of imagery and verbal thinking in the processes and products of composing text about familiar topics. The study replicated and extended a previous study by Reynolds and Paivio (1968) where oral language was used for the definitions. The concrete words in both studies were *library, prisoner, picture, hotel,* and *mother.* The matched abstract words were *crime, science, mind, fun,* and *death.*

The dependent variables involved measures thought to reflect the quality and ease of producing the definitions and the use of imagery and verbal thinking in doing so. These variables included (a) latency (i.e., the time from the presentation of the word to typing on the keyboard), (b) the number of words in the definition, (c) the average length of the words in the definition, (d) the number of T-units (i.e., an independent clause with all its modifiers including dependent clauses), (e) the percentage of T-units with a final modifier (i.e., cumulative constructions, a syntactic variable consistently related to the rated quality of writing), (f) a content score based on the criteria of a good definition, (g) a style score based on the grammaticality and textuality of the definition, (h) the rated use of an imagery strategy (i.e., a 1–4 rating on the amount of using mental pictures of objects, scenes, or events as a composing strategy), and (i) the rated use of a verbal-associative strategy (i.e., a 1–4 rating on the amount of using other words, phrases, and related language as a composing strategy).

Based on DCT and the earlier results of Reynolds and Paivio (1968), the definitions of the concrete words were predicted to exhibit shorter latencies, greater length in number of words, higher quality content, a greater percentage of T-units with cumulative constructions, and more self-reports of an imagery strategy. The definitions of the abstract words were predicted to include longer words and be accompanied by more self-reports of a verbal associative strategy. Two experiments were conducted.

The first experiment used a restricted time limit whereby the students had 90 seconds to write a definition for each of the 10 terms. The predictions of DCT were strongly confirmed. When the students composed definitions for the concrete terms, they began sooner, wrote more, wrote definitions judged higher in quality by reliable ratings, used more cumulative constructions, and reported more use of an imagery strategy. When they composed definitions for abstract terms, they used longer words and reported more use of a verbal-associative strategy. Correlational evidence suggested that concrete words generated more voluble definitions because complex images referentially activated extensive verbal descriptions (cf. Segal, 1976, discussed in Paivio, 1975b; Paivio & Begg, 1981, pp. 208–209).

The second experiment presented each participant with one concrete word and one abstract word from the set and provided a longer time limit (15 minutes per word) together with instructions to write a complete and polished paragraph of definition in that time. Half of the students defined the concrete word first and half defined the abstract word first. This order allowed for an investigation of an extension of the conceptual peg effect to composing. The conceptual peg effect, discussed in chapter 5, accounts for the consistent finding in memory studies that concrete language has the effect of increasing the recall of associated language, thereby serving as a mental "peg" from which associated information can be retrieved.

Predictions from DCT were again confirmed: When the students composed definitions for the concrete terms, they began sooner, wrote more, wrote definitions higher in quality, and reported more use of an imagery strategy. When they composed definitions for abstract terms, they reported more use of a verbal-associative strategy. There was no difference in the use of the cumulative construction in this experiment, but word length in the definitions varied interactively with abstractness and order: Definitions of abstract words defined first had the longest words, whereas definitions of abstract words defined second (after the concrete word) had the shortest words. Also, the definitions of abstract words composed first had the fewest words and T-units, whereas the definitions of abstract words defined second had the most words and T-units. That is, when the abstract words were defined after the concrete words, the definitions were more like the definitions for the concrete words, indicating a transfer effect of concreteness on following material that is interpretable as a conceptual peg effect. However, this effect did not extend to quality ratings, which were uniformly higher for the concrete words.

This experimental test demonstrated that DCT principles can be used to generate testable and accurate experimental predictions about composing. Furthermore, the results replicated those of an earlier study using oral production of definitions, suggesting that common cognitive mechanisms underlie the production of both spoken and written language. Moreover, these mechanisms appear to be those involved in the reception (i.e., reading and listening) of spoken and written language as explained by DCT.

These results are less readily explained by other theories of cognition. For example, theories relying on an abstract, common code for the memory of word concepts (e.g., schema theory) suggest that, because the words were matched for familiarity and meaningfulness, there should have been no significant differences between the definitions of the concrete and abstract sets.

Also, common code theories do not address some specific issues that can be explained by DCT. For example, the definitions of concrete words had more cumulative syntactic constructions (i.e., constructions where modifiers follow the main clause kernel), a consistent characteristic of quality ratings for writing (Hillocks, 1986). The DCT interpretation is that complex, organized images, referentially evoked by the concrete terms, in turn evoked complex, organized language which included such modifiers. Specifically, language evoked by images may contain concrete "peg" words in the main clause of a sentence that tend to attract following modifiers.

To test this assumption, Sadoski and Goetz (1998) investigated the compositions of ninth graders writing on a general topic from a large-scale writing assessment. In the compositions, the use of concrete verbs was associated with significantly more final modifiers than abstract verbs whether or not the verb had an object or complement. Sadoski and Goetz concluded that the results were supportive of the conceptual peg hypothesis, with concrete verbs providing the pegs on which cumulative sentences are composed. Thus, very specific findings at the syntactic level can be explained within the framework of DCT. This degree of explanation is far-reaching for a contemporary theory of writing.

Several other studies provide further support for a DCT view of writing. Tirre, Manelis, and Leicht (1979) assigned undergraduates to read concrete and abstract science passages matched for comprehensibility using either a verbal strategy or an imagery strategy while reading. The verbal strategy involved writing sentences to explain the relationships between sets of words from the passages. The imagery strategy involved drawing a picture to show how the words were related. Students were later asked to explain in a few written sentences how the sets of content words from each passage were related to each other. Passage concreteness had a significant positive effect on writing quality, consistent with a DCT expectation. Strategy assignment did not produce a significant main effect or interaction. However, this may be due to methodological peculiarities in the strategies assigned (e.g., the verbal strategy involved a written production task very similar to the written production task used as the dependent measure and therefore a possible practice advantage; drawing pictorial imagery as a strategy is not identical to using mental imagery as a strategy).

Maes (1997) conducted three experiments with technical school students to determine the effect of the concreteness of referents on establishing and maintaining text coherence with anaphora. In one experiment, participants received a first sentence and were asked to complete a second sentence given only its first word. The referent in the first sentence could be either concrete or abstract, and the second sentence began with either a demonstrative "pointing out" pronoun or a nondemonstrative personal pronoun. For example, the first sentence *The little pin causes an increase in pressure in the cylinder* was followed by the incomplete sentence starters *This_____* or *It_____*. The participants used both types of pronouns to continue a concrete referent, but they generally avoided continuing the abstract referent. Apparently, abstract referents were considered less valid candidates for continuation. In the two other experiments, participants were asked to fill in a blank with the most adequate anaphoric word in two- or three-sentence sequences in which the concreteness of referents was manipulated. In both these experiments, demonstrative pronouns were used significantly more to refer to abstract referents while nondemonstrative pronouns were used significantly more to refer to concrete referents. Maes concluded that abstract referents are more difficult to refer to in writing and require more anaphoric force than concrete referents because of their lower cognitive accessibility and the greater effort required to maintain mental reference to them.

Miller (1994) asked 148 college students to write an expository essay on how they learned best. They were stopped at three points to report about their last few seconds of thought on a written questionnaire. A representative sample was later interviewed in depth about their responses. Across the three trials, thinking occurred in "mostly words" about half the time, in "mostly images" about one fourth of the time, and in "both at the same time" about one fourth of the time. In nearly two thirds of the reports students included some degree of vivid detail. The students reported that at particular points in writing, they experienced a succession of images, with individual images changing from detailed to vague as new images replaced current ones. Moreover, when asked about the key or controlling ideas in their writing, over half reported that key ideas occurred as images, another 10% said key ideas occurred as both images and words. Only 10% responded that thoughts in words could be identified as their thesis idea. Their key images sometimes recurred during writing, apparently sustaining the main idea. This is suggestive of the conceptual peg and motivational aspects of imagery in DCT. As in the thank-you note to Grandma, an image can serve as a motivational and reference point to guide the writing.

Thus, the principles of DCT largely accommodate both experimental and self-report studies of writing. The body of relevant empirical literature in this area is limited at this time, but the convergence of findings from different methodologies is encouraging for the theory. Chapter 8 reviews other studies that are supportive of a DCT view of composing. We will now turn to broader, less technical evidence supporting a DCT view of composing.

ANECDOTAL EVIDENCE OF IMAGERY AS A VEHICLE FOR COMPOSING

DCT has been applied to introspective evidence of the composing of literary and scientific works. For example, Paivio (1983) provided an extensive account of how mental images, in particular, can serve as an inspiration for a work of art or science, how they can serve as recurrent symbols that unify a work thematically, and how they can concretize abstractions that would otherwise be difficult to express. In this section, we present recorded introspective accounts of the composing of written works and show how DCT explains this evidence.

Authors have long reported that imagery serves as both the inspiration and vehicle for composing. Murray (1978) compiled some interesting examples:

> Poets and fiction writers often receive their signals in terms of an *image*. Sometimes this image is static; other times it is a moving picture in the writer's mind. When Gabriel Garcia Marquez was asked what the starting point of his novels was, he answered, "A completely visual image . . . the starting point of *Leaf Storm* is an old man taking his grandson to a funeral, in *No One Writes to the Colonel,* it's an old man waiting, and in *One Hundred Years,* an old man taking his grandson to the fair to find out what ice is." William Faulkner was

quoted as saying, "It begins with a character, usually, and once he stands up on his feet and begins to move, all I do is trot along behind him with a paper and pencil trying to keep up long enough to put down what he says and does." . . . Joyce Carol Oates adds, "I visualize the characters completely; I have heard their dialogue, I know how they speak, what they want, who they are, nearly everything about them." (p. 379)

Other anecdotes are abundantly available. As noted in chapter 2, the poets Blake and Coleridge reported vivid, nearly hallucinogenic mental imagery that inspired and found expression in their works. Mary Shelly's *Frankenstein* took form through a waking image:

My imagination, unbidden, possessed and guided me, sifting the successive images that arose in my mind with a vividness far beyond the usual bounds of reverie. I saw—with shut eyes, but acute mental vision—I saw the pale student of the unhallowed arts kneeling beside the thing he had put together. I saw the hideous phantasm of a man stretched out, and then, on the working of some powerful engine, show signs of life and stir with an uneasy vital half motion. (Shelley, 1963, pp. x–xi)

Other writers have recounted similar experiences. For example, C. S. Lewis (1966) wrote:

One thing I am sure of. All my seven Narnian books, and my three science fiction books, began with seeing pictures in my head. At first they were not a story, just pictures. The *Lion* [the *Witch and the Wardrobe*] all began with a picture of a Faun carrying an umbrella and parcels in a snowy wood. (p. 42)

William Faulkner noted that *The Sound and the Fury* began as an image of a little girl's muddy drawers as she sat in a tree watching her grandmother's funeral (Faulkner, 1959). John Fowles (1977) wrote that the source of his novel *The French Lieutenant's Woman* was an image of a woman on a quay. Virginia Woolf noted that her novel *The Waves* began with an image of a fin cutting through a waste of water (Graham, 1970). Similarly, The central idea of a voluntary change becoming involuntary in *Dr. Jekyll and Mr. Hyde* came to Robert Louis Stevenson in a dream of

Hyde taking the potion in the presence of his pursuers and under-going the change (Woods, 1947). Robert Frost wrote his famous poem "Stopping by Woods on a Snowy Evening" quickly as if he'd "had an hallucination" (Mertins, 1965, p. 82).

Not all such imagery is in the visual modality. Tolouse (citied in Woodworth, 1938), in his psychological analysis of Emile Zola, found that the novelist used olfactory imagery in thinking of per-sons, streets, and houses in terms of odors. The poet Denise Lever-tov claimed that she could smell her poems before she saw them (Murray, 1979).

Not only can imagery serve as the original inspiration of writing, it can also be implicated in the development of the organization of writing. Murray (1978) found that many writers perceived an entire piece of writing as a kind of shape:

> Marge Piercy says, "I think that the beginning of fiction, the story, has to do with the perception of pattern in event." Leonard Gardner, in talking of his fine novel *Fat City,* said, "I had a sense of circle . . . of closing the circle at the end." John Updike says, "I really begin with some kind of solid, coherent image, some notion of the shape of the book and even of its texture. *The Poorhouse Fair* was meant to have a sort of wide shape. *Rabbit, Run* was kind of zigzag. *The Centaur* was sort of a sandwich." (p. 380)

Fleckenstein (1992) examined various drafts of W. B. Yeats' verse drama *Purgatory.* She found evidence that a key image, a light-ning-blasted tree, had been successively revised to increase its def-inition and metaphoric depth as a symbol. There are many other well-known examples of concrete images serving recurrent, sym-bolic functions in literature, such as the albatross in Coleridge's *Rime of the Ancient Mariner* or the white whale in Melville's *Moby Dick.* Coleridge apparently saw the shooting of the albatross as a central, inspirational, and unifying vehicle; Lowes (1927) empha-sized that this symbol "carried in its train the ground plan of the poem" and how it released "thronging images" (p. 228). Likewise, in Howard's (1967) analysis of the composition of *Moby Dick,* he noted that "a symbol is an imaginative bridge between the general and the particular that may be crossed in either direction; and Melville . . . had gradually slipped into the practice of letting his mind play around concrete details until they were made luminous with suggestive implications" (p. 725).

In her analysis of Shakespeare's imagery, Spurgeon (1935) drew special attention to images that dominated a particular work and served as a motif, such as swift and soaring movement as captured specifically in the flights of birds in *Henry V;* the sense of sound throughout *The Tempest;* and the images of light such as the sun, moon, stars, and the reflected light of love that suffuse *Romeo and Juliet.* Other critics (Harrison, 1948) have also noted patterns of imagery in Shakespeare such as blood, water, and darkness in *Macbeth,* and animals in *King Lear.* The recurrence of such images can be interpreted as conceptual pegs serving an organizing and unifying function in composing the works.

C. S. Forester, author of the Captain Horatio Hornblower novels and *The African Queen,* provided this account of the development of scenes in his books:

> What is going on in mind as I write them? I have no doubt that in my case it is a matter of a series of visualizations. Not two-dimensional, as if looking at a television screen; three-dimensional perhaps, as if I were a thin, invisible ghost walking about on a stage while a play is in actual performance. I can move where I like, observe the actors from the back as well as the front, from prompt side as well as opposite prompt, noting their poses and their concealed gestures and their speeches. One might call it four-dimensional, because I am aware of their emotions and their motives as well. So I record what my judgement tells me are the essentials of the scene I am witnessing. (Forester, 1964, p. 77)

The generative and organizational functions of imagery are not restricted to the composing of fictional and poetic writing. Composing expository, persuasive, and technical writing often entails imagery as well (Rutter, 1985). For example, the image of a randomly branching tree not only crystallized Darwin's theory of natural selection but guided him through the writing of it (see Fig. 7.1). His notebooks show only one drawing going through progressive modifications, as if it served as the guiding metaphor for the work (Gruber, 1981).

Minor (1984) examined Einstein's interviews about his composing processes and his actual writings. He concluded that Einstein purposely used much imagery in his writing to reflect how the free variation of mental images in his own thinking revealed anomalies and how this led to his own solutions.

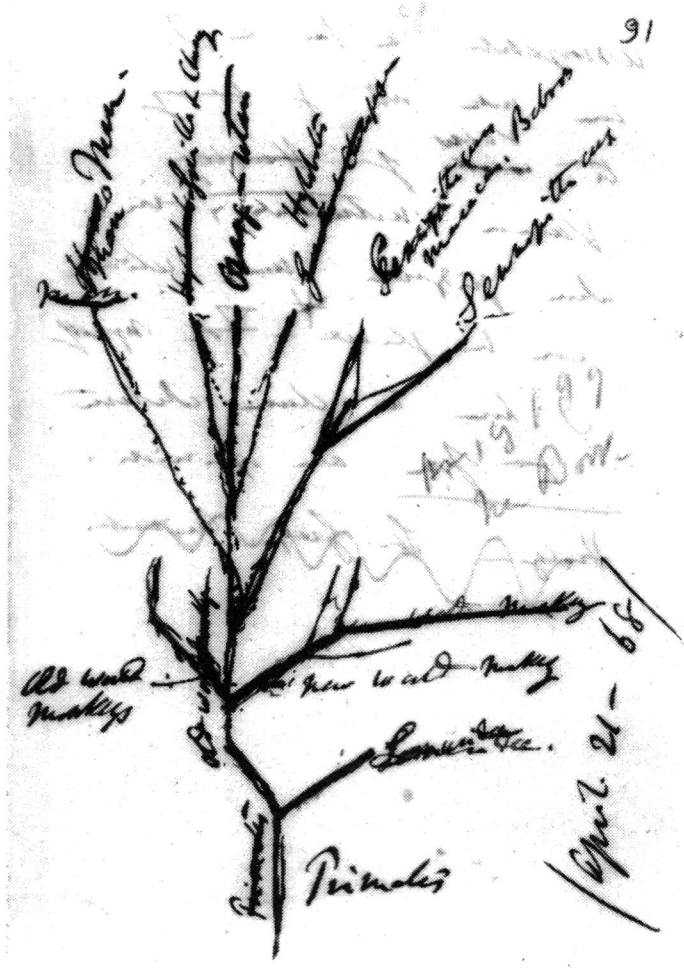

FIG. 7.1. *Darwin's tree of evolution, showing the theoretical relation of humans to other primates. Drawn by Darwin in his journal on April 21, 1868. Various forms of the tree diagram appear throughout the journal; it was apparently the guiding image of his theory of evolution. Reproduced by permission of the Syndics of Cambridge University Library.*

Krippner (1972) recounted that dream imagery produced the inspiration, organization, and first draft of Mendeleev's Periodic Table of the Elements:

> In 1869 D. I. Mendeleev went to bed exhausted after struggling to conceptualize a way to categorize the elements based on their atomic weights. He reported "I saw in a dream a table where all the elements fell into place as required. Awakening, I immediately wrote it down on a piece of paper. Only in one place did a correction later seem necessary." (p. 218)

In sum, anecdotal evidence strongly suggests that imagery can serve as a structural vehicle that inspires, organizes, and carries a written work regardless of its genre. Accordingly, the use of concrete language seems to be a major predictor in evaluating the quality of technical writing. Teklinski (1992) reviewed the elements of style used in technical manuals for computer programming that had won international awards for their professional quality. Concrete nouns were used almost totally, 95% in informational sentences and 98% in instructional sentences.

The DCT explanation of the generative and organizational role of imagery in composing is that images can function as symbols for general ideas. As category exemplars, they can concretize the abstract. More specifically, the conceptual peg hypothesis of DCT explains how symbolic imagery helps to organize and unify the whole for the writer. Certain images can stand for an abstract idea and as a retrieval cue for associated images and language. The creative thinking of the artist or scientist is well served by images that can easily be evoked and at the same time have the property of being an effective reference point around which other images and language can be organized. The content of that image may also evoke an affective state that serves as the "predominant passion" of the work, its guiding emotion.

This could explain, for example, how the shooting of the albatross carried in its train the ground plan of *The Rime of the Ancient Mariner* and released its thronging images to Coleridge. The ground plan was the imagery organized around the albatross scene together with other associated symbolic images, which served as reference points for still other scenes that organized and unified the poem as a whole. The killing of the albatross may have served as the emotional theme for Coleridge as well. Likewise, the image of the branching tree apparently served as the conceptual peg for Darwin's theory of evolution. It was an image from nature that captured the organizational framework of nature and its development, the progressive branchings symbolizing the development produced by natural selection.

It may seem self-evident that language is also a vehicle for the generation and organization of written composition, but an anecdote seems appropriate to illustrate its parallels to imagery. Murray (1978) cited Joseph Heller on the way the inspiration for his novels occured, specifically the inspiration for his novel *Something Happened:*

> I begin with a first sentence that is independent of any conscious preparation. . . . I was alone on a deck [of a cottage]. As I sat there worrying and wondering what to do, one of those first lines suddenly came to mind: "In the office in which I work, there are four people of whom I am afraid. Each of these four people is afraid of five people." Immediately, the lines presented a whole explosion of possibilities and choices—characters (working in a corporation), a tone, a mood of anxiety, or of insecurity. In that first hour . . . I knew the beginning, the ending, most of the middle, the whole scene of that particular "something" that was going to happen. . . . (p. 379)

This anecdote suggests the spreading of activation in the verbal system from the key sentences, followed by activation of images and related affective states. In this case the language is relatively concrete, but abstract language can serve creative and organizing functions as well. Literary scholars have traced the use of abstract language as organizing motif. For example, in *King Lear,* Shakespeare effected an irony throughout the play with the recurrence of two abstract words used in many variations: "nature" and "nothing" (Harrison, 1948).

Thus the two systems cooperate and complement each other in creative writing. The imagery system provides a way to store concrete memories of the world and to transform and manipulate those memories free from the sequential constraints that characterize language. The verbal system more directly symbolizes abstract concepts, and it provides an orderly, sequential flow to thinking that keeps creative effort on track, keeping a rein on associative leaps of imagery that could go off on tangents or lapse into daydreams. In written composition, language is the ultimate code of expression, and its linear, sequential nature serves well to organize and constrain unbridled imaginative thought for clear communication.

While anecdotal evidence is not strictly scientific, its richness must be considered in investigating such a complex phenomenon as composing extended text. These anecdotes serve to further strengthen the case for imagery and language as central to composing at every level.

A KEY STYLE CONCEPT: PERSONA

We last discuss the concept of persona as a central example of how DCT can explain the way writers develop the style of a work. The notion of persona has been discussed by many rhetoricians, but the perspective taken here is that of Gibson (1969). Persona comes from the Latin word for mask—the theatrical masks worn by Roman actors that had megaphonic mouthpieces to carry the voice to the audience. Thus, it has the historical connotation of role-playing. *Persona* is also the root of the words *person* and *personality*. A persona can be seen as a self-image, part of a multitude of personae or self-images that make up an integrated personality. The persona that is adopted in a given act of composing is an aspect of a writer's personality, either real or imagined, that the writer assumes toward the subject and projects to the audience. Hence, this takes the form of a particular "tone of voice" in writing.

For example, Gibson (1969) suggested that writers project an informal, familiar tone of voice to the audience through the use of active verbs, second-person pronouns, cumulative sentence structures, contractions, sentence fragments, and so on. By comparison, a more formal, authorial tone is achieved through more passive voice, periodic sentences, parallel constructions, and the avoidance of contractions, second person pronouns, sentence fragments, and so on.

Persona also affects the language we use toward the subject. Positive attitudes toward the subject suggest the use of honorific language, whereas negative attitudes suggest pejorative language. In certain contexts, terms might be used for reverse effect, or irony (e.g., the mock-heroic tone of *Casey at the Bat,* or the down-home political wit of Will Rogers). Many combinations of attitude toward the subject and tone of voice to the audience are possible that produce many nuances of style.

The concept of persona is central to style in composing because it deeply affects the selection of information from long-term memory, the formation of plans and goals, the imagined audience, and choices of grammar and vocabulary. A different set of personae, complete with different constraints, is adopted for writing a scientific article than for writing a thank-you note to Grandma. Stated differently, persona serves as an inner situational context that monitors and governs the writing process. This is similar to the "monitor" theorized by Flower and Hayes (1981) with the critical difference that the monitor is not necessarily a separate executive; it can be explained by activity within and between representations in the verbal and nonverbal systems as specified in DCT.

Sadoski (1992) explored the concept of persona from philosophical, rhetorical, and cognitive perspectives and argued that DCT could explain much of this concept and its key place in the psychology of writing. Specifically, a writer must adopt (at least) two personae, one for the author and one for the audience. The process would include the evocation of images, language, and affective states associated with the writing situation that establish the two personae. The author persona is a temporary aspect of the writer's cognition, a person the writer is or could imagine, that has a particular perspective toward the subject and the audience. This self-image may be a familiar one or a new one synthesized for the situation. The imagined audience (i.e., the second persona) is construed similarly although it might have quite different perspectives toward the subject and the writer.

The meaning of the subject to be written about presumably exists to some organized degree in long-term memory in verbal and nonverbal form. Language units are selected consistent with the author persona for the initial written expression of that meaning. After some language has been tentatively written, the writer shifts to the perspective of the audience persona for feedback. That is, the writer evaluates those tentative written forms from the perspective of the second persona to see if they seem to succeed in evoking intended images, affects, and language in the imagined audience.

That is, persona is the vehicle by which mental acts are carried out in the minds of both writers and audiences through writers imaginings of themselves as both writers *and* audiences, and the feedback loop of rhetorical decisions required to effect the most desirable written messages. In contrast, feedback in face-to-face conversation is immediate. From moment to moment, speakers adjust their speech by signals received from listeners in order to best communicate. Even in telephone conversations, feedback from the listener is critical; an extended telephone monologue met with silence on the other end soon elicits the query, "Are you still there?" However, writers enjoy no such feedback. They must regularly step out of the persona of writer and into the persona of reader to examine the effect. This often takes the form of pausing and "stepping back" to evaluate a segment of text from the imagined perspective of the reader, as described previously. The shift is subtle, and with accomplished writers it may be simultaneous with the actual writing, an ongoing tension between the two rather than a distinct shifting. But the writer must regularly provide feedback to the author persona from the audience persona.

For example, writing a thank-you note to Grandma may take its persona from the self-image of an appreciative grandchild feeling familiarity and gratitude. The familiarity calls for an informal tone toward the audience and the gratitude calls for an honorific attitude toward the gift. The actual plan for the writing would come from long-term memories of the typical layout of thank-you notes, complete with associated sentence structures and word choices constrained by the gift and the closeness of the relationship. The goal of the writer may take the form of images of Grandma's sentimental response while reading the thank-you note. Language is tentatively generated to be consistent with the plan, and internal feedback from the imagined goal state effects revisions even to the point of replanning. This explanation is consistent with the extended scenario that opened this chapter (for other specific examples, see Sadoski, 1992).

Writing a scientific article would entail a very different persona, but the general process would be the same. The attitude toward the subject would be more clinical and objective, and the tone of voice toward the audience would be very formal, consistent with specific rules laid out by publication style manuals. The images of self and audience would be those of knowledgeable and critical individuals and groups, possibly in professional settings. The generation of plans, forms, and language would be consistent with the image of self as scientist, and the images of an audience of critical peers would provide feedback on effects.

In this way DCT attempts to explain psychologically one of the most profound and mysterious concepts in rhetoric. Research on the topic provides some support. Hillocks (1986) reviewed empirical research on the effect of real or imagined audiences on writing. He found a small body of research indicating that students wrote differently for different assigned audiences, and that, in some cases, this had more effect than the level of knowledge of the topic. The developmental level of the writer also had some effect, suggesting that younger, more egocentric students had more difficulty adapting writing to an audience than older, more developmentally mature students, who could better imagine themselves in the role of others. Chapter 8 reviews other studies carried out since 1986 indicating that compositions are improved by imagining an audience. In a study reported earlier in this chapter, Miller (1994) found that some of the students in her self-report study visualized themselves making a convincing point or speculating on audience reactions. However, our analysis must remain incomplete because direct research from a DCT perspective is lacking.

Summary

As we demonstrated with theories of the reading process, DCT can explain written composition in its own terms. An extended example of the process was provided in both general and theoretical terms. We also demonstrated how an influential theory specific to composing can be reinterpreted in DCT terms, rendering it more consistent with an established general theory of cognition that is applicable to language reception as well as language production, and to nonverbal cognition as well as verbal cognition. Direct experimental research testing DCT predictions was reviewed, along with other supportive empirical research. A rich anecdotal record testifying to the role of imagery and language in composing was presented and interpreted in DCT terms. Finally, the DCT explanation of the concept of persona was examined, indicating that this central and difficult rhetorical concept can be explained in terms of DCT as well.

CHAPTER 8

Educational Implications

This chapter reviews a wide variety of research studies that illustrate the implications of DCT for literacy education. The studies have been selected from more than 30 years of research performed by many researchers on many literacy topics. Topics in reading instruction include decoding, sight word learning, vocabulary acquisition, text comprehension, using text with pictures or animations, engagement and interest, verbal-associative techniques, and selected remedial techniques. Topics in composition instruction include using concrete materials and language, audience effects, imagery instructions, and verbal-associative techniques. Summary conclusions are presented with each topic, but individual studies are reported in some detail for the critical consumer of research.

Chapter 2 chronicled the intellectual history of imagery and verbal processes, including literacy education practices, from antiquity to the mid-20th century. That history revealed a recurrent tension between imagery and verbal processes that was never resolved. The period since then has seen more resolution, and the future seems bright indeed for educational innovations involving the interplay of language and imagery as well as a reconsideration of useful practices from the past. This chapter deals with literacy education issues exclusively, but DCT has been proposed as a unified educational theory including principles of learning, effective instruction, individual differences, and teacher education (Clark & Paivio, 1991).

DECODING OR RECODING

The term *decoding* has been used in reading education to describe the process of converting printed language to spoken language, whether it is understood or not. However, the term *recoding* is preferred by many theorists because it more accurately refers to the process of converting the printed language code to the spoken language code either overtly or as inner speech. In DCT terms, this process involves the activation of associative connections between logogens in the visual modality and logogens in the auditory-motor modality, that is, modality-specific recoding within the verbal system. Learning to recode in reading is widely regarded as one of the central missions of literacy education.

Extensive research on this mission has been carried out by many researchers (Ehri, 1991). Consistent with the DCT interpretation of recoding, Ehri (1978, 1998) referred to the process of word identification in reading as retaining the spellings of words in memory as paired associates of their pronunciations. In this theory, the visual and auditory-motor representations constitute two different parts of a larger amalgamation of associated information about a word. A word's phonological identity is its auditory-motor representation learned through speech, and its orthographic identity is its visual image learned through reading. Grapheme-phoneme knowledge provides a mnemonic system for associating spellings to pronunciations. In reading development, graphemes and phonemes can be merged into larger orthographic and phonological units such as rimes (e.g., *-at, -in, -ook*), affixes, and whole words. These larger units can be more useful in recoding than individual graphemes and phonemes. This is completely consistent with the DCT assumptions that logogens are modality-specific units that vary in size. Also consistent with DCT, these associations are seen as part of a larger associative structure that involves verbal and nonverbal semantic and syntactic information as well.

Several of Ehri's studies show the potent effects of combining imagery with verbal processing in learning to recode. For example, Ehri and Wilce (1979) taught first and second graders a set of consonant-vowel-consonant (CVC) pseudoword pronunciations (e.g., *tib*) with a letter cue standing for each pronunciation (e.g., *T*). In several study conditions, groups of these students (a) were shown visual spellings of the CVC; (b) listened to oral spellings given by the experimenter; (c) listened to phonemic segmentation where the experimenter pronounced each of the three sounds separately; (d) were asked to repeat the correct response once; or (e) were told to imagine the spellings, where the experimenter said the pseudoword's letter sequence while the children formed a mental image of it. Later the children were asked to recall the CVC pronunciation when the cue letter was given aloud.

The CVC pronunciations were learned significantly faster when correct spellings were either seen or imagined. Furthermore, high correlations were found between students' ability to recall psuedowords whose spellings had been seen or imagined and their ability to read familiar words—correlations significantly higher than in the other conditions. Ehri and Wilce concluded that visual images of the spellings of words serve as symbols for their pronunciations in memory. They further suggested that as reading ability develops, these images might come to replace speech pronunciation as a vehicle for accessing semantic, syntactic, and phonological knowledge of the word in memory (i.e., meaningful reading could occur either as print to meaning to pronunciation or as print to pronunciation to meaning).

In another study, Ehri, Deffner, and Wilce (1984) taught prereaders picture mnemonics to assist in learning grapheme-phoneme correspondences. Three conditions were used. In the first condition, students were given pictures where the letter was an integrated part of a drawing (e.g., the letter *f* as the stem of a flower with a drooping head and the crossbar as leaves, or *w* as the bottom of the shape of the wings of a butterfly). A second condition had a separate picture in which the letter was not integrated (e.g., a straight flower without a drooping head with leaves at the base of the stem, an airplane with straight wings). The third condition involved only associations with the names of the pictures, not the pictures themselves. The students were tested on how well they learned the grapheme-phoneme correspondences.

The integrated picture group far outperformed the other groups, learning about twice as many correspondences and remembering more than twice as many of the picture names. The other two groups did not differ significantly. The researchers concluded that integrating the shapes of letters in pictures produced superior learning because the shapes of the letters later evoked images of the pictures with those letter shapes whose names began with the relevant sounds (cf. the keyword method below). Integration with the picture seemed to be the key because the pictures without the letter shapes produced no better results than a control condition without a picture.

Ehri's studies well exemplify how DCT principles can explain learning to recode print to speech. These studies demonstrate the modality-specific nature of the visual and auditory-motor representations and the usefulness of visual imagery as a mnemonic for associating printed letters with pronunciations whether meaningful or not. We have seen that they also have direct educational applications such as using visual imagery for spellings and using letter shapes integrated with keyword pictures for learning grapheme-phoneme correspondence.

SIGHT WORD LEARNING

Learning words as wholes without grapheme-phoneme analysis is a teaching technique often referred to as the sight word method. Whole words are associated with their pronunciations and often their meanings through various educational approaches. Learning sight words in the presence of meaningful pictures is a method dating back to the *Orbis Pictus* that is widely used in basal readers and predictable books, although some researchers have concluded that pictures may distract readers from attention to details of the print (e.g., Samuels, 1970). DCT maintains that building referential links between accurate mental representations of the word forms (word logogens) and mental images of relevant pictures (imagens) is useful in understanding and remembering words.

Arlin, Scott, and Webster (1978–1979) addressed the utility of pictures in sight word reading while controlling for several methodological limitations found in prior research on the topic. Kindergartners were presented with a set of concrete words they did not know in one of three learning conditions: a word and its picture presented together, a word and its pronunciation presented together, or a control condition with the word presented alone. Students were then asked to try to read the word alone, and the cycle continued until the words were learned (control-group students received extra feedback). Learning times were assessed for each group, and students were later tested for retention by reading the words alone. The learning rate for each condition was defined as the number of correct responses on the retention test divided by the time it took to learn the set of words.

The words with pictures condition produced sight word learning at a rate almost 80% faster than words with their pronunciations and faster still than the control condition. The researchers concluded that simultaneous presentation of pictures with concrete words improved sight word learning. Subsequent critique of this study (Singer, 1979–1980) and response and replication (Arlin, 1980) suggested that pictures facilitate learning only when they do not distract from fully learning the printed word form. Although the optimal use of pictures in sight word learning is unresolved (Filippatou & Pumfrey, 1996), the practice enjoys continued popularity in beginning reading materials.

Arlin et al.'s (1978–1979) original findings illustrate the dual coding principle that establishing referential connections between words and images as well as associative connections between printed and spoken words can facilitate word learning. A key point seems to be that accurate learning of the word form is critical in this process; that is, the referential picture adds meaningful and memorable semantic elaboration just as the association to pronunciation provides important connections to speech. A combined technique of learning sight words in which the words are first accompanied by pictures in predictable books and later on charts without pictures has been successfully applied with beginning readers (Bridge, Winograd, & Haley, 1983). In this technique, words are presented first in meaningful contexts with picture cues and then without the picture cues to ensure attention to the word forms.

Word concreteness also plays a role in sight word learning. Hargis and Gickling (1978) taught average-ability kindergartners a set of sight words with high imagery ratings and a set of sight words with low imagery ratings that were matched for length and frequency. The words were unknown to the children and were presented without pictures. The children heard each word used in a sentence, used the word in a sentence of their own, and repeated the word during training. The high-imagery words were learned and retained much better than the low-imagery words.

This research was extended to middle-grade children with reading difficulties by Hargis, Terhaar-Yonkers, Williams, and Reed (1988). They found that (a) high-imagery words from their basal reading books were learned about 12% faster than low-imagery words, (b) words presented in story contexts were learned about 12% faster than words presented in isolation, and (c) decodable (grapho-phonemically regular) words were learned about 6% faster than nondecodable (irregular) words. Significant interactions between these factors indicated that low-imagery words presented in isolation took the longest to be learned regardless of decodability, whereas high-imagery decodable words were learned the fastest regardless of context.

In DCT terms, decodable words (readily activated at the representational level) that were high in imagery (activation at the referential level) were learned fastest even without the benefit of meaningful verbal contexts (activation at associative level). However, words that varied in ease of decodability (representational level) and had less access to imagery (referential level), benefited from meaningful verbal contexts (associative level). Stated more generally, sight word learning benefited from decodability and also from comprehensibility either through word imagery or story context (for similar findings with word recognition by adults, see Strain et al., 1995).

In summary, sight vocabulary learning appears to benefit from pictures that provide a meaningful memory image for the word as long as the word form is well learned. Abstract words appear to be learned better in verbal contexts, whereas concrete, decodable words are more easily learned even in isolation. Because many words taught as sight words are abstract and irregular (e.g., *the, were, there, have*), these words will require the benefit of repeated exposure in context.

VOCABULARY ACQUISITION

Dual coding principles are useful in understanding the acquisition and teaching of vocabulary. Two main sources of vocabulary learning in literacy instruction can be identified: incidental learning from context and direct vocabulary instruction. DCT directly implies that encountering and using words in various contexts establishes a rich set of associative verbal connections and referential nonverbal connections. Such contexts include listening and speaking as well as reading and writing. Little research is available on the acquisition of vocabulary from listening, speaking, and writing, but a meta-analysis of 20 experiments of incidental word learning during normal reading showed that students learn about 15% of the unknown words they encounter (Swanborn & deGlopper, 1999). This rate is influenced by such factors as grade level and partial word knowledge. Using direct instructional techniques in addition can markedly improve that learning rate (Baumann & Kameenui, 1991; Beck & McKeown, 1991; White, Power, & White, 1989).

One of the best researched methods for direct instruction in vocabulary is the keyword method, a method with roots in antiquity that is consistent with DCT. The keyword method requires the learner to form an interactive mental image between the definition of the new vocabulary word and a familiar, concrete word that shares a similar acoustic element. For example, learning the word *carlin,* meaning *old woman,* may be accomplished by using the keyword *car* and having the learner generate an image of an old woman driving a car. When later recalling the definition of *carlin,* the learner retrieves *car* through its acoustic association and then recalls the image, and hence the meaning of *carlin.* This method has been applied widely with powerful results (Levin, 1985; Pressley, Levin, & McDaniel, 1987). It has also been successfully used in teaching foreign language vocabulary (e.g., Atkinson, 1975; Avila & Sadoski, 1996; Rodriguez & Sadoski, 2000).

Levin et al. (1984) experimentally compared the keyword method to semantic mapping and contextual analysis methods to test their relative effects on vocabulary learning and vocabulary comprehension. Both high ability and lower ability middle-grade readers using the keyword method outperformed their counterparts in the groups using the other methods on definition recall after a day. High-ability readers in the keyword group also outperformed the contextual analysis group on appropriateness judgments of sentences and sentence completions. Hence, the keyword method produced better recall of definitions at no cost to vocabulary comprehension as compared to other common school tasks.

Both DCT and empirical data suggest that combining the keyword method with contextual analysis is especially helpful. Such results have been obtained with foreign language vocabulary learning by Rodriguez and Sadoski (2000), who experimentally compared a combined keyword-context method with keyword alone, context alone, and rote memory methods. The combined keyword-context group far outperformed the other groups on definition recall after one week regardless of individual differences in language learning ability.

The use of the keyword method alone has some practical limitations such as the number of words for which a suitable keyword is available and the treatment of words with multiple meanings, so flexible instructional approaches using both imagery and verbal-associative techniques should be best overall. This would be expected from the DCT hypothesis that imagery and verbal processes are independent and additive in their effects on memory (chap. 5).

TEXT COMPREHENSION

Meaningful comprehension is the very essence of reading. The mental imagery that we experience while reading, either spontaneously or induced by instruction, has powerful effects on comprehension. This section is subdivided into sections dealing with (a) selected studies of the spontaneous occurrence of mental imagery in text comprehension, (b) the use of concreteness in enhancing text comprehension, (c) the use of imagery instructions in enhancing text comprehension, and (d) the use of pictures and animations to enhance text comprehension (Sadoski, 1999b; Sadoski & Paivio, 1994).

Spontaneously Occurring Mental Imagery

In two studies, Sadoski (1983, 1985) asked third-, fourth-, and fifth-grade students to read basal reader stories aloud and then complete several comprehension and recall tasks including a report of any mental images they spontaneously experienced. The students in both studies were kept unaware that they would be asked about their imagery. The basal text illustrations were present in the first study (Sadoski, 1983), but not in the second (Sadoski, 1985). Students reading the illustrated story did not discriminate between images of the illustrations and their own spontaneous images; students reading the unillustrated story reported nearly twice as many images. Results of both studies revealed that imagery of a key event in the story, its climax, was related to both total recall and deeper levels of comprehension such as recognition of the story's theme. The natural use of this key image as a conceptual peg for recall was discussed in chapter 5. However, imagery was not found to be related to performance on standardized reading tests, cloze tests, passage-dependent multiple-choice tests, or verbal intelligence tests.

In both studies, oral reading miscues increased significantly during the story event most reported as imaged, providing an objective correlate for the subjective imagery reports and confirming a prediction from dual coding and other imagery-based theories that intensive mental visualization may interfere with the visual processing of print. Figure 8.1 shows the data from Sadoski (1985). The episodes of the story are numbered across the top with their respective numbers of words; Segments A and B are background information that did not contribute to the plot. Down the left side of the figure are scales for mean number of reported images (IM), mean number of miscues per 10 words (MPTW), mean reading time in seconds per 10 words (SPTW), mean propositions (i.e., idea units) per sentence (PPS), mean words per sentence (WPS), and mean syllables per sentence (SPS).

The horizontal lines in the chart show that the high point of miscuing occurred at the same episode as the high point for reported images (Episode 5, the climax), whereas reading times were constant, and idea units, words, and syllables per sentence were all below the average for the story. The increased miscuing cannot be attributed to faster reading or increased difficulty in readability or information load, and can be interpreted as modality-specific interference caused by visual imagery generation during reading. Hence, the formation of imagery is theoretically related to the psycholinguistic phenomenon of oral reading miscues (Goodman, 1969; Goodman & Goodman, 1994; Sadoski, Carey, & Page, 1999).

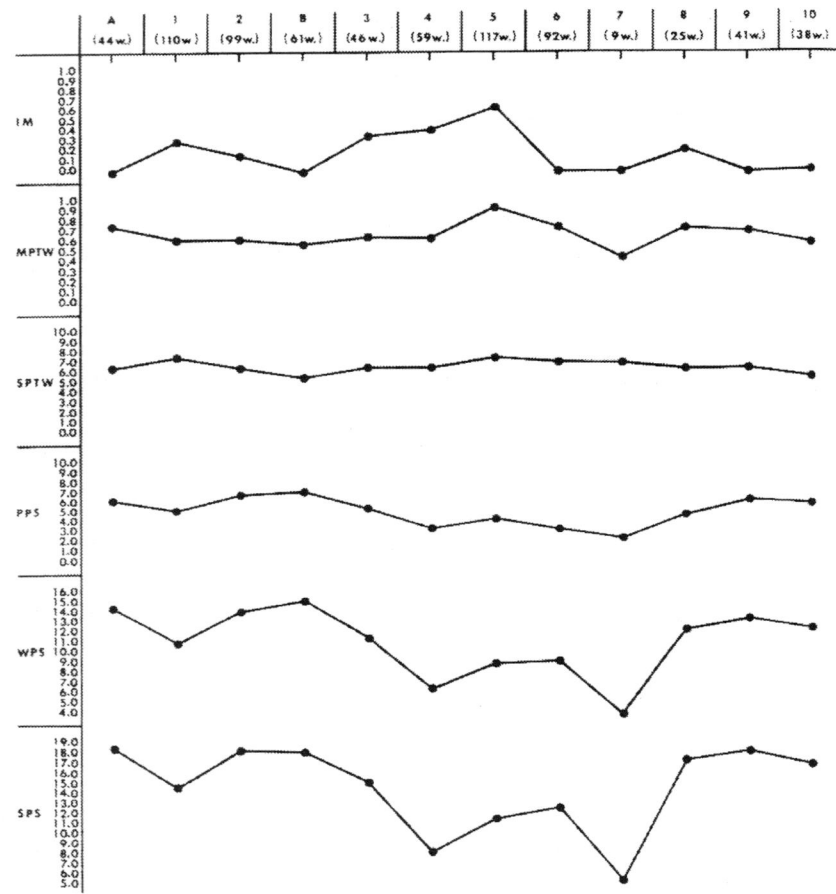

FIG. 8.1. *Diagram showing the relation of reported imagery to oral reading miscues and four text variables across the segments of a story. From Sadoski (1985).*

A converse effect may occur during silent reading. Silent readers are not constrained to maintain a conversational rate in oral reading, and they may slow down at certain points to deal with the conflict between generating images and processing print visually (Denis, 1982; Eddy & Glass, 1981; Giesen & Peeck, 1984; Levin & Divine-Hawkins, 1974). Therefore, teachers might expect readers to produce more oral reading miscues or slow their silent reading rate at points when they are heavily engaging in imagery.

The finding that comprehension of the theme or central idea is related to imagery was confirmed and extended by McCallum and Moore (1999). Students in Grades 2 through 5 read nine expository text passages in science and social studies at three points during a school year: fall, winter, and spring. The students responded to open-ended questions about their generation of mental imagery and their interpretation of the main idea of the passages. Results indicated that reports of images that were consistent with the passage were positively correlated with scores for main idea at all three points in time, whereas imagery that was inconsistent with the passage was negatively correlated with main idea scores during the fall but not during the winter or spring. The researchers concluded that while imagery is not an absolute condition for main idea comprehension, it is positively related and follows a similar pattern of growth over a school year.

Long, Winograd, and Bridge (1989) used think-aloud methodology without any instructions to form images with fifth graders and found that imagery was spontaneously reported at 60% of the think-aloud stops for a poem, a story, and two expository texts taken from school reading materials. Imagery was reported by both students identified as high and low in their propensity to form images as determined by an individual difference measure, with more reported imagery for high imagers. Imagery was reported at points in the text predicted to evoke imagery such as sensory descriptions and figurative language, and also at other times including climactic points. The researchers found no relationships between reported imagery and multiple-choice comprehension or vocabulary tests, suggesting that these measures were insensitive to the imaginal mode of comprehension. They concluded that mental imagery occurs spontaneously and consistently during reading, and that it contributes to interest in reading.

In the most extensive analysis of spontaneous imagery reports yet performed, Sadoski et al. (1990) asked community college students to read a 2,100-word literary story and provide imagery reports immediately and again after 48 hours. Imagery reports were categorized as consistent with a text paragraph, elaborated beyond the paragraph, distortion or contradiction of the paragraph, synthesis of information across paragraphs, or reader-originated. Imagery reports were also categorized by modality: visual, auditory, olfactory, gustatory, kinesthetic, tactile, affective, or multiple modalities. In addition, free verbal recalls obtained immediately and after 48 hours were extensively categorized.

Results indicated that, whereas verbal recall declined after the delay, imagery consistent with the paragraph did not decline. The categories of imagery reports and verbal recall were not highly correlated. A factor analysis of imagery and recall variables produced a set of factors dominated by visual imagery, affective imagery, and reader-originated imagery, suggesting that the experience of reading the story was largely an imaginal one. Other findings indicated a significant correlation between the number of imagery reports for a paragraph and the amount of story grammar macrostructure in the paragraph. Imagery of the climactic episode was by far the most common.

Another set of studies used numerical ratings and self-reports to investigate the spontaneous imagery of undergraduates reading literary short stories (Sadoski, Goetz, & Kangiser, 1988, replicating and extending Sadoski & Goetz, 1985) and feature journalism articles from *Newsweek, Sports Illustrated,* and *National Geographic* (Sadoski & Quast, 1990). In both studies, readers read the entire text and then were asked to go back and rate each paragraph for the degree of imagery experienced, the degree of emotional response, or the importance of the paragraph (one rating type per participant).

Graphs of the ratings for the literary short stories produced the typical pyramid shape of a plot rising to a climax (Fig. 8.2), whereas graphs of the magazine articles showed consistently moderate to high ratings, reflecting a journalistic style that strives for continuous engagement (Fig. 8.3). For both stories and journalism articles, significant correlations between imagery and emotional response ratings were found even when importance ratings were statistically controlled. For the stories, self-reports of the paragraphs rated highest on imagery, emotion, or importance indicated considerable agreement on what was imaged, felt, or held to be important. For the magazine articles, a surprise 16-day delayed recall test determined that paragraphs rated highly for imagery and emotion were still well recalled, but paragraphs rated as important were not. That is, the readers were able to distinguish importance, but they remembered best what they imaged and felt.

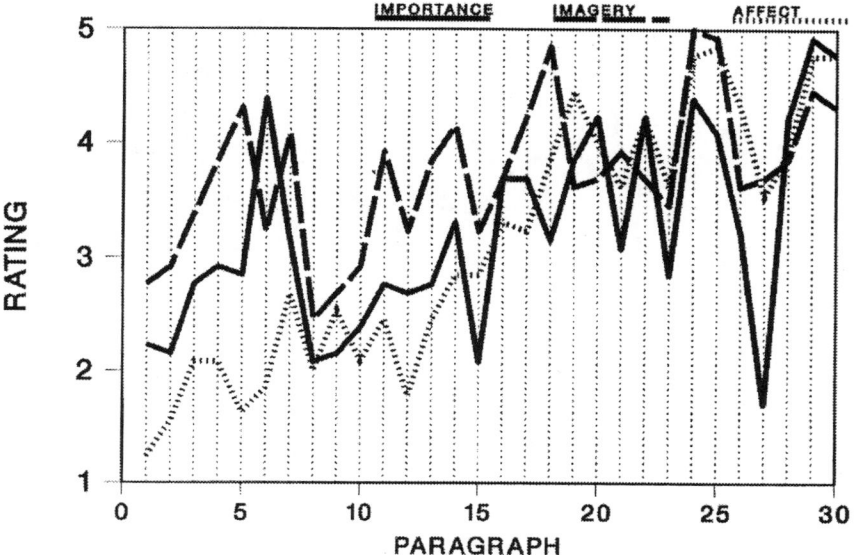

FIG. 8.2. *Diagram of readers' mean ratings for importance, imagery, and affective response across the paragraphs of the short story, "A Secret for Two." The ratings rise to the climax at paragraphs 24-25, drop off, and then rise again at the surprise ending. From Sadoski et al. (1988). Copyright by the International Reading Association. All rights reserved.*

In an extensive correlational study also using rating scales, Goetz, Sadoski, Fatemi, and Bush (1994) assigned undergraduates to read articles selected from the international section of *The New York Times* and then rate them for imagery, emotional response, comprehension, familiarity (general topic and story-specific), importance (general topic and story-specific), interest (general topic and story-specific), and writing quality. Factor analyses revealed that the ratings for imagery, emotional response, interest, comprehension, and writing quality loaded together on one factor, while the ratings for familiarity and importance loaded together on another factor that also received moderate loadings from the interest ratings. The researchers concluded that imagery, interest, emotion, and comprehension (i.e., engagement) are consistently related aspects of reader response that are not necessarily related to familiarity or importance.

The studies reviewed in this section indicate that spontaneous imagery is a natural part of reading that is associated with comprehension of main idea and theme, memory for text, and affective

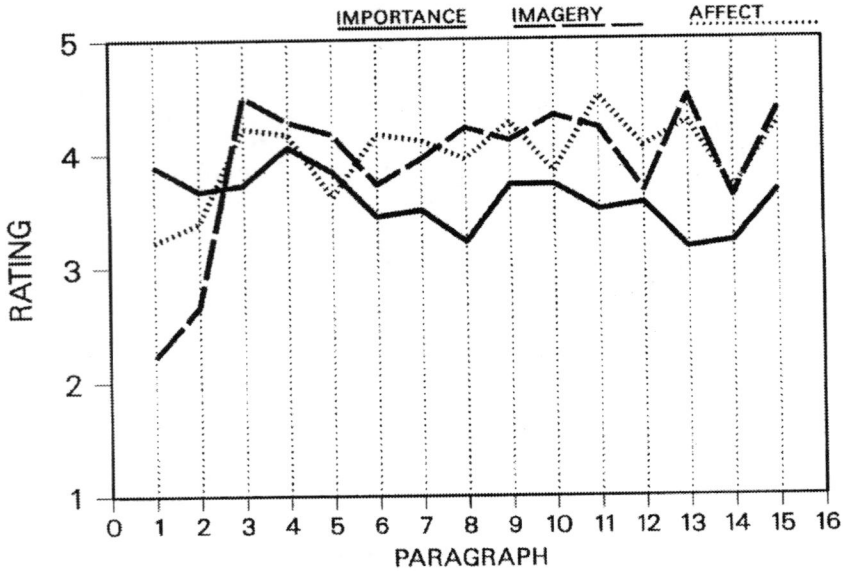

FIG. 8.3. *Diagram of readers' mean ratings for importance, imagery, and affective response across the paragraphs of the feature journalism story, "A Family Down and Out." The introductory paragraphs provided statistics about homeless families. The rest of the paragraphs show a different pattern of ratings from short stories. From Sadoski and Quast (1990). Copyright by the International Reading Association. All rights reserved.*

responses to text. Consistent with the principle of modality-specific interference, spontaneous imagery is related to oral reading miscues and silent reading times. However, traditional measures of comprehension such as multiple-choice tests may be insensitive to the contribution made by imagery; this point will be discussed later in the chapter.

Using Concreteness to Enhance Comprehension

As indicated in chapter 3 and elsewhere, concrete language is a central variable in referential processing, connecting verbal representations with nonverbal images. Throughout this book, we have shown that concreteness produces a variety of effects in both reading and writing. Readability research has consistently found concreteness to be related to ease of reading (Flesch, 1950; Klare,

1974–1975; Teklinski, 1992, discussed in chap. 7). This section reviews selected studies of concreteness effects in the comprehension of texts of various length and kind.

Anderson (1974) asked undergraduates to read simple declarative sentences with general nouns as subjects that had either no modifiers or concrete modifiers (e.g., *The set fell off the table* vs. *The ivory chess set fell off the table*). In subsequent recall, participants remembered 50% more of the sentences with concrete modifiers. A second experiment showed concreteness to be the effective variable because the same results occurred when the sentences were equated for length with either concrete or abstract modifiers (e.g., *The oil-pressure gauge was covered with dust* vs. *The measuring gauge was covered with dust*). Similar results were reported in Anderson et al. (1977, see chap. 5).

In a study also discussed in chapter 5, Sadoski et al. (1993b) investigated the effects of concreteness on the familiarity, comprehensibility, interestingness, and immediate and delayed recall of sentences and paragraphs of historical narrative. The texts were drawn from textbooks and history articles and dealt with historical figures, who varied in familiarity (e.g., Georgia O'Keeffe, Michelangelo, Malvina Hoffman, Robespierre). Concrete and abstract text passages about each figure were selected, and modifications were made to enhance this distinction (i.e., concrete texts were made relatively more concrete and abstract texts more abstract). Results indicated that with readability held constant, concrete text was rated as more comprehensible and interesting than abstract text but not as more familiar. Concrete texts were recalled two to five times better than abstract texts both immediately and after five days. Placing a concrete sentence before an abstract sentence about the same historical figure increased the recall of the abstract sentence by 70%.

A causal model of these data showed that concreteness ratings were by far the best predictor of recall as compared to the ratings for familiarity, comprehensibility, or interestingness (Sadoski, Goetz, & Fritz, 1993a, discussed later). Replication was reported using narrative, literary, persuasive, and expository paragraphs of varying readability in Sadoski et al. (2000). A secondary analysis of that data confirmed that concreteness was an overwhelmingly more powerful predictor than readability as well (Sadoski, 1999b).

Kolker and Terwilliger (1986) measured the concreteness values of 40 passages of 150 to 200 words each from middle-grade social science or general science text. Concreteness was determined by the ratio of concrete words to abstract words for all parts of speech using standard word norms. Although most words tended to be abstract, ten passages were determined to be relatively more concrete and ten passages relatively more abstract (five social science and five science passages each). Over 5 days, 65 average-ability fifth graders silently read the 20 passages and answered six short-answer comprehension questions on each passage, three factual and three inferential. The students correctly answered 42% more questions from the concrete passages. Significant overall increases were found for both factual and inferential questions in both social science and science. The researchers concluded that using concrete text can enhance comprehension and learning in social studies and science.

Wharton (1980) revised narrative passages on wars from American history textbooks to make them more concrete and imagery-evoking while holding readability constant. For example, the sentence *With England in control of the seas and France invincible on land the war became an economic contest* was revised to *With England sweeping the seas and France overrunning the land the war lapsed into an economic tussle.* About one word in eight was changed, and a panel of history professors determined that essential meanings were unaffected. The entire incoming freshman class of a college participated. They scored significantly higher on multiple-choice comprehension questions on the more concrete revised passages than on the original ones. The comprehension questions were at the literal, applied, and critical levels, and test experts judged that the wording of the questions did not favor either treatment. Findings revealed that participants also rated the revised passages as significantly more interesting and image-evoking than the original passages.

The use of advance organizers to enhance comprehension has been advocated for many years, but empirical results are mixed (Barnes & Clawson, 1975; Mayer, 1979). Corkill et al. (1988) conducted two experiments to examine the effects of a concrete advance organizer, an abstract advance organizer, or no advance organizer on learning extended text. In the first experiment, advance organizers that were matched for length and rated comprehensibility but differed in rated concreteness were presented to two separate groups of undergraduates. Students were asked to briefly paraphrase them to show that they had been understood. Then they read and recalled a related 1,200-word passage on astronomy, as did the control group. The concrete organizer group recalled significantly more than the abstract organizer group or the control group. There was no significant difference between the latter two groups. The group that received the concrete organizer recalled more than twice as much as the average of the other two groups. The second experiment successfully replicated the first experiment using an entire 5,000-word textbook chapter on linguistics. Similar results have been reported by other researchers (Mayer, 1983; Royer & Cable, 1975, 1976). Hence, advance organizers may work best when they are concrete.

In summary, the effect of concrete language on text comprehension and interest has been found to be consistently powerful in a variety of text types at the level of sentences, paragraphs, and even textbook chapters. These results are consistent with the theoretical explanation of concreteness effects on comprehension and memory presented in previous chapters.

Induced Imagery

Imagery is typically induced by giving readers instructions to form images or providing training programs on the formation of images. Of the many studies of induced imagery in text comprehension, the following show how induced imagery can have various effects on the comprehension of extended texts in educational settings.

Pressley (1976) taught third-grade children a mental imagery strategy in a classroom to help them remember stories. The children practiced constructing images of progressively longer prose passages (sentences, paragraphs, stories) and were shown good examples of images for the passages in pictures. Controls were told to do whatever they could to remember and did not see the pictures. Then both groups read a 950-word story with alternating printed pages and blank pages. The imagery group was reminded regularly to form images on the blank pages and the control group was reminded regularly to do whatever they could to remember when they saw the blank pages. On a 24-item short answer test, the imagery group outperformed the control group with no significant difference in reading times.

In a somewhat similar study, Gambrell (1982) gave first and third graders short stories to read in segments. Before each segment, the experimental group was told to make pictures in their heads to help remember, whereas the controls were told to think about what they read to remember. After reading each segment, the participants were asked a prediction question, "What do you think is going to happen next?" Responses were scored for factual accuracy and number of accurate predictions. Third graders in the imagery group reported twice as many facts and made twice as many accurate predictions as controls. First-grade imagers also tended to outperform controls on both measures, but the differences were not statistically significant.

Gambrell, Pressley, and other researchers have proposed that with beginning readers, the burden of verbal processing may inhibit forming images simultaneously. This is consistent with the principle of modality-specific interference, which may pose particular difficulty for beginning readers who must spend much time grappling with unfamiliar print. Perhaps very early readers do better reading and forming images successively, as in the Pressley study.

Anderson and Kulhavy (1972) presented high school seniors a 2,190 word text about a fictitious primitive tribe. The experimental group was instructed to read the text and form vivid images, whereas the control group received only instructions to read carefully. Analysis of multiple-choice and short-answer comprehension tests showed no difference between the groups, but analysis of a postexperimental questionnaire revealed that a majority of the control group reported forming images during reading. Therefore, the participants could now be classified by the amount of reported imagery rather than as belonging to the experimental or control group. Reanalysis of the data showed that comprehension was an increasing function of the amount of imagery reported. In a subsequent study with a similar passage, Kulhavy and Swenson (1975) found that fifth and sixth graders directly benefited from instructions to form imagery placed after every paragraph in a 20-paragraph text.

Steingart and Glock (1979) asked undergraduates to use either a mental imagery strategy or a verbal repetition strategy to comprehend and recall descriptive passages that were organized in three different ways. Each passage dealt with a variety of objects such as shelters, vehicles, or plants. In the first organization, each of the objects was described completely in a separate paragraph. In the second organization, all the objects were described by one attribute per paragraph (i.e., one paragraph for their shapes, another paragraph for their colors, and so on). In the third organization, the information was scrambled across paragraphs. Regardless of text organization, the participants using the imagery strategy answered more questions and recalled more than those using a repetition strategy. Imagery also resulted in more higher level inferences and better organized recalls.

Gambrell and Bales (1986) studied the effects of mental imagery training on the comprehension monitoring performance of fourth- and fifth-grade poor readers. An experimental group received a short training session in which they were encouraged to make pictures in their minds to help them understand and remember while reading. A control group was told to do whatever they could to understand and remember. Both groups then read passages in which either explicit or implicit inconsistencies had been embedded. They were instructed to read to determine if there was anything that was not clear and easy to understand. Questions and probes revealed that the imagery group identified both types of inconsistencies more than twice as well as the controls. Follow-up interviews revealed that few control group students reported using any imagery, suggesting that poor readers use little imagery. Giesen and Peeck (1984) found similar results with embedded inconsistencies with college students.

In summary, using induced imagery in educational settings has a strong record of promoting various aspects of text comprehension. Interested readers can find more information in reviews by Denis (1984), Suzuki (1985), and Alesandrini (1985). For additional reviews of the use of imagery in problem-solving situations, see Kaufmann (1990) and Kaufmann and Helstrup (1985).

Combinations of Text With Pictures or Animations

The use of pictures to assist with comprehending and learning from text has a long history. Chapter 2 provides evidence of the use of pictures in learning basic concepts and vocabulary in school materials in medieval times and earlier. Contemporary textbooks are replete with dazzling illustrations. Learning by visualization, which implies both internal mental imagery and such external representations as pictures, graphs, animations, and virtual reality has been historically reviewed by Rieber (1995). The following selected studies provide examples of the effective use of pictures and animations to enhance text comprehension and learning in education.

In a study with 120 fourth graders reading a 925-word basal reader story with five text-relevant illustrations, Gambrell and Jawitz (1993) investigated the relative effectiveness of induced mental imagery, attention to story illustrations, and both together. The group instructed to form mental images read an unillustrated version of the story. The group instructed to attend to illustrations read the standard illustrated version of the story. The group instructed to do both also read the illustrated version. Finally, a control group was instructed to read and remember the unillustrated version. The group instructed to form their own mental images as well as attend to illustrations significantly outperformed all the other groups on several measures of comprehension and recall including inferential comprehension. The group that only imaged outperformed the illustrations-only group on recall of story structure elements and complete recall of the story. The control group had the lowest performance on all recall tasks although it was the only group explicitly instructed to read to remember. The researchers concluded that mental images and illustrations independently enhanced reading performance, and that, in combination, these two strategies produced impressive increases in children's comprehension and recall of stories. They proposed an imagery-illustration theory that is completely consistent with DCT.

Kulhavy, Lee, and Caterino (1985) likewise proposed a "conjoint retention" hypothesis, which they noted was essentially a rendition of DCT. Fifth graders were shown a map of a small town with a railroad, streets, buildings, a pond, and other features. One group wrote a geographical description of the map, another wrote a short story about life in the town. Both groups were later given an incomplete map and asked to fill in as many features as they could recall. The story group remembered more features and located them more accurately. The researchers concluded that the verbal elaboration provided in writing the story was superior to writing a simple description of the map. In a second experiment, fifth graders either saw the map or read a verbal description of it and listened to a story about the history of the town. Then they were asked to recall both the story and the map. The learners who saw the map recalled more events from the story, and their recall was dependent on whether they remembered the geographic features associated with the events. Again, conjoint availability of the information in spatial form and elaborated verbal form provided better recall. Similar results were obtained by Schwartz and Kulhavy (1987) and Kealy and Webb (1995).

Purnell and Solman (1991) conducted five experiments to examine the use of illustrations in the comprehension of technical material by high school students. Some students received text alone, some students received an illustration of the same content alone, and others received both the text and the illustration of the same content. For example, one set of materials explained the water cycle of condensation, precipitation, percolation, and evaporation either as an extended text or in a labeled illustration of clouds, rain, a body of land, and a body of water. Comprehension was measured by 20 multiple-choice questions. Comprehension performance was superior when the same content was given both in text and illustration over (a) a single reading of the text, (b) a single exposure of the illustration, (c) repeated readings of the text, (d) repeated exposure of the illustration, or (e) seeing an illustration that contained related, but not identical, information to the text. When text and illustration of the same content were compared alone, comprehension was superior for the illustration. The researchers noted that their results were completely consistent with DCT.

Mayer (1999) reviewed his extensive program of studies on educational multimedia explanations including text and illustrations in books or animations and narrations on computers. His materials dealt with such topics as the operation of pumps, the respiratory system, the formation of lightning, and so on. The combined results of these studies suggested the following set of design principles for multimedia learning (a) use words and pictures rather than words alone; (b) place words close to corresponding pictures on a page or present narrations concurrently with corresponding animations; (c) minimize extraneous words, pictures, and sounds; (d) present words as speech rather than on-screen text in animations (presumably to minimize modality-specific interference); and (e) use these design principles in light of individual differences, particularly with low-experience, high-imagery learners.

Mayer noted that in every experimental test in his research program, the multimedia group outperformed the single representation group. For example, in measures of problem-solving, the median improvement for the multiple-representation group over the single-representation group was 97% for books (five studies) and 65% for computers (four studies). These empirically based design principles are consistent with the results of Gambrell and Jawitz (1993), Kulhavy et al. (1985), and Purnell and Solman (1991), and are completely consistent with DCT principles.

The studies reviewed in the preceding four subsections illustrate the powerful role of combining imagery and language in text comprehension in educational materials and settings. Whether imagery is spontaneous or induced, it has impressive consequences for comprehending text either alone or together with pictures and multimedia.

ENGAGEMENT, APPRECIATION, AND INTEREST

Comprehension and recall may be essential to education, but educational goals go beyond comprehension and recall. Affective responses including engagement, interest, and emotional response are highly valued educational outcomes when combined with learning. Considerable research has indicated that educational text that evokes mental imagery also tends to evoke more engagement, interest, and emotional response as well as better understanding and recall, particularly long-term recall.

Several studies reviewed earlier in the chapter point to the relationship between mental imagery and affect in text appreciation (Goetz et al., 1994; Long et al., 1989; Sadoski & Goetz, 1985; Sadoski & Quast, 1990; Sadoski et al., 1988, 1993a, 1993b, 2000; Wharton, 1980). These studies generally indicate that as student readers experience mental imagery, they tend to find text more interesting as well as more comprehensible and more memorable. Similar findings were reported by Nell (1988).

The causal nature of these relationships has been investigated. For example, Sadoski et al. (1993a) used causal modeling to test the effects of concreteness and familiarity on comprehensibility, the effects of concreteness, familiarity, and comprehensibility on interestingness, and the effects of all those variables on immediate and delayed recall. The findings indicated that (a) concreteness makes text more comprehensible than familiarity; (b) familiar, comprehensible text is more interesting; (c) concrete, interesting text is recalled better soon after reading; and (d) concreteness has an even more pronounced benefit on delayed recall. These causal modeling results with narrative sentences were replicated with paragraphs of various text types (Sadoski et al., 2000).

The results of these causal analyses are consistent with other correlational studies involving imagery, affect, and long-term recall (e.g., Sadoski & Quast, 1990) as well as experimental studies. For example, Hidi and Baird (1988) modified a school science text about famous inventors and their inventions to promote interest for fourth- and sixth-grade students. Modifications included descriptive elaborations of main ideas. Results showed that students recalled more of the modified text both immediately and after a delay than students in earlier, comparable studies recalled of standard science and social studies texts. Further, the students tended to recall concrete, active, personally engaging material better than abstract material that was rated as more important because it expressed main ideas. However, when concrete elaboration was added to abstract main idea sentences, the students recalled some of these sentences better.

Wade and Adams (1990) asked undergraduates of higher or lower reading ability to rate and recall the sentences of an encyclopedia article on the life of admiral Horatio Nelson. Regardless of the students' reading ability, information rated as interesting was better recalled both immediately and after a delay than information rated as important. Information rated as interesting was generally concrete, vivid, and personally engaging. Wade et al. (1993) replicated these findings with immediate recall and students' strategy reports. Wade, Buxton, and Kelly (1999) used texts on dinosaurs and found that a variety of factors promoted recall and self-reports of interest including comprehensibility, importance, and imagery.

A series of studies used history textbook passages on the wars in Vietnam and Korea rewritten by expert author teams in order to increase comprehension and recall (Britton, Van Dusen, Gulgoz, & Glynn, 1989; Duffy et al., 1989; Graves et al., 1988; Graves et al., 1991). The various author teams revised the original text through improved coherence, organization, vivid description, and other text factors. In a general synthesis of all the studies, Graves et al. (1991) concluded that text revisions that added interest, concreteness, novelty, character identification, and other engaging content best promoted comprehension and recall over the original versions.

Another text revision technique involved giving voice to fourth graders' history textbooks by revising them to incorporate more concrete action, conversational language, and emphasis on human relationships (Beck, McKeown, & Worthy, 1995). For example, the sentence *So their motto became "No taxation without representation"* was revised to *As the colonists' anger swept across the land, you could hear the cry, "No taxation without representation"* (cf. Wharton, 1980). Revisions also enhanced the coherence of the text by more directly explaining the connections between information such as the American colonists' opposition to taxes and the principle of participatory government. Comprehension was measured by open-ended questions and recall. The version revised for voice and coherence was comprehended better both immediately and after a delay than the original text or versions modified for voice only or coherence only. A related technique in which students are asked to imagine a textbook author as a real person to whom questions should be addressed has also been associated with improved engagement and comprehension in children's reading of both fiction and nonfiction (McKeown & Beck, 1998).

Taken together, these studies show that text concreteness and mental imagery play a role in active engagement with, and appreciation of, educational text through facilitating its comprehensibility, interestingness, and memorability. Most of the studies used narrative and expository text, but some used persuasive and literary text as well. The role of imagery and affect in the appreciation of literary text is of great intuitive appeal and has been studied still further.

In literary education, text material is approached more aesthetically (Rosenblatt, 1994). The goal of studying imaginative literature is to grow through its intelligent enjoyment, to appreciate its artistry through experiencing in the imagination the world evoked by the text, and to keenly perceive the significance of its insights. Students learn from stories, poems, and plays through their experience of them and their reflections on them. The role of imagery and affect is obviously central to this educational goal.

Many studies have demonstrated the relationships between imagery and affect in literary response. In a factor-analytic study of 68 items covering a broad spectrum of aspects of literary response, Miall and Kuiken (1995) found factors for imagery and empathy that formed parts of a second-order factor they labeled *Experiencing;* that is, the degree to which a reader becomes absorbed in a fictional work. Several other studies showing this relationship were reviewed earlier in this chapter (e.g., Long et al., 1989; Sadoski et al., 1988, 1990).

In a causal model, Sadoski (1984) found that children's imagery and affective responses to a story were equally predictive of how well they summarized the plot of a story, which in turn was highly predictive of their total recall of the story. These results were interpreted as extending the structural-affect theory of stories (Brewer & Lichtenstein, 1982), which states that particular structural features of stories (e.g., surprise endings) are related to particular affective responses in readers. Such features may be frequently imaged as well.

Goetz and Sadoski (1996) reviewed their program of research using a variety of literary stories and multivariate research methods demonstrating that (a) readers' imagery and emotional responses can be reliably and validly measured; (b) imagery and affect are consistently correlated, even when other relevant variables are controlled; and (c) imagery and affect are related to literary understanding. For example, Goetz, Sadoski, and Olivarez (1991) showed that ratings of imagery and affect by one group of students were highly significant predictors of the recall of the same story by a second, independent group of students after variance due to individual differences and readability was statistically removed.

In summary, the role of imagery in bringing both expository and literary text to life is not only intuitively obvious but empirically supported as well. We next turn to the verbal side of the picture.

VERBAL-ASSOCIATIVE ASPECTS OF READING INSTRUCTION

Although this chapter focuses especially on using imagery procedures and concrete language in reading instruction (i.e., dual coding), educational techniques involving verbal-associative relationships have been shown to improve reading as well. Some of these include elements of dual encoding because they implicate imagery to some extent. For example, a research review of graphic organizers that array related vocabulary concepts from a text in an organized diagram showed that they promote vocabulary growth, especially when used after reading (Moore & Readence, 1984).

A more purely verbal-associative educational technique is morphological analysis, where students break an unfamiliar word into parts such as roots and affixes and then recombine the parts into a meaningful whole. This technique has been estimated to nearly double the understanding of affixed words seen in context over the use of context alone (White et al., 1989). The technique was recommended for students in fourth grade and above; primary-grade children see far fewer affixed words and would be familiar with fewer root words. Prefix meaning instruction was estimated to be especially potent.

Other more purely verbal-associative techniques have received mixed research support in reading. For example, sentence combining, the merging of shorter related sentences into longer, more syntactically mature sentences, was designed to develop syntactic fluency. The results of sentence combining on reading are mixed, with several studies showing significant gains on one set of comprehension measures, but no significant results on others (Hillocks & Smith, 1991). Further research is warranted to determine the most appropriate application of sentence combining to improving reading.

PREVENTING AND REMEDIATING READING PROBLEMS

A remedial and preventive reading program by Lindamood and Bell (Bell, 1991; Lindamood, Bell, & Lindamood, 1997) makes use of principles that were independently developed but are closely related to DCT. Separate aspects of the technique focus on multisensory instruction for decoding and reading comprehension.

For example, phonemic awareness is taught through associating phonemes to motor acts and pictures of the mouth. Bilabial plosives such a /p/ or /b/ are taught as "lip poppers," lingual alveolar plosives such as /t/ or /d/ are (tongue) "tip tappers," and so on. Comprehension is taught through a program of visualizing and verbalizing that is explicitly based on DCT. Instruction entails progressive buildup (guided instruction) of imagery to larger and larger text segments—words, phrases, sentences, texts—with learners being guided by the clinician to describe their images in increasing detail. Higher order comprehension such as inference, prediction, and evaluation is dealt with through imagination and linguistic elaboration as well. Lindamood et al. (1997) provide clinical evidence of the effectiveness of these programs with reading disabled individuals of various ages.

Other remedial techniques, such as those developed by Monroe (1932), Fernald (1943), and Oakhill and Patel (1991) have also shown success using multisensory approaches or imagery approaches. The multisensory methods of Montessori, discussed in chapter 2, have also been adapted for remedial reading instruction. In summary, multisensory approaches have gained considerable attention in preventing and remediating reading difficulty (Johnston & Allington, 1991).

The sections above show that using imagery, concreteness, and verbal-associative educational techniques to improve reading has a broad and growing research base. The many studies reviewed in the sections above can be consistently interpreted in DCT terms.

SOME CHALLENGES TO DCT IN TEXT COMPREHENSION

Measurement Issues and Problems

The dual coding view of text comprehension in education has impressive support, but it faces some challenges as well. One challenge is the way in which imagery variables are sensitive to measurement.

For example, Durrell and Murphy (1963) reviewed an early series of studies on mental imagery in reading conducted at Boston University. Although the imagery reports of students from primary grades through college were reliable and detailed, low correlations were found between imagery reports and standardized tests of reading achievement or intelligence. Even though Durrell concluded that imagery was difficult to measure, he included it in his widely used diagnostic test of reading ability (Durrell & Catterson, 1980).

Several studies already reviewed in this chapter also have found that imagery reports were unrelated to standardized reading or verbal intelligence tests, cloze tests, or some multiple-choice tests on specific passages (e.g., Long et al., 1989; Sadoski, 1983, 1985; but for positive relationships between pictorial imagery or text concreteness and passage-specific multiple-choice tests, see Purnell & Solman, 1991; Wharton, 1980). Similar small or nonsignificant findings using standardized reading tests with imagery questionnaires or induced imagery have been reported as well (e.g., Cramer, 1980; Lesgold, McCormick, & Golinkoff, 1975; Long et al., 1989; Miccinati, 1982; Whitehead, 1990). The general pattern seems to be that imagery variables are related to free or cued recall, comprehension ratings, and various forms of comprehension assessment that allow for open-ended responses (e.g., Gambrell, 1982; Gambrell & Bales, 1986; Gagne & Memory, 1978; Kolker & Terwilliger, 1986; McCallum & Moore, 1999; Pressley, 1976; Sadoski, 1983, 1985; Sadoski et al., 1993a, 2000; Steingart & Glock, 1979) but imagery variables are less related to the formats used in most standardized achievement tests (i.e., multiple choice and modified cloze). When imagery or concreteness variables are tapped by multiple-choice measures, it may be when the questions are more inferential, critical, and applied (e.g., Wharton, 1980) rather than more literal and passage dependent (e.g., Sadoski, 1983, 1985).

DCT suggests a plausible interpretation for this pattern. Measures such as verbal IQ, cloze, and standardized achievement tests load heavily on a general verbal factor and appear to heavily favor the verbal system. Because the nonverbal code is theoretically distinct, little relationship between imagery variables and such measures might be expected. Measures that allow free responses or responses less constrained by verbal patterns might gain better access to the nonverbal system than measures that are more constrained by the verbal patterns of the test items. Measurement in imagery research is an area where further study is needed.

"Seductive Details"

Another challenge to a DCT approach to text modification for improved recall has come from the "seductive details" studies. The term *seductive details* is used to describe the putative effect of adding vivid but irrelevant details to a text to make it more interesting with the result that the vivid details are recalled at the expense of more important abstract generalizations (e.g., Garner, Gillingham, & White, 1989; Wade et al., 1993). A critical review of these studies (Goetz & Sadoski, 1995a) questioned this effect on two grounds (for a response, see Wade, Alexander, Schraw, & Kulikowich, 1995, and the rejoinder by Goetz & Sadoski, 1995b).

First, the conclusion that concrete details detract from learning important abstractions was unfounded due to inadequate experimental controls in these studies. Specifically, a control condition without seductive details was not used in most of these studies to show that the abstract material would be remembered even if such details were not present (i.e., abstract material is poorly remembered in any case).

Second, in the single experiment where such a control was present and the concrete details appeared to detract, the addition of the new concrete content added nearly 40% to the length of the text. That is, the coherence of the text was quantitatively and qualitatively altered so that what should be recalled as main ideas and irrelevant details was questionable. Goetz and Sadoski concluded that DCT could explain the results interpreted as showing the seductive details effect as well as results that ran counter to this hypothesis.

Subsequent experimental studies have confirmed the absence of a seductive details effect. Schraw (1998) used a control condition without seductive details in the passage on Horatio Nelson used in two of the studies critiqued by Goetz and Sadoski (1995a). He found no difference in the recall of important abstractions or total recall between the control and seductive detail conditions. Similar results with other texts were reported by Hegarty (1995).

Harp and Mayer (1997, 1998) claimed a seductive details effect, but the addition of substantial concrete material both quantitatively and qualitatively substantially altered the original text in ways that confound interpretation. The original text of six paragraphs dealt with the physical principles causing a lightning strike. The altered text added almost 30% new material about the dramatic effects of lightning strikes. The first paragraph was about equally divided between material on causes and effects, and material about effects was included in each of the remaining paragraphs. Furthermore, in several experiments, illustrations of the content of each paragraph were also used. A black-and-white line drawing showing positive and negative electrical forces (plus and minus signs) between objects was included to the left of each paragraph and matched by color photograph from *National Geographic* of an actual lightning strike to the right of each paragraph. Rather than adding irrelevant seductive details about the effects of lightning to a discussion on the causes of lightning, the coherence of these texts was altered so that the naive reader might interpret their main ideas as both the causes and effects of lightning. In fact, Harp & Mayer (1998) scored 12 idea units as seductive details about effects, but only nine idea units as casual information. For further discussion see Sadoski (in press).

Another study by Spooren, Mulder, and Hoeken (1998) found that varying text organization from simple listing to problem solution can have larger effects than increasing interestingness through increased character identification, activity level, or topic provocativeness (e.g., a hotel vs. a brothel). Using sentence recognition and reading time as comprehension measures, the results of three experiments with undergraduates showed that the manipulation of text organization had effects either on reading time or recognition, whereas the manipulation of interestingness was inconsistent. That is, students read the more structured text better regardless of the interestingness of the text or its topic. However, these results pose no problem for DCT because context effects are prominently included in the theory. Moreover, concreteness was not manipulated in the study; all the texts were about concrete objects and actions, but some were rated more interesting (but not necessarily more concrete) than others.

In summary, there appears to be no harm, and some benefit, in adding concrete detail to well-structured text to promote interest unless enough is added so that a new text with a different coherence emerges. Although it may be hypothetically possible to disrupt the learning of important abstractions by the inclusion of competing concrete details, the evidence at present does not provide reason to warn against the general practice of using concreteness to promote comprehension, interest, and recall. Perhaps concreteness is best used judiciously to support desired learnings (Sadoski, 1999c). Theoretically, DCT can consistently explain the results of these studies in terms of abstractness–concreteness and contextual organization effects in comprehension and memory.

WRITTEN COMPOSITION

Concreteness Effects

Practical guidelines for the use of concreteness in composing informational text were compiled in Sadoski (1999c). One of these is Strunk and White's (1979) classic maxim for writers: "Use definite, specific, concrete language" (p. 21). Strunk and White maintained that those who have studied writing are in agreement on this point more than any other, and they admonish writers that even in the case of general, abstract principles, concrete examples should be provided. Both DCT and empirical research provide support for this maxim.

Studies already reviewed indicate that the use of concrete language in text is related to improved ratings for comprehensibility, interest, recall, and writing quality (e.g., Goetz et al., 1994; Sadoski et al., 1993b, 2000; Wharton, 1980). For example, studies detailed in chapter 7 showed that (a) writing definitions of concrete concepts produced more and better writing than definitions of abstract concepts (Sadoski et al., 1997); (b) writing about the relationships between concepts in a concrete passage produced better writing than in an abstract passage (Tirre et al., 1979); (c) the use of concrete referents produced more text coherence through anaphora and final modifiers (Maes, 1997; Sadoski & Goetz, 1998); and (d) imagery often serves as the guiding idea in composing (Miller, 1994). Also relevant is the DCT interpretation of the concept of the writer's persona discussed in chapter 7.

Educational practices in writing instruction have also provided support for using concrete materials. In a meta-analysis of 73 experimental-control interventions, Hillocks (1986) found that instructional techniques using inquiry were by far the most robust in improving writing quality, twice as effective as the average intervention. He defined inquiry as focusing on immediate and concrete data during writing instruction in order to generate and apply criteria for describing, narrating, defining, or persuading.

For example, Hillocks (1995) contended that writing careful, analytic definitions is an important educational activity because such definitions are at the heart of analysis, argument, and dialectical processes that drive inquiry in every field. Sadoski et al. (1997) found that writing definitions of concrete concepts produced an effect size in quality ratings of defining abstract concepts (.36) that was larger than the mean effect size for the 73 interventions in Hillocks' meta-analysis (.28). Classroom activities requiring students to write definitions of abstract terms using concrete data sets have produced improved writing quality in both quantitative and qualitative studies (e.g., Hillocks, Kahn, & Johannessen, 1983; Johannessen, 1989). Hillocks et al. (1983) assigned students to define concepts such as *courageous action* that were presented in concrete scenarios of actions where someone may or may not have been courageous. The use of concrete data resulted in more accurate defining criteria and supporting examples and higher quality scores overall than did a control procedure.

Audience Effects

Butterfield et al. (1996) reviewed the research evidence on audience effects and concluded that various ways of conveying concrete information about an audience improve writing. For example, Roen and Willey (1988) investigated the effects of writers' attending to audience in drafting and revising. Undergraduates in freshman composition classes were assigned to one of three conditions: (a) no attention to audience, (b) attention to audience before and during drafting, and (c) attention to audience before and during revising. Those instructed to attend to audience either during drafting or revising produced higher quality compositions. Attention to audience during revision was most effective.

Redd-Boyd and Slater (1989) asked undergraduates in an intermediate composition course to write a persuasive essay on a proposed campus drug policy to either (a) a real assigned audience (their essays were actually read and rated for persuasiveness by a university administrator prior to implementing the policy), (b) an imaginary assigned audience (their grade was based on convincing their teacher that they could convince the administrator), or (c) an unspecified audience. Interviews, questionnaires, and writing samples indicated that assigning an audience increased motivation, effort, and the use of persuasive rhetorical strategies. The researchers also found an audience effect across groups. That is, some students in all groups reported writing to a university administrator, whereas some students in the real audience group reported writing to someone else (cf. Anderson & Kulhavy, 1972).

When persuasiveness ratings were analyzed accordingly, students who said they imagined the administrator while writing were twice as likely to persuade the real administrator as students who did not.

Traxler and Gernsbacher (1992, 1993) also investigated the way writers envision their readers. Undergraduates wrote and then revised descriptions of complex, unfamiliar geometric shapes. Both the original and revised descriptions were read by peers, who were to select the described figure from a set of similar looking figures; selection accuracy was used as the writing criterion. In Traxler and Gernsbacher (1992), half of the writers received feedback on their original description only regarding how well their peer readers selected the right shape. The half who received this minimal feedback revised their descriptions better than those who did not. Further, the writers who received such feedback wrote better descriptions of a new set of geometric figures. Traxler and Gernsbacher (1993) used a similar methodology. Half of the writers were "put in the shoes" of their readers by being asked to identify figures from descriptions written by others (i.e., they were asked to perform their readers' task). Writers who gained their readers' perspective this way revised their descriptions better than those who did not. When students both performed their readers' task and received feedback on how well their peer readers selected the right shape, they revised their descriptions even better.

Imagery Instructions

Imagery instructions in composing have also been effective. For example, Long and Hiebert (1985) investigated an imagery technique to improve the creative writing of gifted elementary students. The students were assigned to either a visualization training group that practiced writing with specific instructions to visualize or a story listening group that practiced writing without instructions. After three weekly lessons, the visualization group wrote longer, more original compositions than the control group.

Jampole, Konopak, Readence, and Moser (1991) refined and extended the study by Long and Hiebert (1985) with another sample of gifted students. The imagery training consisted of listening to 1,200 to 1,500 word passages written to evoke imagery in various modalities (e.g., "A musty dry smell arises from the brown leaves under foot that crackle as you walk on them"); the group then discussed their images. The control group listened to children's stories and discussed literal and interpretive comprehension questions. Four sessions were held in a two-week period. Identical creative writing prompts were given to each group. The imagery group wrote more original compositions using more sensory descriptions, although their compositions were no longer.

An instructional approach to composition that uses both verbal and nonverbal techniques and cites DCT as one of its theoretical bases was developed by Schultz (1982). The Story Workshop approach involves a multisensory approach to invention and group interactions for audience response. Students, led by an instructor, recall images relevant to a writing topic, images from assigned readings, images from topic word associations, or other sources. Students describe their images vividly and specifically, using language and gesture. This invention serves as a basis for drafting. Subsequent oral reading of student drafts or exemplary published works is included. Schultz (1987) reported a pre–post increase in composition length of 60% after a 30-hour program with remedial high school students. Improvements in invention, concrete expression, individual voice, and fluency were also reported.

Verbal-Associative Instructional Techniques

The previous sections have focused on using imagery and concrete language in written composition instruction (i.e., dual coding); however, more purely verbal-associative educational techniques have been effective also. For example, Anderson, Bereiter, and Smart (1980) asked sixth graders simply to list all the relevant single words they could think of that might be used in writing about a chosen topic. After 12 one-hour sessions in which they practiced with a variety of expository and opinion topics, the children wrote essays twice as long and used three times as many uncommon words as students in a control group. In an opinion essay, the experimental group advanced an average of three arguments on the issue, as compared to two for the controls, and elaborated their arguments significantly more. Interestingly, there were no differences in the quality of the compositions for the two groups. In DCT terms, organizing knowledge into networks of verbal associations can produce more voluble, organized composition, but these verbal organizations do not necessarily produce more meaningful writing.

Other more purely verbal-associative techniques also have research support. For example, sentence combining practice consistently produces both increased syntactic fluency (i.e., writing more syntactically mature clauses) and improved holistic scores of writing quality across many studies (Hillocks, 1986; Hillocks & Smith, 1991). Perhaps practice in dealing with sentences and contexts, as provided in sentence combining, invites more meaningful processing than dealing with networks of word associations.

In summary, using imagery, concreteness, and verbal-associative educational techniques to improve writing also has a broad and growing research base. As with reading, the numerous studies reviewed here can be consistently interpreted in DCT terms.

Summary

This chapter reviewed selected contemporary studies that illustrate the implications of DCT for literacy education. These studies were primarily peer-reviewed research efforts published in journals or edited volumes with rigorous standards. They come from a host of researchers using a wide variety of methods.

DCT principles can account for a spectrum of reading phenomena including phonological recoding, sight word learning, vocabulary learning, text comprehension, and text appreciation. Readers' spontaneous, relevant mental imagery of text material is positively related to comprehension across age groups and text types. Imagery appears to be related to the deeper comprehension of text as indicated by measures of theme, main idea, inference, and problem-solving. Behavioral corroboration for these findings has been found in both oral and silent reading. Using concreteness in educational text material can lead to impressive gains in the comprehension of sentences, paragraphs, and extended texts up to whole textbook chapters. Induced imagery produces similar gains. DCT principles also provide a clear account of impressive learning gains from combining text with pictures and multimedia. The appreciation of both literary and nonfiction texts is positively related to the experience of imagery and related affect. Remedial reading techniques consistent with DCT have a promising record of clinical success.

DCT principles can likewise account for a variety of findings related to written composition and its teaching. The use of concrete language and concrete materials is associated with better writing quality. Imagining concrete audiences in various ways produces gains in writing quality, as does direct instruction including imagery training or more verbal-associative methods such as sentence combining. Instructional practices informed by established theory are a goal throughout education, and the theoretical mechanisms of DCT permit a unified explanation of many literacy practices, although unresolved issues remain.

The often tangled history of mental imagery and verbal processes may be approaching resolution as theorists, researchers, and educators unravel its connections. The future seems promising for merging general cognitive theory, theories of reading and writing, and corresponding educational practices. DCT provides one framework for such a unification.

REFERENCES

Abrams, M. H. (1993). *A glossary of literary terms* (6th ed.). Fort Worth, TX: Harcourt, Brace, Jovanovich College.

Adams, M. J. (1990). *Beginning to read: Thinking and learning about print*. Cambridge, MA: MIT Press.

Adler, M. J. (1940). *How to read a book: The art of getting a liberal education*. New York: Simon & Shuster.

Alba, J. W., & Hasher, L. (1983). Is memory schematic? *Psychological Bulletin, 2,* 203–231.

Alesandrini, K. L. (1985). Imagery research with adults: Implications for education. In A. A. Sheikh & K. S. Sheikh (Eds.), *Imagery in education: Imagery in the educational process* (pp. 199–221). Farmingdale, NY: Baywood.

Anderson, R. C. (1974). Concretization and sentence learning. *Journal of Educational Psychology, 66,* 179–183.

Anderson, R. C., Goetz, E. T., Pichert, J. W., & Halff, H. M. (1977). Two faces of the conceptual peg hypothesis. *Journal of Experimental Psychology: Human Learning and Memory, 3,* 142–149.

Anderson, R. C., & Kulhavy, R. W. (1972). Imagery and prose learning. *Journal of Educational Psychology, 63,* 242–243.

Anderson, R. C., & Nagy, W. E. (1991). Word meanings. In R. Barr, M. L. Kamil, P. B. Mosenthal, & P. D. Pearson (Eds.), *Handbook of reading research* (Vol. II, pp. 690–724). New York: Longman.

Anderson, V., Bereiter, C., & Smart, D. (1980, April). *Activation of semantic networks in writing: Teaching students how to do it themselves.* Paper presented at the annual meeting of the American Educational Research Association, Boston, MA.

Arlin, M. (1980). Commentary: A response to Harry Singer. *Reading Research Quarterly, 15,* 550–558.

Arlin, M., Scott, M., & Webster, J. (1978–1979). The effects of pictures on rate of learning sight words: A critique of the focal attention hypothesis. *Reading Research Quarterly, 14,* 645–658.

Atkinson, R. C. (1975). Mnemotechnics in second-language learning. *American Psychologist, 30,* 821–828.

Avila, E., & Sadoski, M. (1996). Exploring new applications of the keyword method to acquire English vocabulary. *Language Learning, 46,* 379–395.

Baddeley, A. D. (1986). *Working memory.* New York: Oxford University Press.

Barnes, B. R., & Clawson, E. U. (1975). Do advance organizers facilitate learning? Recommendations for further research based on an analysis of 32 studies. *Review of Educational Research, 45,* 637–659.

Bartlett, F. C. (1995). *Remembering.* Cambridge, UK: Cambridge University Press. (Original work published in 1932)

Baumann, J. F., & Kameenui, E. J. (1991). Research on vocabulary instruction: Ode to Voltaire. In J. Flood, J. M. Jensen, D. Lapp, & J. R. Squire (Eds.), *Handbook of research on teaching the English language arts* (pp. 604–632). New York: Macmillan.

Beck, I. L., & McKeown, M. (1991). Conditions of vocabulary aquisition. In R. Barr, M. L. Kamil, P. B. Mosenthal, & P. D. Pearson (Eds.), *Handbook of reading research* (Vol II, pp. 789–814). New York: Longman.

Beck, I. L., McKeown, M. G., & Worthy, J. (1995). Giving text a voice can improve students' understanding. *Reading Research Quarterly, 30,* 220–238.

Bell, N. (1991). Gestalt imagery: A critical factor in language comprehension. *Annals of Dyslexia, 41,* 246–260.

Black, J. B., Turner, T. J., & Bower, G. H. (1979). Spatial reference points in language comprehension. *Journal of Verbal Learning and Verbal Behavior, 18,* 187–198.

Bransford, J. D., & Franks, J. J. (1971). The abstraction of linguistic ideas. *Cognitive Science, 2,* 331–350.

Bransford, J. D., Barclay, J. R., & Franks, J. J. (1972). Sentence memory: A constructive vs. interpretive approach. *Cognitive Psychology, 3,* 193–209.

Brazil, D. (1995). *A grammar of speech.* New York: Oxford University Press.

Brewer, W. F., & Lichtenstein, E. H. (1982). Stories are to entertain: A structural-affect theory of stories. *Journal of Pragmatics, 6,* 473–486.

Bridge, C., Winograd, P., & Haley, D. (1983). Using predictable materials vs. preprimers to teach beginning sight words. *Reading Teacher, 36,* 884–891.

Britton, B. K., & Gulgoz, S. (1991). Improving text learning. *Journal of Educational Psychology, 83,* 329–345.

Britton, B. K., Van Dusen, L., Gulgoz, S., & Glynn, S. M. (1989). Instructional texts rewritten by five expert teams: Revisions and retention improvements. *Journal of Educational Psychology, 81,* 226–239.

Britton, J., Burgess, T., Martin, N., McLeod, A., & Rosen, H. (1975). *The development of writing abilities (11-18).* London, UK: Macmillan Education Ltd.

Bronowski, J. (1977). The reach of imagination. *A sense of the future: Essays in natural philospohy* (pp. 22–31). Cambridge, MA: MIT Press.

Bronowski, J. (1978). *The origins of knowledge and imagination.* New Haven, CT: Yale University Press.

Brooks, L. R. (1967). The suppression of visualization in reading. *The Quarterly Journal of Experimental Psychology, 19,* 289–299.

Brooks, L. R. (1968). Spatial and verbal components of the act of recall. *Canadian Journal of Psychology, 22,* 349–368.

Broudy, H. S., & Palmer, J. R. (1965). *Exemplars of teaching method.* Chicago, IL: Rand McNally.

Bryant, M. M. (1993). History of the English language. In *New Webster's dictionary and thesaurus of the English language* (pp. xi–xviii). Danbury, CT: Lexicon.

Bugelski, B. R. (1971). *The psychology of learning applied to teaching.* Indianapolis, IN: Bobbs-Merrill.

Bundy, M. W. (1927). *The theory of imagination in classical and medieval thought.* Urbana: University of Illinois Press.

Butterfield, E. C., Hacker, D. J., & Albertson, L. R. (1996). Environmental, cognitive, and metacognitive influences on text revision: Assessing the evidence. *Educational Psychology Review, 8,* 239–297.

Caplan, H. (Trans.). (1944). *Rhetorica ad Herennium.* Cambridge, MA: Harvard University Press.

Carroll, J. B. (1993). *Human cognitive abilities: A survey of factor-analytic studies.* New York: Cambridge University Press.

Carruthers, M. J. (1990). *The book of memory: A study of memory in medieval culture.* New York: Cambridge University Press.

Chafe, W. L. (1977). The recall and verbalization of past experience. In R. W. Cole (Ed.), *Current issues in linguistic theory* (pp. 215–246). Bloomington: Indiana University Press.

Chafe, W. L. (1994). *Discourse, consciousness, and time: The flow and displacment of conscious experience in speaking and writing.* Chicago, IL: University of Chicago Press.

Chaytor, H. J. (1950). *From script to print: An introduction to medieval vernacular literature.* Cambridge, UK: W. Heffer.

Chomsky, N. (1965). *Aspects of the theory of syntax*. Cambridge, MA: MIT Press.

Clanchy, M. T. (1979). *From memory to written record: England, 1066-1307*. Cambridge, MA: Harvard University Press.

Clark, J. M. (1983). Representational memory: Paivio's levels of meaning as experiential model and conceptual framework. In J. C. Yuille (Ed.), *Imagery, memory, and cognition: Essays in honor of Allan Paivio* (pp. 211–231). Hillsdale, NJ: Lawrence Erlbaum Associates.

Clark, J. M., & Paivio, A. (1987). A dual coding perspective on encoding processes. In M. A. McDaniel & M. Pressley (Eds.), *Imagery and related mnemonic processes: Theories and applications* (pp. 5–33). New York: Springer-Verlag.

Clark, J. M., & Paivio, A. (1991). Dual coding theory and education. *Educational Psychology Review, 3*, 149–210.

Corkill, A. J., Glover, J. A., & Bruning, R. H. (1988). Advance organizers: Concrete vs. abstract. *Journal of Educational Research, 82*, 76–81.

Count-van Manen, G. (1991). George Herbert Mead on mental imagery: A neglected nexus for interdisciplinary collaboration with implications for social control. *Journal of Mental Imagery, 15*, 1–15.

Cornoldi, C., & Paivio, A. (1982). Imagery value and its effects on verbal memory: A review. *Archivio di Psicologica Neurologia e Psichiatria, 2*, 171–192.

Covino, W. A. (1994). *Magic, rhetoric, and literacy*. Albany: State University of New York Press.

Cramer, E. H. (1980). Mental imagery, reading attitude, and comprehension. *Reading Improvement, 17*, 135–139.

Crowley, S. (1993). Modern rhetoric and memory. In J. F. Reynolds (Ed.), *Rhetorical memory and delivery: Classical concepts for contemporary composition and communication* (pp. 31–44). Hillsdale, NJ: Lawrence Erlbaum Associates.

Daneman, M. (1991). Individual differences in reading skills. In R. Barr, M. L. Kamil, P. B. Mosenthal, & P. D. Pearson (Eds.), *Handbook of reading research* (Vol. II, pp. 512–538). New York: Longman.

Davies, W. J. F. (1974). *Teaching reading in early England*. New York: Barnes & Noble.

Denis, M. (1982). Imaging while reading text: A study of individual differences. *Memory & Cognition, 10*, 540–545.

Denis, M. (1984). Imagery and prose: A critical review of research on adults and children. *Text, 4*, 381–401.

Dewey, J. (1916). *Democracy and education*. New York: Macmillan.

Duffy, T. M., Higgins, L., Mehlenbacher, B., Cochran, C., Wallace, D., Hill, C., Haugen, D., McCaffrey, M., Burnett, R., Sloane, S., & Smith, S. (1989). Models for design of instructional text. *Reading Research Quarterly, 24,* 434–457.

Durrell, D. D., & Catterson, J. H. (1980). *Analysis of reading difficulty* (3rd ed.). New York: The Psychological Corporation.

Durrell, D. D., & Murphy, H. A. (1963). Boston University research studies in reading. *Journal of Education, 146,* 1–53.

Eddy, J. K., & Glass, A. L. (1981). Reading and listening to high and low imagery sentences. *Journal of Verbal Learning and Verbal Behavior, 20,* 333–345.

Ehri, L. C. (1978). Beginning reading from a psycholinguistic perspective: Amalgamation of word identities. In F. B. Murray (Ed.), *The development of the reading process* (IRA monograph No. 3, pp. 1–33). Newark, DE: International Reading Association.

Ehri,, L. C. (1991). Development of the ability to read words. In R. Barr, M. L. Kamil, P. B. Mosenthal, & P. D. Pearson (Eds.), *Handbook of reading research* (Vol. II, pp. 383–417). New York: Longman.

Ehri, L. C. (1998). Research on learning to read and spell: A personal-historical perspective. *Scientific Studies of Reading, 2,* 97–114.

Ehri, L. C., Deffner, N. D., & Wilce, L. S. (1984). Pictorial mnemonics for phonics. *Journal of Educational Psychology, 76,* 880–893.

Ehri, L. C., & Wilce, L. S. (1979). The mnemonic value of orthography among beginning readers. *Journal of Educational Psychology, 71,* 26–40.

Eliot, T. S. (1960). Hamlet and his problems. *Selected essays* (pp. 121–126). New York: Harcourt, Brace.

Elson, W. H., & Runkel, L. E. (1914). *Elson-Runkel primer*. Chicago, IL: Scott, Foresman.

Enkvist, N. E. (1978). Coherence, pseudo-coherence, and non-coherence. In J-O Ostman (Ed.), *Reports on text linguistics: Semantics and cohesion* (pp. 109–128). Abo, Finland: Publications of the Research Institute of the Abo Akademi Foundation.

Faulkner, W. (1959). William Faulkner. In M. Cowley (Ed.), *Writers at work: The Paris Review interviews*. New York: Viking Press.

Fernald, G. (1943). *Remedial techniques in basic school subjects*. New York: McGraw-Hill.

Filippatou, D., & Pumfrey, P. D. (1996). Pictures, titles, reading accuracy, and reading comprehension: A research review (1973–1995). *Educational Research, 38,* 259–291.

Fillmore, C. J. (1977). The case for case reopened. In P. Cole & J. M. Sadock (Eds.), *Syntax and semantics* (Vol. 8, pp. 59–81). New York: Academic Press.

Fillmore, C. J. (1984). Lexical semantics and text semantics. In J. E. Copeland (Ed.), *New directions in linguistics and semiotics* (pp. 123–147). Houston, TX: Rice University Studies.

Fillmore, C. J., & Kay, P. (1983). *Final report to NIE: Text semantic analysis of reading comprehension tests* (Grant No. G-790121). Washington DC: National Institute of Education.

Fleckenstein, K. S. (1992). The writer's eye on image: Revising for definition and depth. *Journal of Mental Imagery, 16,* 109–116.

Flesch, R. (1950). Measuring the level of abstraction. *Journal of Applied Psychology, 34,* 384–390.

Flower, L., & Hayes, J. R. (1981). A cognitive process theory of writing. *College Composition and Communication, 32,* 365–387.

Flower, L., & Hayes, J. R. (1984). Images, plans, and prose: The representation of meaning in writing. *Written Communication, 1,* 120–160.

Forester, C. S. (1964). *The Hornblower companion.* London, UK: Michael Joseph Ltd.

Fowles, J. (1977). Notes on an unfinished novel. In M. Bradbury (Ed.), *The novel today.* London, UK: Fontana.

Fries, C. C. (1962). *Linguistics and reading.* New York: Holt, Rinehart & Winston.

Fyfe, W. H. (Trans.) (1960). *Aristotle; "Longinus"; Demetrius.* Loeb Classical Library. Cambridge, MA: Harvard University Press.

Gagne, E. D., & Memory, D. (1978). Instructional events and comprehension: Generalization across passages. *Journal of Reading Behavior, 10,* 321–335.

Gambrell, L. B. (1982). Induced mental imagery and the text prediction performance of first and third graders. In J. A. Niles & L. A. Harris (Eds.), *New inquiries in reading research and instruction* (pp. 131–135). *Thirty-first Yearbook of the National Reading Conference.* Rochester, NY: National Reading Conference.

Gambrell, L. B., & Bales, R. J. (1986). Mental imagery and the comprehension-monitoring performance of fourth- and fifth-grade poor readers. *Reading Research Quarterly, 21,* 454–464.

Gambrell, L. B., & Jawitz, P. B. (1993). Mental imagery, text illustrations, and children's story comprehension and recall. *Reading Research Quarterly, 28,* 264–276.

Garner, R., Gillingham, M. G., & White, C. S. (1989). Effects of "seductive details" on macroprocessing and microprocessing in adults and children. *Cognition and Instruction, 6,* 41–57.

Garrett, M. F. (1975). The analysis of sentence production. In G. H. Bower (Ed.), *Psychology of learning and motivation* (Vol. 9, pp. 133–178). New York: Academic Press.

Gernsbacher, M. A. (1984). Resolving 20 years of inconsistent interaction between lexical familiarity and orthography, concreteness, and polysemy. *Journal of Experimental Psychology: General, 113,* 256–281.

Gibson, W. (1969). *Persona: A style study for readers and writers.* New York: Random House.

Giesen, C., & Peeck, J. (1984). Effects of imagery instruction on reading and retaining a literary text. *Journal of Mental Imagery, 8,* 79–90.

Goetz, E. T., & Sadoski, M. (1995a). The perils of seduction: Distracting details or incomprehensible abstractions? *Reading Research Quarterly, 30,* 500–511.

Goetz, E. T., & Sadoski, M. (1995b). The perils of seduction revisited: A reply to Wade, Alexander, Schraw, and Kulikowich. *Reading Research Quarterly, 30,* 518–519.

Goetz, E. T., & Sadoski, M. (1996). Imaginative processes in literary comprehension. In R. J. Kreuz & M. S. MacNealy (Eds.), *Empirical approaches to literature and aesthetics* (pp. 221–240). Norwood, NJ: Ablex.

Goetz, E. T., Sadoski, M., Fatemi, Z., & Bush, R. (1994). That's news to me: Readers' responses to brief newspaper articles. *Journal of Reading Behavior, 26,* 125–138.

Goetz, E. T., Sadoski, M., & Olivarez, A., Jr. (1991). Getting a reading on reader response: Relationships between imagery, affect, and importance ratings, recall and imagery reports. *Reading Psychology, 12,* 13–26.

Goff, L. M., & Roediger, H. L. (1998). Imagination inflation for action events: Repeated imaginings lead to illusory recollections. *Memory & Cognition, 26,* 20–33.

Goodman, K. S. (1969). Analysis of reading miscues: Applied psycholinguistics. *Reading Research Quarterly, 5,* 9–13.

Goodman, Y. M., & Goodman, K. S. (1994). To err is human: Learning about language processes by analyzing miscues. In R. B. Ruddell, M. R. Ruddell, & H. Singer (Eds.), *Theoretical models and processes of reading* (4th ed., pp. 104–123). Newark, DE: International Reading Association.

Gough, P. B. (1972). One second of reading. In J. F. Kavanagh & I. G. Mattingly (Eds.), *Language by ear and by eye* (pp. 331–358). Cambridge, MA: MIT Press.

Gough, P. B. (1985). One second of reading: Postscript. In H. Singer & R. B. Ruddell (Eds.), *Theoretical models and processes of reading* (3rd ed., pp. 687–688). Newark, DE: International Reading Association.

Graham, J. W. (1970). Point of view in the waves: Some services of the style. *University of Toronto Quarterly, 39,* 193–211.

Graves, M. F., Prenn, M. C., Earle, J., Thompson, M., Johnson, V., & Slater, W. H. (1991). Improving instructional text: Some lessons learned. *Reading Research Quarterly, 26,* 110–122.

Graves, M. F., Slater, W. H., Roen, D., Redd-Boyd, T., Duin, A. H., Furniss, D. W., & Hazeltine, P. (1988). Some characteristics of memorable expository writing: Effects of revisions by writers with different backgrounds. *Research in the Teaching of English, 22,* 242–265.

Gray, W. S., Artley, A. S., Arbuthnot, M. H., & Gray, L. (1951). *Guidebook to accompany the three preprimers.* New York: Scott, Foresman.

Green, J. A. (1969). *The educational ideas of Pestalozzi.* New York: Greenwood Press.

Grendler, P. F. (1989). *Schooling in Renaissance Italy: Literacy and learning, 1300-1600.* Baltimore, MD: Johns Hopkins University Press.

Gruber, H. E. (1981). *Darwin on man: A psychological study of scientific creativity* (2nd ed.). Chicago, IL: University of Chicago Press.

Guilford, J. P., & Hoepfner, R. (1971). *The analysis of intelligence.* New York: McGraw-Hill.

Halliday, M. A. K., & Hasan, R. (1976). *Cohesion in English.* London: Longman.

Hargis, C. H., & Gickling, E. E. (1978). The function of imagery in word recognition development. *Reading Teacher, 31,* 870–874.

Hargis, C. H., Terhaar-Yonkers, M., Williams, P. C., & Reed, M. T. (1988). Repetition requirements for word recognition. *Journal of Reading, 31,* 320–327.

Harp, S. F., & Mayer, R. E. (1997). The role of interest in learning from scientific text and illustrations: On the distinction between emotional interest and cognitive interest. *Journal of Educational Psychology, 89,* 92–102.

Harp, S. F., & Mayer, R. E. (1998). How seductive details do their damage: A theory of cognitive interest in science learning. *Journal of Educational Psychology, 90,* 414–434.

Harrison, G. B. (Ed.). (1948). *Shakespeare: The complete works.* New York: Harcourt, Brace, & World.

Harste, J. C., Woodward, V. A., & Burke, C. L. (1984). *Language stories and literacy lessons.* Portsmouth, NH: Heinemann Educational Books.

Hayes, J. R. (1996). A new framework for understanding cognition and affect in writing. In C. M., Levy, & S. Ransdell (Eds.), *The science of writing: Theories, methods, individual differences, and applications* (pp. 1–27). Mahwah, NJ: Lawrence Erlbaum Associates.

Hayes, J. R., & Flower, L. S. (1980). Identifying the organization of writing processes. In L. Gregg & E. Steinberg (Eds.), *Cognitive processes in writing: An interdisciplinary approach* (pp. 3–30). Hillsdale, NJ: Lawrence Erlbaum Associates.

Hayes, J. R., Flower, L., Schriver, K. A., Stratman, J. F., & Carey, L. (1987). Cognitive processes in revision. In S. Rosenberg (Ed.), *Advances in applied psycholonguistics (Vol. II.) Reading , writing, and language learning* (pp. 176–240). Cambridge, UK: Cambridge University Press.

Hegarty, P. (1995, April). *Seductive details re-examined: The effects of interesting details on learning from text.* Paper presented at the annual meeting of the American Educational Research Association, San Francisco, CA.

Hermann, D. J., & Chaffin, R. (Eds.). (1988). *Memory in historical perspective: The literature before Ebbinghaus.* New York: Springer-Verlag.

Hidi, S., & Baird, W. H. (1988). Strategies for increasing text-based interest and students' recall of expository texts. *Reading Research Quarterly, 23,* 465–483.

Hillocks, G., Jr. (1986). *Research on written composition: New directions for teaching.* Urbana, IL: ERIC Clearinghouse on Reading and Communication Skills and the National Conference on Research in English.

Hillocks, G., Jr. (1995). *Teaching writing as reflective practice.* New York: Teachers College Press.

Hillocks, G., Jr., & Smith, M. (1991). Grammar and usage. In J. Flood, J. M. Jensen, D. Lapp, & J. R. Squire (Eds.), *Handbook of research on teaching the English language arts* (pp. 591–603). New York: Macmillan.

Hillocks, G., Jr., Kahn, E. A., & Johannessen, L. R. (1983). Teaching defining strategies as a mode of inquiry: Some effects on student writing. *Research in the Teaching of English, 17,* 275–284.

Hockett, C. F. (1963). The problem of universals in language. In J. H. Greenburg (Ed.), *Universals of language* (pp. 1–22). Cambridge, MA: MIT Press.

Holcomb, P. J., Kounios, J., Anderson, J. E., & West, W. C. (1999). Dual-coding, context-availability, and concreteness effects in sentence comprehension: An electrophysiological investigation. *Journal of Experimental Psychology: Learning, Memory, and Cognition, 25,* 721–742.

Howard, L. (1967). The composition of Moby Dick. In H. Hayford & H. Parker (Eds.), *Norton critical edition of Moby Dick* (pp. 709–727). New York: W. W. Norton.

Hubel, D. H., & Wiesel, T. N. (1962). Receptive fields, binocular interaction, and functional architecture in the cat's visual cortex. *Journal of Physiology, 160,* 106–154.

Huey, E. B. (1908). *The psychology and pedagogy of reading.* New York: Macmillan. (Reprinted 1968, Cambridge, MA: MIT Press).

Intons-Peterson, M. J. (1993). Imagery's role in creativity and discovery. In B. Roskos-Ewoldsen, M. J. Intons-Peterson, & R. E. Anderson, (Eds.), *Imagery, creativity, and discovery: A cognitive perspective* (pp. 1–37). New York: North-Holland.

Jacob, S. H. (1976). Contexts and images in reading. *Reading World, 15,* 167–175.

Jampole, E. S., Konopak, B. C., Readence, J. E., & Moser, E. B. (1991). Using mental imagery to enhance gifted elementary students' creative writing. *Reading Psychology, 12,* 183–197.

Johannessen, L. R. (1989). Teaching writing: Motivating inquiry. *English Journal, 78,* 64–66.

Johnson, C. (1904). *Old-time schools and school-books.* New York: Macmillan. (Reprinted 1963, Glouster, MA: Peter Smith).

Johnson-Laird, P. N. (1983). *Mental models.* Cambridge, MA: Harvard University Press.

Johnston, P., & Allington, R. (1991). Remediation. In R. Barr, M. L. Kamil, P. B. Mosenthal, & P. D. Pearson (Eds.), *Handbook of reading research* (Vol. II, pp. 984–1012). New York: Longman.

Just, M. A., & Carpenter, P. A. (1980). A theory of reading: From eye fixations to comprehension. *Psychological Review, 87,* 329–354.

Just, M. A., & Carpenter, P. A. (1987). *The psychology of reading and language comprehension.* Boston, MA: Allyn & Bacon.

Kaufmann, G. (1990). Imagery effects in problem solving. In P. J. Hampson, D. F. Marks, & J. T. E. Richardson (Eds.), *Imagery: Current developments* (pp. 169–196). London: Routledge.

Kaufmann, G., & Helstrup, T. (1985). Mental imagery and problem solving: Implications for the educational process. In A. A. Sheikh & K. S.

Sheikh (Eds.), *Imagery in education: Imagery in the educational process* (pp. 113–144). Farmingdale, NY: Baywood.

Kealy, W. A., & Webb, J. M. (1995). Verbal learning with maps and diagrams. *Contemporary Educational Psychology, 20,* 340–358.

Kieras, D. (1978). Beyond pictures and words: Alternative information-processing models for imagery effects in verbal memory. *Psychological Bulletin, 85,* 532–554.

Kintsch, W. (1988). The role of knowledge in discourse comprehension: A construction-integration model. *Psychological Review, 95,* 163–182.

Kintsch, W. (1998). *Comprehension: A paradigm for cognition.* Cambridge, UK: Cambridge University Press.

Klare, G. (1974–1975). Assessing readability. *Reading Research Quarterly, 10,* 62–102.

Klausmeier, H. J., Ghatala, E. S., & Frayer, D. (1974). *Conceptual learning and development: A cognitive view.* New York: Academic Press.

Kolker, B., & Terwilliger, P. N. (1986). Visual imagery of text and children's processing. *Reading Psychology, 7,* 267–277.

Kosslyn, S. M. (1980). *Image and mind.* Cambridge, MA: Harvard University Press.

Kosslyn, S. M. (1994). *Image and brain: A resolution of the imagery debate.* Cambridge, MA: MIT Press.

Kounios, J., & Holcomb, P. J. (1994). Concreteness effects in semantic processing: ERP evidence supporting dual-coding theory. *Journal of Experimental Psychology: Learning, Memory, and Cognition, 20,* 804–823.

Krippner, S. (1972). The creative person and nonordinary reality. *Gifted Child Quarterly, 16,* 203–228.

Kulhavy, R. W., Lee, B. J., & Caterino, L. C. (1985). Conjoint retention of maps and related discourse. *Contemporary Edcuational Psychology, 10,* 28–37.

Kulhavy, R. W., & Swenson, I. (1975). Imagery instructions and the comprehension of text. *British Journal of Educational Psychology, 45,* 47–51.

Kutas, M. (1993). In the company of other words: Electrophysiological evidence for single-word and context effects. *Language and Cognitive Processes, 8,* 533–572.

LaBerge, D., & Samuels, S. J. (1974). Toward a theory of automatic information processing in reading. *Cognitive Psychology, 6,* 293–323.

Lakoff, G. (1977). Linguistic gestalts. In *Papers from the thirteenth regional meeting.* Chicago: Chicago Linguistics Society.

Lakoff (1993). Contemporary theory of metaphor. In A. Ortony (Ed.), *Metaphor and thought* (2nd ed., pp. 202–251). Cambridge, UK: Cambridge University Press.

Lakoff, G., & Johnson, M. (1980). *Metaphors we live by.* Chicago, IL: University of Chicago Press.

Lakoff, G., & Johnson, M. (1999). *Philosophy in the flesh.* New York: Basic Books.

Lang, P. J. (1979). A bio-informational theory of emotional imagery. *Psychophysiology, 16,* 495–512.

Langer, S. K. (1962). Speculations on the origin of speech and its communicative function. *Philosophical sketches* (pp. 26–53). Baltimore, MD: Johns Hopkins University Press.

Laurie, S. S. (1972). *John Amos Comenius.* New York: Lenox Hill.

Lesgold, A. M., McCormick, C., & Golinkoff, R. M. (1975). Imagery training and children's prose learning. *Journal of Educational Psychology, 67,* 663–667.

Leventhal, H. (1980). Toward a comprehensive theory of emotion. In L. Berkowitz (Ed.), *Advances in experimental social psychology* (Vol. 13). New York: Academic Press.

Levin, J. R. (1985). Educational applications of mnemonic pictures: Possibilities beyond your wildest imagination. In A. A. Sheikh & K. S. Sheikh (Eds.), *Imagery in education: Imagery in the educational process* (pp. 63–87). Farmingdale, NY: Baywood.

Levin, J. R., & Divine-Hawkins, P. (1974). Visual imagery as a prose learning process. *Journal of Reading Behavior, 6,* 23–30.

Levin, J. R., Johnson, D. D., Pittelman, S. D., Hayes, B. L., Levin, K. M., Shriberg, L. K., & Toms-Bronowski, S. (1984). A comparison of semantic- and mnemonic-based vocabulary-learning strategies. *Reading Psychology, 5,* 1–15.

Lewis, C. D. (1948). *The poetic image.* London, UK: Jonathan Cape.

Lewis, C. S. (1954). *English literature in the sixteenth century excluding drama.* Oxford, UK: Clarendon.

Lewis, C. S. (1966). It all began with a picture .... In W. Hooper (Ed.), *Of other worlds: Essays and stories* (p. 42). New York: Harcourt, Brace, & World.

Ley, R. G. (1983). Cerebral laterality and imagery. In A. A. Sheikh (Ed.), *Imagery: Current theory, research, and application* (pp. 252–287). New York: Wiley.

Liberman, A. M., & Mattingly, I. G. (1985). The motor theory of speech perception revisited. *Cognition, 21,* 1–36.

Lindamood, P., Bell, N., & Lindamood, P. (1997). Sensory-cognitive factors in the controversy over reading instruction. *Journal of Developmental and Learning Disorders, 1,* 143–182.

Long, S., & Hiebert, E. H. (1985). Effects of awareness and practice in mental imagery on creative writing of gifted children. In J. A. Niles & R. V. Lalik (Eds.), *Issues in literacy: A research perspective. Thirty-fourth Yearbook of the National Reading Conference* (pp. 381–385). Rochester, NY: National Reading Conference.

Long, S. A., Winograd, P. A., & Bridge, C. A. (1989). The effects of reader and text characteristics on reports of imagery during and after reading. *Reading Research Quarterly, 24,* 353–372.

Lowes, J. L. (1927). *The road to Xanadu.* London, UK: Constable.

MacAllister, A. T. (1954). Introduction. In D. Alighieri, *The inferno* (J. Ciardi, Trans.). New York: Mentor Books.

Maes, A. (1997). Referent ontology and centering in discourse. *Journal of Semantics, 14,* 207–235.

Mandler, G. (1975). *Mind and emotion.* New York: Wiley.

Marks, D. F. (1997). Paivio, Allan Urho. In N. Sheehy, A. J. Chapman, & W. A. Conroy (Eds.), *Biographical dictionary of psychology* (pp. 432–434). New York: Routledge.

Marschark, M., & Hunt, R. R. (1989). A reexamination of the role of imagery in learning and memory. *Journal of Experimental Psychology: Learning, Memory, and Cognition, 15,* 710–720.

Marschark, M., Katz, A. N., & Paivio, A. (1983). Dimensions of metaphor. *Journal of Psycholinguistic Research, 12,* 17–40.

Marschark, M., & Paivio, A. (1977). Integrative processing of concrete and abstract sentences. *Journal of Verbal Learning and Verbal Behavior, 16,* 217–231.

Mathews, M. M. (1966). *Teaching to read: Historically considered.* Chicago, IL: University of Chicago Press.

Mayer, R. E. (1979). Can advance organizers influence meaningful learning? *Review of Educational Research, 49,* 371–383.

Mayer, R. E. (1983). Can you repeat that? Qualitative and quantitative effects of repetition and advance organizers on learning from science prose. *Journal of Educational Psychology, 75,* 40–49.

Mayer, R. E. (1999). Research-based principles for the design of instructional messages: The case of multimedia explanations. *Document Design, 1,* 7–20.

McCabe, B. J. (1971). The composing process: A theory. In G. Hillocks, B. J. McCabe, & J. F. McCampbell (Eds.), *The dynamics of*

English instruction: Grades 7-12 (pp. 516–529). New York: Random House.

McCallum, R. D., & Moore, S. (1999). Not all imagery is created equal: The role of imagery in the comprehension of main ideas in exposition. *Reading Psychology, 20,* 21–60.

McGill-Franzen, A. (1993). *Shaping the preschool agenda: Early literacy, public policy, and professional beliefs.* Albany: State University of New York Press.

McKeown, M. G., & Beck, I. L. (1998). Talking to an author: Readers taking charge of the reading process. In N. Nelson & R. C. Calfee (Eds.), *The reading-writing connection, Ninety-seventh Yearbook of the National Society for the Study of Education* (pp. 112–130). Chicago, IL: National Society for the Study of Education.

McKellar, P. (1957). *Imagination and thinking.* New York: Basic Books.

Mead, G. H. (1934). *Mind, self, and society.* Chicago, IL: University of Chicago Press.

Meltzer, B. N. (1991). Mead on mental imagery: A complement to Count-van Manen's views. *Journal of Mental Imagery, 15,* 17–33.

Mertins, L. (1965). *Robert Frost: Life and times- walking.* Norman: University of Oklahoma Press.

Meyer, B. J. F., & Rice, G. E. (1989). Prose processing in adulthood. In L. W. Poon, D. C. Rubin, & B. A. Wilson (Eds.), *Everyday cognition in adulthood and late life* (pp. 157–194). Cambridge, UK: Cambridge University Press.

Miall, D. S., & Kuiken, D. (1995). Aspects of literary response: A new questionnaire. *Research in the Teaching of English, 29,* 37–58.

Miccinati, J. L. (1982). The influence of a six-week imagery training program on children's reading comprehension. *Journal of Reading Behavior, 14,* 197–203.

Miller, A. I. (1984). *Imagery in scientific thought: Creating 20th century physics.* Boston, MA: Birkhauser.

Miller, G. A. (1979). Images, models, similes, and metaphors. In A. Ortony (Ed.), *Metaphor and thought* (pp. 202–250). London: Cambridge University Press.

Miller, H. (1994). Sites of inspiration: Where writing is embodied in image and emotion. In A. G. Brand & R. L. Graves (Eds.), *Presence of mind: Writing and the domain beyond the cognitive* (pp. 113–124). Portsmouth, NH: Boynton/Cook.

Minor, D. E. (1984). Albert Einstein on writing. *Journal of Technical Writing and Communication, 14,* 13–18.

Moeser, S. D., & Bregman, A. S. (1972). The role of reference in the acquisition of a miniature artificial language. *Journal of Verbal Learning and Verbal Behavior, 11,* 759–769.

Moeser, S. D., & Bregman, A. S. (1973). Imagery and language acquisition. *Journal of Verbal Learning and Verbal Behavior, 12,* 91–98.

Monroe, M. (1932). *Children who cannot read.* Chicago, IL: University of Chicago Press.

Moore, D. W., & Readence, J. E. (1984). A quantitative and qualitative review of graphic organizers research. *Journal of Educational Research, 78,* 11–17.

Morton, J. (1979). Facilitation in word recognition: Experiments causing change in the logogen model. In P. A. Kolers, M. Wrolstead, & H. Bouma (Eds.), *Processing of visible language* (Vol. 1). New York: Plenum Press.

Murphy, J. J. (1990). Quintilian's influence on the teaching of speaking and writing in the Middle Ages and Renaissance. In R. L. Enos (Ed.), *Oral and written communication: Historical approaches* (pp. 158–183). Newbury Park, CA: Sage.

Murray, D. M. (1978). Write before writing. *College Composition and Communication, 29,* 375–381.

Murray, D. J., Leung, C., & McVie, D. F. (1974). Vocalization, primary memory, and secondary memory. *British Journal of Psychology, 65,* 403–413.

Nash-Webber, B. (1975). The role of semantics in automatic speech understanding. In D. G. Bobrow & A. Collins (Eds.), *Representation and understanding* (pp. 351–382). New York: Academic Press.

Nell, V. (1988). The psychology of reading for pleasure: Needs and gratifications. *Reading Research Quarterly, 23,* 6–50.

Nelson, D. L., & Schreiber, T. A. (1992). Word concreteness and word structure as independent determinants of recall. *Journal of Memory and Language, 31,* 237–260.

Oakhill, J., & Patel, S. (1991). Can imagery training help children who have comprehension problems? *Journal of Research in Reading, 14,* 106–115.

Osgood, C. E. (1953). *Method and theory in experimental psychology.* New York: Oxford University Press.

Paivio, A. (1965). Abstractness, imagery, and meaningfulness in paired-associate learning. *Journal of Verbal Learning and Verbal Behavior, 4,* 32–38.

Paivio, A. (1969). Mental imagery in associative learning and memory. *Psychological Review, 76,* 241–263.

Paivio, A. (1971). *Imagery and verbal processes*. New York: Holt, Rinehart, and Winston. (Reprinted 1979, Hillsdale, NJ: Lawrence Erlbaum Associates).

Paivio, A. (1975a). Coding distinctions and repetition effects in memory. In G. Bower (Ed.), *The psychology of learning and motivation* (Vol. 9, pp. 179–214). New York: Academic Press.

Paivio, A. (1975b). Imagery and synchronic thinking. *Canadian Psychological Review, 16*, 147–163.

Paivio, A. (1983). The mind's eye in arts and science. *Poetics, 12*, 1–18.

Paivio, A. (1986). *Mental representations: A dual coding approach*. New York: Oxford University Press.

Paivio, A. (1991a). *Images in mind: The evolution of a theory*. New York: Harvester Wheatsheaf.

Paivio, A. (1991b). Dual coding theory: Retrospect and current status. *Canadian Journal of Psychology, 45*, 255–287.

Paivio, A. (1996). Imagery and memory. In M. S. Gazzaniga (Ed.), *The cognitive neurosciences*. Cambridge, MA: MIT Press.

Paivio, A., & Begg, I. (1971). Imagery and comprehension latencies as a function of sentence concreteness and structure. *Perception & Psychophysics, 10*, 408–412.

Paivio, A., & Begg, I. (1981). *The psychology of language*. Englewood Cliffs, NJ: Prentice–Hall.

Paivio, A., & Clark, J. M. (1986). The role of topic and vehicle imagery in metaphor comprehension. *Communication and Cognition, 19*, 367–388.

Paivio, A., & O'Neill, B. J. (1970). Visual recognition thresholds and dimensions of word meaning. *Perception & Psychophysics, 8*, 273–275.

Paivio, A., & te Linde, J. (1982). Imagery, memory, and the brain. *Canadian Journal of Psychology, 36*, 243–272.

Paivio, A., & Walsh, M. (1993). Psychological processes in metaphor comprehension and memory. In A. Ortony (Ed.), *Metaphor and thought* (2nd ed., pp. 307–328). Cambridge, UK: Cambridge University Press.

Paivio, A., Walsh, M., & Bons, T. (1994). Concreteness effects in memory: When and why? *Journal of Experimental Psychology: Learning, Memory, and Cognition, 20*, 1196–1204.

Patterson, K. E., & Coltheart, V. (1987). Phonological processes in reading: A tutorial review. In M. Coltheart (Ed.), *Attention and performance XII: The psychology of reading*. Hillsdale, NJ: Lawrence Erlbaum Associates.

Paulson, E. J., & Goodman, K. S. (1999). Influential studies in eye-movement research. *Reading Online* [electronic journal of the International Reading Association]. Available: http://www.readingonline.org/research/eyemove.html.

Perfetti, C. A. (1985). *Reading ability*. New York: Oxford University Press.

Perrig, W., & Kintsch, W. (1985). Propositional and situational representations of text. *Journal of Memory and Language, 24,* 503–518.

Petrucci, A. (1995). *Writers and readers in medieval Italy: Studies in the history of written culture* (C. A. Radding, Trans.). New Haven, CT: Yale University Press.

Pichert, J. W., & Anderson, R. C. (1977). Taking different perspectives on a story. *Journal of Educational Psychology, 69,* 309–315.

Pollatsek, A., Lesch, M., Morris, R. K., & Rayner, K. (1992). Phonological codes are used in integrating information across saccades in word identification and reading. *Journal of Experimental Psychology: Human Perception and Performance, 18,* 148–162.

Pressley, G. M. (1976). Mental imagery helps eight-year-olds remember what they read. *Journal of Educational Psychology, 68,* 355–359.

Pressley, M. (1977). Imagery and children's learning: Putting the picture in developmental perspective. *Review of Educational Research, 47,* 585–622.

Pressley, M., Levin, J. R., & McDaniel, M. A. (1987). Remembering versus inferring what a word means: Mnemonic and contextual approaches. In M. G. McKeown & M. E. Curtis (Eds.), *The nature of vocabulary acquisition* (pp. 107–127). Hillsdale, NJ: Lawrence Erlbaum Associates.

Purnell, K. N., & Solman, R. T. (1991). The influence of technical illustrations on students' comprehension of geography. *Reading Research Quarterly, 26,* 277–299.

Quintilian, M. F. (1921). *Institutio Oratoria* (H. E. Butler, Trans.). New York: G. P. Putnam's Sons.

Rasinski, T. V. (1985). Picture this: Using imagery as a reading comprehension strategy. *Reading Horizons, 25,* 280–288.

Rayner, K. (1997). Understanding eye movements in reading. *Scientific Studies of Reading, 1,* 317–339.

Rayner, K., & Pollatsek, A. (1989). *The psychology of reading*. Englewood Cliffs, NJ: Prentice-Hall.

Redd-Boyd, T. M., & Slater, W. H. (1989). The effects of audience specification on undergraduates' attitudes, strategies, and writing. *Research in the Teaching of English, 23,* 77–108.

Renninger, K. A., Hidi, S., & Krapp, A. (1992). *The role of interest in learning and development*. Hillsdale, NJ: Lawrence Erlbaum Associates.

Reynolds, A., & Paivio, A. (1968). Cognitive and emotional determinants of speech. *Canadian Journal of Psychology, 22,* 164–175.

Richards, I. A. (1950). *Coleridge on imagination*. New York: W. W. Norton.

Richardson, A. (1994). *Individual differences in imaging: Their measurement, origins, and consequences*. Amityville, NY: Baywood.

Rieber, L. P. (1995). A historical review of visualization in human cognition. *Educational Technology Research & Development, 43,* 45–56.

Rodriguez, M., & Sadoski, M. (2000). Effects of rote, context, keyword, and context/keyword methods on retention of vocabulary in EFL classrooms. *Language Learning, 50,* 385–412.

Roen, D. H., & Willey, R. J. (1988). The effects of audience awareness on drafting and revising. *Research in the Teaching of English, 22,* 75–88.

Rosenblatt, L. M. (1994). The transactional theory of reading and writing. In R. B. Ruddell, M. R. Ruddell, & H. Singer (Eds.), *Theoretical models and processes of reading* (4th ed., pp. 1057–1092). Newark, DE: International Reading Association.

Royer, J. M., & Cable, G. W. (1975). Facilitated learning in connected discourse. *Journal of Educational Psychology, 67,* 116–123.

Royer, J. M., & Cable, G. W. (1976). Illustrations, analogies, and facilitative transfer in prose learning. *Journal of Educational Psychology, 68,* 205–209.

Ruddell, R. B., Ruddell, M. R., & Singer, H. (Eds.). (1994). *Theoretical models and processes of reading* (4th ed.). Newark, DE: International Reading Association.

Rumelhart, D. E. (1977). Toward an interactive model of reading. In S. Dornic (Ed.), *Attention and performance VI* (pp. 573–603). New York: Academic Press.

Rupley, W. H., Willson, V. L., & Nichols, W. D. (1998). Exploration of the developmental components contributing to elementary school children's reading comprehension. *Scientific Studies of Reading, 2,* 143–158.

Rutter, R. (1985). Poetry, imagination, and technical writing. *College English, 47,* 698–712.

Sadock, J. M. (1993). Figurative speech and linguistics. In A. Ortony (Ed.), *Metaphor and thought* (2nd ed., pp. 58–70). Cambridge, UK: Cambridge University Press.

Sadoski, M. (1983). An exploratory study of the relationships between reported imagery and the comprehension and recall of a story. *Reading Research Quarterly, 19,* 110–123.

Sadoski, M. (1984). Text structure, imagery, and affect in the recall of a story by children. In J. A. Niles & L. A. Harris (Eds.), *Changing perspectives in research in reading/language processing and instruction* (pp. 48–53). *Thirty-third Yearbook of the National Reading Conference.* Washington, DC: National Reading Conference.

Sadoski, M. (1985). The natural use of imagery in story comprehension and recall: Replication and extension. *Reading Research Quarterly, 20,* 658–667.

Sadoski, M. (1992). Imagination, cognition, and persona. *Rhetoric Review, 10,* 266–278.

Sadoski, M. (1999a). Comprehending comprehension [Essay review of the book *Comprehension: A paradigm for cognition*]. *Reading Research Quarterly, 34,* 493–500.

Sadoski, M. (1999b). Mental imagery in reading: A sampler of some significant studies. *Reading Online* [electonic journal of the International Reading Association]. Available: http://www.readingonline.org/research/Sadoski.html

Sadoski, M. (1999c). Theoretical, empirical, and practical considerations in designing informational text. *Document Design, 1,* 25–34.

Sadoski, M. (in press). Resolving the effects of concreteness on interest, comprehension, and learning important ideas from text. *Educational Psychology Review.*

Sadoski, M., Carey, R. F., & Page, W. D. (1999). Empirical evidence for the validity and reliability of miscue analysis as a measure of reading comprehension. In A. M. Marek & C. Edelsky (Eds.), *Reflections and connections: Essays in honor of Kenneth S. Goodman's influence on language education* (pp. 123–144). Cresskill, NJ: Hampton Press.

Sadoski, M., & Goetz, E. T. (1985). Relationships between affect, imagery, and importance ratings for segments of a story. In J. A. Niles & R. Lalik (Eds.), *Issues in literacy: A research perspective* (pp. 180–185). *Thirty-fourth Yearbook of the National Reading Conference.* Washington, DC: National Reading Conference.

Sadoski, M., & Goetz, E. T. (1998). Concreteness effects and syntactic modification in written composition. *Scientific Studies of Reading, 2,* 341–352.

Sadoski, M., Goetz, E. T., & Avila, E. (1995). Concreteness effects in text recall: Dual coding or context availability? *Reading Research Quarterly, 30,* 278–288.

Sadoski, M., Goetz, E. T., & Fritz, J. B. (1993a). A causal model of sentence recall: Effects of familiarity, concreteness, comprehensibility, and interestingness. *Journal of Reading Behavior, 25,* 5–16.

Sadoski, M., Goetz, E. T., & Fritz, J. B. (1993b). Impact of concreteness on comprehensibility, interest, and memory for text: Implications for dual coding theory and text design. *Journal of Educational Psychology, 85,* 291–304.

Sadoski, M., Goetz, E. T., & Kangiser, S. (1988). Imagination in story response: Relationships between imagery, affect, and structural importance. *Reading Research Quarterly, 23,* 320–336.

Sadoski, M., Goetz, E. T., Olivarez, A., Lee, S., & Roberts, N. M. (1990). Imagination in story reading: The role of imagery, verbal recall, story analysis, and processing levels. *Journal of Reading Behavior, 22,* 55–70.

Sadoski, M., Goetz, E. T., & Rodriguez, M. (2000). Engaging texts: Effects of concreteness on comprehensibility, interest, and recall in four text types. *Journal of Educational Psychology, 92,* 85–95.

Sadoski, M., Kealy, W. A., Goetz, E. T., & Paivio, A. (1997). Concreteness and imagery effects in the written composition of definitions. *Journal of Educational Psychology, 89,* 518–526.

Sadoski, M., & Paivio, A. (1994). A dual coding view of imagery and verbal processes in reading comprehension. In R. B. Ruddell, M. R. Ruddell, & H. Singer (Eds.), *Theoretical models and processes of reading* (4th ed., pp. 582–601). Newark, DE: International Reading Association.

Sadoski, M., Paivio, A., & Goetz, E. T. (1991). A critique of schema theory in reading and a dual coding alternative. *Reading Research Quarterly, 26,* 463–484.

Sadoski, M., & Quast, Z. (1990). Reader response and long term recall for journalistic text: The roles of imagery, affect, and importance. *Reading Research Quarterly, 25,* 256–272.

Samuels, S. J. (1970). Effects of pictures on learning to read, comprehension, and attitudes. *Review of Educational Research, 40,* 397–407.

Samuels, S. J. (1977). Introduction to theoretical models of reading. In W. Otto, C. Peters, & N. Peters (Eds.), *Reading problems: A multidisciplinary perspective* (pp. 7–41). Reading, MA: Addison-Wesley.

Samuels, S. J. (1994). Word recognition. In H. Singer & R. B. Ruddell (Eds.), *Theoretical models and processes of reading* (3rd ed., pp. 256–275). Newark, DE: International Reading Association.

Saussure, F. de. (1974). *Course in general linguistics* (W. Baskin, trans.; C. Bally & A. Sechehaye, Eds.). Glasgow: Fontana. (Original work published 1915)

Schneider, E. (1953). *Coleridge, opium, and Kubla Kahn.* Chicago, IL: University of Chicago Press.

Schraw, G. (1998). Processing and recall differences among seductive details. *Journal of Educational Psychology, 90,* 3–12.

Schultz, J. (1982). *Writing from start to finish.* Upper Montclair, NJ: Boynton/Cook.

Schultz, J. (1987, March). *The power of acceptance of mixed diction—of the student's voice—in the teaching of composition.* Paper presented at the annual meeting of the Conference on College Composition and Communication, Atlanta, GA.

Schwartz, N. H., & Kulhavy, R. W. (1987). Map structure and the comprehension of prose. *Educational and Psychological Research, 7,* 113–128.

Segal, A. U. (1976). *Verbal and nonverbal encoding and retrieval differences.* Unpublished doctoral dissertation, University of Western Ontario, London.

Seidenberg, M., & McClelland, J. L. (1989). A distributed, developmental model of word recognition and naming. *Psychological Review, 96,* 523–586.

Shelley, M. (1963). *Frankenstein.* New York: Penguin Books.

Shepard, R. N. (1978). Externalization of mental images and the act of creation. In B. S. Randhawa & W. E. Coffman (Eds.), *Visual learning, thinking, and communication* (pp. 133–189). New York: Academic Press.

Shepard, R. N., & Cooper, L. A. (1982). *Mental images and their transformations.* Cambridge, MA: MIT Press.

Shuster, G. N. (1979). Introduction. In *The confessions of St. Augustine* (J. G. Pilkington, Trans.). Norwalk, CT: Easton Press.

Singer, H. (1979–1980). Sight word learning with and without pictures: A critique of Arlin, Scott, and Webster's research. *Reading Research Quarterly, 15,* 290–298.

Skemp, R. R. (1987). *The psychology of learning mathematics.* Hillsdale, NJ: Lawrence Erlbaum Associates.

Smith, E. E., & Medin, D. L. (1981). *Categories and concepts.* Cambridge, MA: Harvard University Press.

Smith, J. D., Reisberg, D., & Wilson, M. (1992). Subvocalization and auditory imagery: Interactions between the inner ear and the inner voice. In D. Reisberg (Ed.), *Auditory imagery* (pp. 95–120). Hillsdale, NJ: Lawrence Erlbaum Associates.

Smith N. B. (1986). *American reading instruction*. Newark, DE: International Reading Association.

Soloman, K. O., Medin, D. L., & Lynch, E. (1999). Concepts do more than categorize. *Trends in Cognitive Sciences, 3,* 99–104.

Speidel, G. E., & Troy, M. E. (1985). The ebb and flow of mental imagery in education. In A. A. Sheikh & K. S. Sheikh (Eds.), *Imagery in education: Imagery in the educational process* (pp. 11–38). Farmingdale, NY: Baywood.

Spooren, W., Mulder, M., & Hoeken, H. (1998). The role of interest and text structure in professional reading. *Journal of Research in Reading, 21,* 109–120.

Spurgeon, C. F. E. (1935). *Shakespeare's imagery and what it tells us.* New York: Cambridge University Press.

Stahl, W. J., Johnson, R., & Burge, E. L. (1971). *Martianus Capella and the seven liberal arts* (Vols. 2 & 3). New York: Columbia University.

Stanovich, K. E. (1991). Word recognition: Changing perspectives. In R. Barr, M. L. Kamil, P. B. Mosenthal, & P. D. Pearson (Eds.), *Handbook of reading research* (Vol. II, pp. 418–452). New York: Longman.

Steingart, S. K., & Glock, M. D. (1979). Imagery and the recall of connected discourse. *Reading Research Quarterly, 15,* 66–83.

Strain, E., Patterson, K., & Seidenberg, M. S. (1995). Semantic effects in single-word naming. *Journal of Experimental Psychology: Learning, Memory, & Cognition, 21,* 1140–1154.

Strunk, W., Jr., & White, E. B. (1979). *The elements of style* (3rd ed.). New York: Macmillan.

Sulzby, E., & Teale, W. (1991). Emergent literacy. In R. Barr, M. L. Kamil, P. B. Mosenthal, & P. D. Pearson (Eds.), *Handbook of reading research* (Vol. II, pp. 727–758). New York: Longman.

Suzuki, N. S. (1985). Imagery research with children: Implications for education. In A. A. Sheikh & K. S. Sheikh (Eds.), *Imagery in education: Imagery in the educational process* (pp. 179–198). Farmingdale, NY: Baywood.

Swanborn, M. S. L., & deGlopper, K. (1999). Incidental word-learning while reading: A meta-analysis. *Review of Educational Research, 69,* 261–285.

Teklinski, B. (1992). Style analysis of award winning technical manuals. *Journal of Technical Writing and Communication, 22,* 415–423.

Tirre, W. C., Manelis, L., & Leicht, K. L. (1979). The effects of imaginal and verbal strategies on prose comprehension by adults. *Journal of Reading Behavior, 11,* 99–106.

Tomasello, M. (Ed.). (1998). *The new psychology of language: Cognitive and functional approaches to language structure*. Mahwah, NJ: Lawrence Erlbaum Associates.

Trabasso, T., & van den Broek, P. W. (1985). Causal thinking and the representation of narrative events. *Journal of Memory and Language, 24,* 612–630.

Traxler, M. W., & Gernsbacher, M. A. (1992). Improving written communication through minimal feedback. *Language and Cognitive Processes, 7,* 1–22.

Traxler, M. W., & Gernsbacher, M. A. (1993). Improving written communication through perspective-taking. *Language and Cognitive Processes, 8,* 311–334.

van den Broek, P. W., Rohleder, L., & Narvaez, D. (1996). Causal inferences in the comprehension of literary texts. In R. J. Kruez & M. S. MacNealy (Eds.), *Empirical approaches to literature and aesthetics* (pp. 179–200). Norwood, NJ: Ablex.

van Dijk, T. A., & Kintsch, W. (1983). *Strategies of discourse comprehension*. New York: Academic Press.

Van Petten, C. (1993). A comparison of lexical and sentence-level context effects in event-related potentials. *Language and Cognitive Processes, 8,* 485–531.

Wade, S. E., & Adams, R. B. (1990). Effects of importance and interest on recall of biographical text. *Journal of Reading Behavior, 22,* 331–353.

Wade, S. E., Alexander, P., Schraw, G., & Kulikowich, J. (1995). The perils of criticism: A response to Goetz and Sadoski. *Reading Research Quarterly, 30,* 512–515.

Wade, S. E., Buxton, W. M., & Kelly, M. (1999). Using think-alouds to examine reader-text interest. *Reading Research Quarterly, 34,* 194–216.

Wade, S. E., Schraw, G., Buxton, W. M., & Hayes, M. T. (1993). Seduction of the strategic reader: Effects of interest on strategies and recall. *Reading Research Quarterly, 28,* 92–114.

Waller, R. (1991). Typography and discourse. In R. Barr, M. L. Kamil, P. B. Mosenthal, & P. D. Pearson (Eds.), *Handbook of reading research* (Vol. II, pp. 341–380). New York: Longman.

West, W. C., O'Rourke, T. B., & Holcomb, P. J. (1998). Event-related brain potentials and language comprehension: A cognitive neuroscience approach to the study of intellectual functioning. In S. Soraci & W. J. McIlvane (Eds.), *Perspectives on fundamental processes in intellectual functioning* (pp. 131–168). Stamford, CT: Ablex.

Wharton, W. P. (1980). Higher imagery and the readability of college history texts. *Journal of Mental Imagery, 4,* 129–147.

White, T. G., Power, M. A., & White, S. (1989). Morphological analysis: Implications for teaching and understanding vocabulary growth. *Reading Research Quarterly, 24,* 283–304.

Whitehead, D. W. (1990). *Imagery and reading comprehension: An exploratory study.* Unpublished master of philosophy thesis, University of Waikato.

Wilkins, A., & Moscovitch, M. (1978). Selective impairment of semantic memory after temporal lobectomy. *Neuropsychologia, 16,* 73–79.

Wittrock, M. C. (1977). Generative processes in memory. In M. C. Wittrock (Ed.), *The human brain* (pp. 153–184). Englewood Cliffs, NJ: Prentice-Hall.

Woods, R. L. (1947). *The world of dreams.* New York: Random House.

Woodworth, R. S. (1938). *Experimental psychology.* New York: Holt.

Yates, F. A. (1966). *The art of memory.* London: Routledge & Kegan Paul.

Yuille, J. C., & Paivio, A. (1969). Abstractness and recall of connected discourse. *Journal of Experimental Psychology, 82,* 467–471.

Zajonc, R. B., Murphy, S. T., & McIntosh, D. N. (1993). Brain temperature and subjective emotional response. In M. Lewis & J. M. Haviland (Eds.), *Handbook of emotions* (pp. 209–220). New York: Guilford Press.

Zholkovsky, A. (1984). *Themes and texts.* Ithaca, NY: Cornell University Press.

AUTHOR INDEX

Goetz, E. T., 6, 63, 64, 101, 103, 105, 107, 108, 110, 133, 136, 147, 150, 173, 174, 175, 177, 184, 185, 187, 190, 191, 193
Goff, L. M., 92
Golinkoff, R. M., 190
Goodman, K. S., 117, 171
Goodman, Y. M., 171
Gough, P. B., 117
Graham, J. W., 153
Graves, M. F., 185, 186
Gray, L., 39
Gray, W. S., 39
Green, J. A., 30
Grendler, P. F., 24
Gruber, H. E., 155
Guilford, J. P., 146
Gulgoz, S., 129, 185

H

Hacker, D. J., 147, 194
Haley, D., 167
Halff, H. M., 107
Halliday, M. A. K., 61, 83, 97, 129
Hargis, C. H., 168
Harp, S. F., 191, 192
Harrison, G. B., 155, 158
Harste, J. C., 118
Hasan, R., 61, 83, 97, 129
Hasher, L., 100
Haugen, D., 185
Hayes, B. L., 169
Hayes, J. R., 142, 143, 144, 145, 147, 160
Hayes, M. T., 185, 191
Hazeltine, P., 185
Hegarty, P., 191
Helstrup, T., 181
Hermann, D. J., 14
Hidi, S., 89, 185

Hiebert, E. H., 195
Higgins, L., 185
Hill, C., 185
Hillocks, G., Jr., 150, 162, 188, 193, 194, 197
Hockett, C. F., 146
Hoeken, H., 192
Hoepfner, R., 146
Holcomb, P. J., 46, 92, 103, 117
Howard, L., 154
Hubel, D. H., 118
Huey, E. B., 5, 25, 29, 34, 37
Hunt, R. R., 102

I

Intons-Peterson, M. J., 65

J

Jacob, S. H., 6
Jampole, E. S., 195
Jawitz, P. B., 182, 184
Johannessen, L. R., 194
Johnson, C., 27
Johnson, D. D., 169
Johnson, M., 7, 87
Johnson, R., 17
Johnson, V., 185, 186
Johnson-Laird, P. N., 79
Johnston, P., 189
Just, M. A., 117, 124

K

Kahn, E. A., 194
Kameenui, E. J., 169
Kangiser, S., 174, 184, 187
Katz, A. N., 87
Kaufmann, G., 181
Kay, P., 81, 97, 126
Kealy, W. A., 108, 147, 183, 193
Kelly, M., 64, 185

Walsh, M., 86, 102
Webb, J. M., 183
Webster, J., 167
West, W. C., 46, 92, 103, 117
Wharton, W. P., 178, 184, 186, 190, 193
White, C. S., 191
White, E. B., 193
White, S., 169, 188
White, T. G., 169, 188
Whitehead, D. W., 190
Wiesel, T. N., 118
Wilce, L. S., 165
Wilkins, A., 92
Willey, R. J., 194
Williams, P. C., 168
Willson, V. L., 118
Wilson, M., 120
Winograd, P., 167, 173, 184, 187, 190

Wittrock, M. C., 23
Woods, R. L., 154
Woodward, V. A., 118
Woodworth, R. S., 154
Worthy, J., 186

Y

Yates, F. A., 12, 21, 22, 23, 25, 27
Yuille, J. C., 109

Z

Zajonc, R. B., 89
Zholkovsky, A., 97

SUBJECT INDEX